D0988808

Breaking Out of Prison

To DJ —
May we all be
free to be our full
& deep self

A pleasure to meet
you & hear your
words.

Dean

Breaking Out of Prison

a guide to consciousness, compassion, and freedom

Bernice Mennis

iUniverse, Inc.
New York Bloomington Shanghai

Breaking Out of Prison
a guide to consciousness, compassion, and freedom

Copyright © 2008 by Bernice Mennis

All rights reserved. No part of this book may be used or reproduced by any means, graphic, electronic, or mechanical, including photocopying, recording, taping or by any information storage retrieval system without the written permission of the publisher except in the case of brief quotations embodied in critical articles and reviews.

iUniverse books may be ordered through booksellers or by contacting:

iUniverse
1663 Liberty Drive
Bloomington, IN 47403
www.iuniverse.com
1-800-Authors (1-800-288-4677)

Because of the dynamic nature of the Internet, any Web addresses or links contained in this book may have changed since publication and may no longer be valid.

The views expressed in this work are solely those of the author and do not necessarily reflect the views of the publisher, and the publisher hereby disclaims any responsibility for them.

ISBN: 978-0-595-44691-9 (pbk)
ISBN: 978-0-595-89014-9 (ebk)

Printed in the United States of America

Dedicated to all my students
to all my teachers

Table of Contents

Dropping Keys...ix

Chapter One: To Begin 1

Chapter Two: Tools for Survival: making lemonade from lemons................5

Chapter Three: Space to saunter...11

Chapter Four: Going into the prison...17

Chapter Five: Humanizing the Demon 20

Chapter Six: The acorn and the seed 24

Chapter Seven: Marvelous error 30

Chapter Eight: The unwanted guest and the welcoming host 42

Chapter Nine: Seeing and Not Seeing 49

Chapter Ten: What to do with all this energy: explosion and implosion.....54

Chapter Eleven: More on violence and language. Or how, when everything is
        connected, there is no one beginning but only a circle turning............66

Chapter Twelve: The inquiring mind, the believing heart and the voice of cynicism.71

Chapter Thirteen: A Stranger in a New Land: Some Guidelines 80

Transition Chapter 88

Chapter Fourteen: The Journal..92

Chapter Fifteen: The difficulty of looking at what is right in front of us.................104

Chapter Sixteen: Looking out, looking in, the same process 115

Chapter Seventeen: Narration, telling the stories of our lives................122

Between Seventeen and Eighteen: How to get from there to here................132

Chapter Eighteen: In between narration and definition …...................135

Chapter Nineteen: Redefining the word and the world.................139

Chapter Twenty: A very long way into "Comparison"................163

A Brief Interlude: losing one's way and how to return................180

Chapter Twenty-one: Analysis, part one................183

Chapter Twenty-two: Analysis, continued................191

Chapter Twenty-three: Making connection after so many years................201

Chapter Twenty-four: Still analysis, but making the web more intricate................216

Chapter Twenty-five: A Poetic Interlude................250

Chapter Twenty-six: My letter to them................254

Chapter Twenty-seven: Patterns................257

Chapter Twenty-eight: Grace Abounding................260

Chapter Twenty-nine: Where were they? How to locate?................265

Chapter Thirty: Those who survived................270

Chapter Thirty-one: July 14, Tom's Birthday and Bastille Day................274

Chapter Thirty-two: Happy Birthday, Tom................279

Chapter Thirty-three: The end of one cycle................291

Acknowledgments................293

Bibliography................295

DROPPING KEYS

The small man

Builds cages for everyone

He

Knows.

While the sage,

Who has to duck his head

When the moon is low,

Keeps dropping keys all night long

For the

Beautiful

Rowdy

Prisoners.

(Daniel Ladinsky, *The Gift: Poems by Hafiz*)

CHAPTER ONE:

TO BEGIN

The beginning of the Jewish New Year.

There was a storm on Thursday. Wind and rain knocked down many trees in the Adirondack woods in which I live. It was four days before Niagara Mohawk could restore electricity to my road, serving first the more concentrated populations in Saratoga, Glens Falls, and Lake George. People deeper in the woods still have no electricity. Power was returned one hour before sunset on the day of Yom Kippur. A good way to end the old year and bring in the new. My nephew Aaron and I sat and watched the sunset over the beaver pond, each of us trying to blow the shofar, the ram's horn, to mark the year's passing, I managing only a few notes, my nephew blowing until the sounds came out strong, eerie, other worldly. The New Year beginning. A chance, again, to act like a free and conscious human being.

My neighbor and friend, Raphael, talks to Aaron and me about the Hebrew alphabet. The aleph, the first letter of the alphabet, he explains, does not actually begin the Bible but, rather, the bet, the second letter. The aleph is silent, before the beginning, without form. The bet has a wall on its left side. All that lay to the left of that wall is "ein sof"—the unknown, the time before, when there was nothing and when there was everything. On the right of the bet is the opening, the big bang, the creation, the beginning of form.

This book will be about forms—the forms that imprison and the forms that free, the struggle with form, with our own edges and borders, with the bars which confine and constrict and, even (and these are harder) with the ones that

1

comfort, that give security and identity and meaning. This book is—presumptuous as it sounds, and it is strange to even write this—about ways to break out of prisons—those constructed by others and those internalized by us and, even, created by us. It is about how to be free.

And how did I come to write this book? And why? In my twenty five years teaching writing I have always encouraged students to write as a way of revealing their own thoughts and feelings to themselves, their own memories, images and stories. I know the process works, the writing taking us somewhere that our mind alone—without a pen creating the path—cannot, the writing like a rope which allows us to go forward into a dark cave knowing we have a way to return. Writing as tether, lifeline, parachute. Writing as process.

In *Writing the Australian Crawl*, the poet William Stafford talks about the process of writing as one of gently following the threads of one's own mind, the golden threads which will lead us, if followed gently and without judgment, to "Jerusalem," to the holy land. I think of Thoreau's essay "Walking," the word "saunter" coming from the pilgrim's journey to Saint Tierre, sauntering as a pilgrimage to the holy land. Writing is a way of sauntering, of moving slowly, not rushing too soon to a known goal nor allowing our journey to be interrupted by others. It is a sacred journey. One of the reasons for writing this book is to allow my mind the space I have always nurtured within my students, to do what I have preached. Even more, it is to do what I know "works" in terms of expanding my own boundaries and understanding.

There are other reasons.

The most compelling is the many students I have encountered in my twelve years teaching in prisons for Skidmore College's ironically titled "University Without Walls"—the "inmates," students, learners whose words and lives have stretched me beyond my own prisons and boundaries. I have saved some copies of some of their papers from their Freshman Composition classes, and I do not want to hoard my treasures. It is puzzling to me why most of us do not share our "saunterings" to the holy land but, instead, speak of what is peripheral and inessential. I have, for a long time, wanted to disperse these writings from the prison, to acknowledge, to honor, to reflect back to the writers the depth of their own words and lives, to have others partake in the richness.

With the so called Anti-crime bill on the Federal Level and with Pataki defeating Cuomo for Governor of New York, funds that financially helped students to participate in higher education within prisons were withdrawn despite evidence that the programs worked to lessen recidivism and change people's lives.

With no funds Skidmore withdrew its program. The very few open windows within a very closed and suffocating prison system were closed. In anger at our society for its ignorance, in sadness for the inmates and their loss of that potential that comes with higher education, and in my own grief at the drying up of one of my own sources for growth and deeper understanding, I felt a need to write about my experiences within the prisons and to give space to the writings of many of my students.

That feels particularly important now, when everything in the larger society reflects back to the people in prison that they are "bad" and that those who put them in prison are "good." I think of the denial, the arrogance of the judgment of those of us on the outside who build more and more prisons—literally, metaphorically, psychologically—in order to keep us safe from "them." More prisons per population than any other country in our world, more metal and concrete bars around "them" and more mental bars around "us," limiting our ability to really see and understand both ourselves and the larger forces in the society and the world. Burdening some people with the entire weight of "evil," we keep others in a state of false "innocence," unable to acknowledge or take responsibility for misdeeds, unable to feel remorse with its possibility of growth and freedom.

I come back to Yom Kippur, the day of Atonement, the day which allows, encourages, and forces us to take on the "sins" we have projected onto others, to let in where and how we ourselves have "missed the mark." The fasting and the prayers are ways of breaking down our own resistance and denial.

I also think of my own life's journey, of how each of us has certain questions that keep recurring in different forms throughout our lives—certain repeated motifs around which our lives revolve. Looking back, I can remember my small child self in that tiny Bronx apartment wondering how I could escape its narrow confines. I think of the different talks I have given and the essays I have written, of my twenty five years teaching, of my practice of meditation, of Buddhism and mindfulness, of my political actions around civil rights, women's rights, and gay rights. I see that for me a recurring motif has to do with imprisonment and freedom and the continual question: How can I (we) be free.

And so this book *Breaking Out of Prison*—to bring together the many strands that have been woven into my life, to give each space to speak; to saunter in this holy land, which is intimately connected to our very earth, and to see if, at the end, I could enlarge my own understanding, my own boundaries, and, through that process, help others explore more deeply their edges; to bring together what I have learned from meditation, Buddhism, feminism, from teaching and from life about the process of awareness as a way to break out of the prisons that confine ourselves and others in spaces much too small for our spirit.

And so I begin, this day after Yom Kippur, September 21, 1999.

Chapter Two:

Tools for Survival: Making Lemonade from Lemons

In the beginning is another beginning. My students joke about my favorite marginalia: "Go further, go deeper here, move more slowly. Between these two sentences there is a whole world you need to enter." And so I enter the world of my childhood.

I grew up in a small three room apartment in the Bronx. When I was eleven, my family moved from 5E to 6B, the apartment where I then lived for the next nine years, and where my mother and father lived till they died. When my mother died, at 87, she had lived in that building for over fifty years. I still visit there, visit those old ones I knew when I was young, the parents of the kids I played with, still take Peggy, the neighbor in 6A, shopping on Lydig Avenue, sometimes take Francis, downstairs in 5B, to the cemetery where her relatives and my parents are buried. And I always go to the Bronx Botanical Gardens, my refuge as a child, the place where I had space to breathe and be.

Even when I was a child I knew that the move from the fifth floor to the sixth, from three rooms to four, couldn't provide that space "to be." My parents were too watchful, too fearful. For them, a closed door was merely a door to be opened—no sense of knocking, no sense of a separate individual leading her own life apart from them, no sense that if you were reading or writing or talking or doing Yoga or meditating or crying or staring at the wall … that they couldn't or shouldn't just interrupt. No sense of the inviolability of space. And as I write that word "inviolability," I realize that I have never used it before and do not even know if it is a word.

"Inviolable": "secure from violation or profanation, secure from assault or trespass." As a child, I couldn't secure my boundaries without my parents feeling hurt, rejected. It's interesting that so much of my teaching now has to do with challenging and crossing boundaries, moving beyond the walls that restrict, "trespassing" on property others have declared "inviolable." But I also realize how much of my teaching—and my life—has to do with respect for boundaries, for the space around others and around ourselves, not imposing on that space, protecting space and not carelessly giving it away, not allowing everything and everyone to impose and interrupt, keeping our power and focus. I try to train my students to train their friends and family to respect the space and time required to do concentrated, deep and meaningful work, to value the sacredness of quiet space.

But as a child I knew I could not train my parents. And since I couldn't control them, I learned other ways of taking space, ways that were in my control. Because my parents woke up early, my father leaving for work at six a.m. every morning, I tried to stay up later and later, the night hours becoming the uninterrupted and inviolable space, the time where I could be. And on days I wasn't in school, I would go to the Bronx Botanical Gardens, crossing a bridge that went over the Bronx River Parkway, entering through an unofficial and always open gate. I felt totally safe, knew every section, every tree, knew where to go in order to dwell in or amplify what I was feeling, where to write or read or think or lie in the sun, or shade. For me then, and now, nature was an open space able to receive whatever and whoever came, able to receive me.

But I also needed to find a way to be within that apartment, with my family. So I learned to listen closely, to observe. As the second child, I could see my sister trying to get from my parents what they clearly could not give. And I saw them demanding her to be who she was not. I learned about subjectivity, about different points of view, about not banging one's head against that same hard and painful wall again and again. I learned protection and repression, but also lessons in consciousness and freedom.

Our skills get sharpened and honed early in life. Those beginning tools of survival were useful and necessary. But some of those sharp tools can, later in our lives, cause self-inflicted wounds when wielded unconsciously. As children, even in the best and most loving of homes, we are all "imprisoned"—born into a certain family, in a certain place and time, with very little control over our own lives. We are totally dependent for everything, powerless. And all of us, in various degrees, find ways to escape some of our early "prisons"—ways to survive, to ameliorate conditions that are painful or constricting. The ways we escape prison as children, however, can become what imprison us as adults. We become caught in triggered reactions that plummet us back to our childhood pain and defense—the protection over what is soft, the hardening that keeps us locked in small and rigid forms, the early training from our past that disables us from imagining and choosing healthier and more conscious ways of being in our present, our habitual defenses often totally inappropriate for our present survival.

Clearly some of those "tools" are no longer useful. But just as clearly some still are. My skills as a teacher were, I believe, forged in that very small, very confined Bronx apartment in the 1940's. The ways I tried to break out of that prison provided many of the skills that later helped me in freeing students. But one of our challenges as adults is to consciously recognize and claim skills forged unconsciously and often against our will in circumstances not chosen by us: to transform a defensive reaction into a chosen tool, allowing it to be expansive (in terms of growth) rather than defensive (in terms of protection). This chapter will explore that process of reclaiming and transforming our learned skills of survival.

A close friend is a long time meditation student; she has taken extensive meditation retreats and knows the practice well. The other day, she spoke of her early experiences doing Vipassana or insight meditation and how easy it was for her to focus on her breadth. It was only within the last few years that she understood the early experience that honed that skill—how her ability to focus intently on breath came from her childhood mechanism of dissociation.

It's a long story—as are most of our stories with their intricate and complex connections of cause and effect—but a small part of the story goes like this: At a certain stage of her life she "lost it"—became almost catatonic, had fearful visions, was unable to work. During that period she was exorcized by the Catholic Church to rid herself of the "demons" who seemed to possess her. She also saw a therapist who defined her condition as catatonic and schizophrenic. It was only many years later, with the growing societal consciousness about childhood sexual abuse, that my friend and many others were able to resee and rename what had happened, not only in her early childhood but also in her early adulthood. As a very small child she had been sexually abused by her father. As a way of escaping the pain, she left her body, focusing her mind elsewhere. Later in life the different parts of herself from which she had disassociated—particularly the very young, hurt and enraged child—began to emerge within her, not outside demons possessing her but parts of herself which she had silenced.

She talked about how the escape through dissociation—the ability to totally cut off from the world around her and focus her mind elsewhere—was her survival mechanism as a child. She simply left her body when it was being hurt. As an adult, it was that same mechanism that allowed her to focus strongly on her breath and learn the skill of breath awareness, undistracted by the outside world. The problem, however, was that she was not learning awareness and mindfulness, but, rather, dissociating from her self. Her ability to focus was sharp, like a laser beam, but she needed to work consciously with intention in order to make it an instrument of freedom rather than escape.

My story is less dramatic.

As a teacher, I feel that one of my skills is my ability to focus in on what is deep and essential in someone else's writing. A ferret, tenacious, I am relentless, asking questions to help students to find their way back to the source, to the gold that I sense hidden in the mountain, in the stream, in their mind and heart. Whether they are writing critically or creatively, a research essay or memoir, I insist that they move slowly and deeply into their own experiences and their research, that they reflect and make connections. I am interested, curious, want to hear and understand. Since I do not know the shape or the location or the way to get to their richness, there is no way I can possibly impose my view or vision.

As a teacher I can spot when they are going astray, circling, avoiding, moving too quickly, making too many jumps, becoming too abstract, and I can help them see "the problem," trusting my own intuitive response to their words, following my senses, picking up the scent of something deep, powerful, true, real, authentic. Give me even a small morsel of active thought, of genuine feeling, and I am happy. And what is true now, as an adult, was true when I was a child.

A childhood friend recalls how I would constantly try to stir some engaged conversation with my mother or father, asking a question, trying to find a thread that would save me from sinking in passivity and would enable me to be present with them. As a child I think I knew that they could not really hear me or my life. I also knew that I loved focused attention, loved being present.

I realized that the only way to be present with them was to find something in their words with which my own mind could engage in an honest and real way: Tell me about you childhood in your small Russian village? Why did you come over with your uncle and aunt and not your parents? And why didn't you work with your brother and parents at their fruit stand? Tell me about some of your customers today—what they said, how they acted. Tell me about your father, mom—about his small grocery store. How did it feel to be taken from your family, to be with dad's mother? What did you know about what was happening to Jews in Europe during World War II? And with McCarthy and the House Unamerican Activities Committee, did you know some of the neighbors who were blacklisted? And not just "big questions" about the past, about life, but a thread within any story that held the promise of something real and genuine—a feeling, a thought, a memory, a connection. I knew that unless I found real nourishment, it would be hard to be there, in the flesh, in that family.

As an "enthusiast" (in the Enneagrams), I am, literally, in love with this sensory world, with the incredible bounty of diverse forms in the natural world and, also, in our human world. As a teacher, I genuinely want to hear each individual's unique voice. Wildflowers proliferating, seeds spreading—what cannot be controlled or imposed from the outside but generates from within. It is a skill honed from childhood. But there is, I believe, something more.

I think students pick up my love for the rough edges and true lines that delineate us, my openness to what is true and real. They also, I think, know they can speak about what is not knowable, make leaps that feel strange and irrational, write about scraps of paper with strange scribbles, nestled in their pocket, that showed them the secret way home. As a child I held secret so much of what I knew and felt. As an adult, I remember.

Our childhoods shape us—all the unmet needs with their vast hungers, all the questions which play themselves out continually throughout our lives in different forms. All my teaching, I believe, has been to find answers to the questions I asked as a child, to find teachers to help me learn how to break out of prison and be free. Those endless and quiet and passive years in that very small Bronx apartment were my beginning school for learning.

And there was something else I learned. My family would have big political arguments all the time. While my mother would try to maintain some peace, my father would constantly bait me. I learned how to debate, to think clearly, to follow points logically. But it didn't seem to matter because each time I would "win" my father would switch the argument and change the playing field; I would have to answer some new argument on different grounds. And I would. But I would still not win because, really, it was a question of power, of his having the power; it didn't really matter what I said, how effective or clear or logical my argument. Through those arguments, with all their frustration, I learned something about clarity and logic but, even more, about power and powerlessness. I also learned something which was confirmed when I taught argumentative prose as part of English Composition—that the skill of persuasion and argument, while important, does not always provide space for a more slow, deep and complex reflection. It was only recently, however, that I learned another "lesson."

When I read Barbara Myerhoff's *Number Our Days* I saw something else about those frustrating debates with my father, saw what my clear and direct vision was unable to see. Myerhoff talks about old Jewish immigrants in a Senior Citizen Center and how they loved debate, often bringing into their meetings totally inessential and irrelevant material in order to engage, debate, and connect. A new member, more assimilated and wanting a more well run meeting, imposed rules to limit the discussion to make it move more efficiently. Myerhoff describes the people leaving the now well organized meeting. They are passive and quiet, lifeless. Reading her words, I realized, for the first time, that my immigrant father's "baiting" was not so much an arrogant assertion of power but, even more, his way of engaging with his young daughter, a way to have emotional and vital contact in the only way he knew. In some way it was a question of power: it didn't matter what I said; my father had the power to change the argument and win. That was true. But it was also true that he, someone who worked six days a week, twelve hours a day, wanted to engage with his daughter, and political arguing was a way he could hold me there, with him, at that small kitchen table, in that tiny apartment in the Bronx. One way, he could be free—to be in relationship.

CHAPTER THREE:

SPACE TO SAUNTER

Open space. Nowhere to go and nothing to do. Meditating. Sitting by the flowing stream. The desert. Moving on the river day after day. Being in the body. T'aiChi. The Sabbath, lighting the candles. Rituals. Placing one stone carefully on the earth. Eating one grape slowly. Listening to the sound of Tibetan bells. Feeling the breath of someone lying next to you. Touching your own deep heart.

The child uninterrupted in play. The adult uninterrupted in work he or she loves. Being unrushed. Being.

When I visited Tunisia, there was very little to do. In the morning, in the small local hotel, a knock on the door and someone would bring in a small tray with bread, butter, hot coffee, hot milk. Quiet, not imposing. A walk through a village. The market, the sounds of animals, the mounds of spices, smells and color. Old buildings, parched and living stone, the sound of the call to prayers. The hammans, the baths, silent hours with women and children, steam and water.

At night, walking slowly through the village. Men sitting around a small table, smoking, drinking coffee, talking quietly. Going back to the hotel early in the evening. Writing in my journal, the words coming as images, experiences coming as poems and dreams coming as visions, the boundary between conscious and unconscious permeable, fluid. I was in my body, in tune with my body, attuned to something larger, the body of this earth. It was that way, too, on a nine day river trip a few years later, moving down the San Juan with its steady flow of water, like breath, carrying me.

In Tunisia, I would write in my journal every night:

It is easy to sink into sand so deep
it is the same as staying so still
that the sand moves over you
and you become part of the dune.
Or the deepest end of the cave
where the light glows purple
at the furthest point in the sky
during the day.
Now I see why they twirl.
Because the swirl is the same as the still light
in the center, but the heat sizzles it
into a curve which dances
in the wind like fire.

She rose, her belly arched, her body uplifted
like the dunes blown by the wind. The source cavernous
flowing with life. The undercurrent beating like the tom tom.
The Berber chant moving along the contour of the mounds until it
disappears, fading into the horizon. And when you mount the dunes
it comes again, the song in the wind, the granular texture
velvet to touch.
Dry and wet the same here. The desert, the sun, the source constant.

The flow of wind, water.

And the women came to the desert to sing
their prayers in the hot sun. And it was good.
The heat was good. It blossomed in the wilderness
into ripe fruit. It burst with golden laughter.

The women came with their Tozuer black or Kairouan white.
Vivid color underneath the veil and underneath the color the body, naked.
In the film in my mind's eye
I see the women in the hammams.
It is called "before the separation."
Women moving, as if in a dream, carrying pails of hot water.

The steam, the haze, the movement, the stillness. All silent.
Each taking stone and slowly scrubbing cheek, forehead, neck.
down legs, down breasts, and across belly.
Taking cloth and moving across another—child, sister, friend—
touching shoulder, arm, back, stretching across continents.
Water. Steaming water. Then cold. Again and again.

The film is long and slow, a stretch of pendulous bodies.

And then the women move from that center
leave hot pool and pulsing navel.
And out of the silence come soft sounds
of Arabic, Berber, French, Italian, Yiddish, English, Russian.
And over their warm and radiant bodies they slowly wrap
bright red and purple cloth, the orange silk sari,
tight skirt, worn dungarees.
And over that the heavy black or red or blue muslin.

The bare feet move slowly out the door
into separate worlds.

At night we walked into the oasis
fragrant with jasmine and rose, citron and orange blossom.
You took off the scarf that had been carefully wound round
your head during the hot day and held it out so I could see
how long it stretched, more than your length, your hair
now black and wavy.

We sat on a bridge and you began to sing softly, an ancient song,
and I, who could not speak nor understand your language,
knew what you sang and said, please sing that again.
And your voice, trembling and loud, moved through the air
like a deep river opening itself to its own dark swells.
And in English you translated: I am an orphan
alone in the world. I am alone. Without father, mother, or brother.
And after the song you sat silent and then said: "It is all true.
I am an orphan. I have told you my life."
And you wept.

And I heard, in that Berber tongue, an ancient Jewish melody
my father sang in a language I did not know about a people
wandering alone, without a home.
The voice and the river, the past and the present,
the Berber and the Jew now become one,
that one night, a bridge
in the darkness filled with deep and subtle fragrance.

In Tunisia I fell in love—with the mosaics, the tiles, the art. I wondered how so many different designs placed side by side could feel spacious and pleasing rather than cluttered. I thought of borders and boundaries and how a simple framing or border around a complex design provided space for the eye to rest, and the mind. God commanded the Sabbath, a day of rest. If we left a space for rest in our daily lives, who knows what art, wisdom and compassion could flow.

When we were building our house, working from early morning into darkness in hard physical labor, I knew that I could continue to work if, each night, I stopped to watch the sun set on the pond and if, each morning, I jogged down to the waterfall; if I preserved a small empty space in my busy mind.

And yesterday, jogging, I had that space. Going up the big hill before the waterfall, a thought or, really, a question, entered that space: How do we really know whether Sisyphus' fate was, indeed, so terrible? How do we know what went on within his mind as he rolled that heavy stone up and down? How do we know if he were free or imprisoned?

And I thought—as I jogged—of jogging this same road every morning. It's different, I know, my "labor" not imposed on me from the outside. I can choose, could do something else, and will, the rest of the day. But I think of chopping wood and carrying water, of ironing and washing dishes, and of all those repeated tasks which are often calming, providing a space for my own deeper thoughts which do not seem to come when I am involved in my "important and productive work." In her *Second Sex*, Simone deBeauvoir contrasts men's "transcendent" labor—the creation of a product that lasts in time—to women's "immanent" labor—work that is repetitive, constant, with little to show at the end of the day. The clean house becomes dirty, the food prepared is eaten. A Sisyphysian task. Hopeless. And yet …

On the meditation retreat, we sit and walk in silence, sit and walk and sit and walk and sit and walk. We eat lunch, silently, then sit and walk, and sit, and walk until it is tea time. Then we hear a one hour talk, and sit, and walk. And in that space, our mind becomes Rumi's "guest house," where all thoughts and feelings come, where there is room for everything to enter, where all that has been kept out and denied has room to be.

This being human is a guest house.
Every morning a new arrival.

A joy, a depression, a meanness,
some momentary awareness comes
as an unexpected visitor.

Welcome and entertain them all!
Even if they're a crowd of sorrows,
who violently sweep your house
empty of its furniture,
still, treat each guest honorably.
He may be clearing you out
for some new delight.

The dark thought, the shame, the malice,
meet them at the door laughing,
and invite them in.

Be grateful for whoever comes,
because each has between sent
as a guide from beyond.

("The Guest House," trans. Coleman Barks)

I know there is a vast difference between a task imposed on another and one chosen by oneself, but I am attempting to see is if even imposed prisons—imposed by "god," by birth, by gender socialization, by the courts, by abusive and unjust powers and/or by fate or circumstance—if even those can be spaces of freedom. How do we know? How can we assume? About Sisyphus or about ourselves?

Wordsworth has a sonnet "Nuns fret not at the convent walls" about the seeming confinement of the sonnet form, about chosen restrictions which, in some way, free the spirit. Raphael talks about how the restrictions of keeping a Kosher home and following a more orthodox way of life actually free him by simplifying his life. I turn my own ball of assumptions around, my own prejudices, in order to see all the different surfaces and textures of freedom and imprisonment. "Immanent": "to remain in place. Remaining within a domain of reality. Inherent. Existing in consciousness and not in an extramental world." And what I am thinking now is that the space of immanent reality can be a very good place for understanding all that lay within us.

Prison is, clearly, a way of stopping someone in their tracks. And while it is terrible to be stopped by another, forbidden to live our chosen lives, what is not terrible is to be able to look around, to actually see, to move consciously rather than habitually, to choose our life. The irony is that through being stuck in prison, some people actually break into freedom. A parallel irony is that when people are told they are going to die, they are sometimes catapulted into life, into a life of their own choosing.

It is hard in this society—so shaped with noise, movement, bombarding sensations, consumer goods—to have the space and time to actually look around and see where we are. If I were looking from outside—which space and time allow—I might almost see this speed and sensory bombardment as a conspiracy by those in power to keep people from consciousness, a way of keeping us entrapped in a whirl of consumer frenzy from which a sentence of imprisonment or death or rolling a stone up and down a mountain could, actually, free us. In fact, if someone were up above looking down on our frenetic movement, I am not sure they could distinguish our "chosen movement" from Sisyphus' endless punishment. What they would see are people accumulating more and more money to buy more and more unnecessary things, having less time with family, friends, and self, blindly destroying all that gives them life—the air, water, earth—and spending vast sums of money creating weapons to destroy and kill one another. A vision much worse than the vision of Sisyphus who, at the worst, is just wasting his time doing nothing.

But at his best, Sisyphus could be wasting his time being free, being present and aware and conscious and compassionate, finally having the space to see what he could not see when he was imprisoned in the world and had the illusion he was free.

CHAPTER FOUR:

GOING INTO THE PRISON

Why would anyone voluntarily go into a prison? Actually we all, unconsciously, "choose" to enter different prisons throughout our lives. But perhaps "choose" is the wrong word here, since what is unconscious lacks the possibility of choice. It's only from hindsight that we question: Why did I do that? And why did I do that again, and again? In a later chapter, I will explore the conscious choice of restraint and limitation as a path towards freedom, but here I want to look more directly at the much smaller question of why I chose to enter a concrete and steel prison once a week for over twelve years. It is a question many students have actually asked me.

When I teach analysis, I ask students to think of the layers of possible "answers" to any question of cause and effect, to not simplify what is complex and multilayered, to go beyond the immediate or superficial or symptomatic, to allow in seeming contradictions and all that is real, to know that there are often personal, psychological, political, economic … and all kinds of "reasons," reasons that our rational mind or our ethical ideals might not approve or recognize. When we want to persuade or influence or manipulate, when we write argumentative prose, we often simplify. But when we want to understand, to write as a way of exploring and coming to a deeper understanding, than we have to open ourselves to all that enters when we ask the question "Why."

Why did I teach in the prison? I needed work, Skidmore paid well, and the prison was very near my house. That is all true. But I also traveled to a Bedford Hills Women's Prison, three hours away, for a very small salary, and when Skidmore ended their prison program, I continued to volunteer and would have gladly taught for free had the program continued. I did not miss the convenience. What I did miss was the richness of my learning during those years.

Part of why I chose to teach in the prison was that I was interested in having contact with people whose lives were very different from mine, who could tell me something about life from an angle and a history that I did not know. Also, I wanted to do some kind of "good," some service. I have lived a relatively easy and comfortable life, have been very fortunate, know the reality of "there but for fortune go you and I." The Jewish word "tzadik" is often translated as "charity"; Jews are commanded to give tzadik on different occasions. But Raphael told me that the more accurate translation is "justice." We give to others as a way of doing justice in the world, of balancing the uneven scales. Teaching in a prison was a very small way, I felt, that I could balance the scales. Also, in a strange but real way, I missed some of the political comradery I felt in New York City, the progressive and left vision I shared with friends. I thought that perhaps the politics of the men in prison might be closer to mine than the politics of my neighbors in this very conservative upstate rural New York area to which I had moved twenty years earlier. I wanted to connect with people who, I thought, might actually speak my language, who had similar NYC consciousness, who had awareness of race, economic class, and oppression. The strongest conscious reason, however, for teaching in the prison was my feeling that those who had been cut off from the distractions of life in the outside world might have knowledge inaccessible to those of us living our lives "outside" the prison bars; I wanted to learn what I did not know.

Looking now, from hindsight, I think that there was another motivation, a deeper and more specific understanding for which I have searched, both consciously and unconsciously, throughout my life. I wanted to understand how one can survive and, even, flourish, within a prison, any prison, and how one can be free even when physically confined and seemingly powerless.

When I would read about the Holocaust I would try to transport myself, as a Jew, back to that time and place, thinking how I might act in those circumstances, knowing that I could never really know, but still imagining. In my mind, I believed I probably would not have been one of the survivors. I wasn't thinking about whether I would have been assigned to the left line or the right, or shot, or starve to death, the forces outside of my control. Rather, I was thinking of my own psychological state and whether the experience of cruelty, betrayal, pain, and death would lead me to fight for survival or, instead, sink me into despair. I would have liked to image myself as a resistance fighter, but I could not conceive of being able to keep my spirit alive.

I could also not conceive how I could survive in a mental institution or an old age home, or any institution in which others had a great deal of power over my life, especially if that power were abusive and irrational. Just seeing people bully someone else, take more than their share, act arrogant and self-righteous, use their power to belittle, humiliate, and control rouses rage. Who knows the deeper sources of this rage, the projection, the shadow; I know enough now to realize that these hated parts must be part of me. But I also know that the rage entraps me, whether it was getting angry at my fifth grade teacher who humiliated a very vulnerable boy in my class, or screaming at a young Vermont State Trooper who had given me a two hundred dollar ticket and then followed me, pulling me over again because I splashed his car with mud when I pulled out. I felt a rage against him as I did against the politicians talking about the need for "welfare reform," or talking against gun control, or quoting the Bible about the perversity of gays and how the "gay agenda" was destroying the moral fabric of society. If I had been a slave during slavery, a black person during Jim Crow, a Jew during the Holocaust, a person put into a mental institution, someone in Great Meadows Correctional Institution, I don't know if or how I could survive. I thought, perhaps, that the men in the prison, having been in that crucible, could show me some possible ways.

I learn through inspiration and example. I wanted to teach where I could learn. I am writing this book to teach others what I have learned during those years. It is a way of giving back the richness that I have received, of doing tzadik or justice, of letting the men speak of their reality in their own words, so that what has been distorted and simplified can be seen in its more complex and real and human form.

CHAPTER FIVE:

HUMANIZING THE DEMON

What happens to our self image and concept of the world when we recognize the humanity of those we have demonized? I'm not talking about romanticizing or idealizing or seeing "the other" as perfect or ideal, another form of simplification, another way of not seeing. Rather, I'm talking about being able to let in another's full being, expanding our view to allow in all we have not wanted or not been able to see. And what does it mean for those who have seen themselves as bad, as monsters, to let in other possibilities, to not see themselves through the limited and distorted lens of another's negative judgment?

I think of two stories.

At the last supper, Jesus looked at his disciples and said, "One of you will betray me." What struck me for the first time when I recently heard a friend read this section of the New Testament was not what Jesus said but how each of the disciples responded: "Is it I, Lord?" Not, "I could never, maybe him or him," but a question allowing in a most terrible possibility. The realization that we really do not know and that anything is possible ... because life is complex and mysterious, because we are tried and challenged in ways we cannot imagine, because we are human and imperfect. I think how, in allowing in the possibility of doing a terrible act, each disciple was able to deepen and expand rather than limit his own humanity.

And another story. Monks in a monastery were having quarrels. Unable to live with each other, they called in a rabbi to help them. The Rabbi said that he did not know how to solve their conflict but that he did know that one of the monks residing there was the messiah. According to the story, from that day forth, the monks lived in peace.

Imagine the possibility that "the other" could be the messiah. Imagine that you, yourself, might be the messiah. What would that do to your relationship with others and to yourself? What would that do for the world?

In allowing in all the possibilities of doing both good and evil, we acknowledge that both ourselves and others live within the same human community. Nothing and no one is beyond the pale. Clearly that acknowledgment is not easy: the desire to deny the shadow parts of ourselves and project them onto others, to blame "them" in order to preserve our own sense of innocence and goodness, is part of our human condition, is "natural." The small child wanting to ward off punishment blames her sibling: "She did it. Not me." It's natural, innocent really. But later the stakes get higher, the denial more unconscious, the concept of self more vulnerable, the image of self and other more rigid, the societal and culture infrastructure of racism, anti-Semitism, sexism, homophobia more available, a fixed and accessible structure to support our denial, a prison to protect our concept of self and of world and a prison into which we can put the other.

I once gave a talk about why I teach. Exploring the different layers in my own mind, I found one less conscious, surprising, honest and very real reason: I teach so that I will not be killed as a Jew, woman, lesbian … I know that is naive. Clearly very educated people do acts of great cruelty; there seems to be no real correlation between the amount of years one spends in higher education and the moral fabric of one's life. Many of Hitler's top advisors had Ph.D.'s. There are highly educated people who are sexist, racist, anti-Semitic, who supported the institutions of slavery, imperialism, and colonization, who built and dropped bombs, who experiment on animals, beat wives and abuse children. I think of the Jewish immigrant Anzia Yezierska's words, "Education without a heart is a curse," and know that is true. Much of our education can be a curse, refining and developing our technical and intellectual skills without cultivating our emotions, spirit, heart, or compassion. In fact, much of the role of education has been to separate us from our heart, to train us to be "objective," defining objectivity as the elimination of all we know through our own experience, all that we feel through our own hearts. To disconnect in order to "know" is a curse.

But what I meant when I gave my talk—and what I honestly (although perhaps still naively) think—is that education which cultivates consciousness will save me and will save the earth. Education that demands close observation, questioning, re-membering our past, careful and slow reflection, noticing connections, seeing cause and effect, understanding on complex and multiple levels, education that cultivates the imagination, that allows in possibilities beyond our fixed and rigid borders, that allows in the thought that we and "the other" could be both betrayer and messiah, education which forces us to acknowledge and own all the parts of ourselves so that we do not strew our garbage and toxins all over the world, forcing others to carry the burdens of our sins—that education, I believe, would save me and our world.

English Composition 101 is one way of cultivating that consciousness. It is a simple beginning, a way of training the mind to see beyond inherited concepts and indoctrination, to ask questions and to reflect. Teaching English Composition within the prison was a way of freeing people locked behind bars, giving them one way to break out of prison.

In a writing exercise in which I asked students to come to their own definition of a word by looking closely at their actual experiences, one student, Tom, spoke of "compassion" as coming from the consciousness of one's own ability to do malevolent acts. And I thought: Yes, this is what many of those in prison know—their own ability to do malevolent acts. Not only can they imagine the possibility of being a betrayer, but they know it as a reality, intimately and painfully. But many of us in the outside world do not know and do not want to know our own capacity for malevolence, cannot ask, "Is it I?" Needing to deny any possibility of our doing "evil," we need to put "them" in more and more prisons, keeping them separate from us, denying that they could be part of us, thinking ourselves angels who do no wrong. But angels do not have free choice; they can only do good. In viewing ourselves as angels we, ironically, deny the very gift of our humanity: the continual possibility to choose good or evil, to fail, to fall, to learn, and to grow. The reality and the good news is that none of us are angels.

This book is partly about the prison of those of us on the outside who cannot let in realities that go against our concept of self and world. It is about how we are kept small and rigid by our need to protect and defend and how, through writing and reflecting, we can begin to free ourselves from those confining conceptual prisons. But it is also about those who are in the inside of the prisons, who have been defined by others as bad and evil, who see themselves as monsters, and how they, through the simple act of writing, began to see their larger possibilities, their deeper humanity, and their own capacity to do great good.

Prisons are created to break the spirit of the inmate, not just to punish for a crime done—to have the prisoner make amends for wrong doing—but to make him/her feel dehumanized, cast out of the human community. The writing I had students do within the prison was one way for them to retrieve those parts of self that the prison kept locking out, to have them experience, again, their own fullness of mind and heart. Not angels, not devils, but complex human beings capable of both good and bad. It was education with a heart.

CHAPTER SIX:

THE ACORN AND THE
SEED

Though I do not believe that a plant will spring up where no seed has been, I have great faith in a seed. Convince me that you have a seed there, and I am prepared to expect wonders …

(Thoreau, *Faith in the Seed*)

It is mid October here in the Adirondacks. The leaves have fallen. Squirrels and chipmunks and mice are all busy, preparing for the winter, gathering and harboring, creating the ever changing shape of our woods, their food droppings becoming our future trees. Hurricane Floyd did its part, its winds felling large white pine, poplars, and Maples. It was hard to experience the damage. The sky though, I can see more sky and more light, and who knows what other kinds of growth that open space will allow. I do my own winter scurrying, my own preparation, cutting and splitting the wood that has fallen.

Today, jogging, I did what I often do in windy Autumn days, in bright sun and under deep blue sky. I, another animal, "assisted" the milkweed seeds in their flight. The timing has to be right, as with all seed dispersal. When the pod is not ready, all my breath results in no motion. The white soft body with brown peacock speckled tail stays compact and intact, still fish rather than bird. But when the tendrils start to loosen, become like airy cotton, my breath becomes the other wind, and I watch the white parachute become a soft prism of color, carrying the brown seed further and further. The motion is peaceful, mesmerizing. I am a spreader of seeds. I move from one plant to another, scattering what seems dry and dead—black eyed Susans, lupine, and primrose.

My uncle, a survivor of the Holocaust, was the only member of our family who planted a garden. Every summer he would bring bags full of cucumber, pepper, tomatoes from his New Jersey suburban home to my grandparents' apartment in the Southeast Bronx, each of his Bronx relatives getting a small brown bag of vegetables. He was allergic to tomatoes but still grew them, loved to see their succulent growth, loved to see all growth.

Now I am in my fifties and he is in his seventies, still at his same job selling furniture in Newark. At the end of last summer, I visited his home and saw purple flowers everywhere. I hadn't known that he planted flowers as well as vegetables. Two years before, he told me, he had bought a light purple plant because it was very beautiful; he didn't know its name. At the end of the summer he harvested the seeds, tiny black dots, and the next spring planted those seeds in small planters, moving the seedlings from small to larger containers until it was warm enough to put the small plants outside in the earth. That second summer he had twelve plants. What I saw that third summer was a field of purple.

In his drawer he took out an envelope containing thousands of black poppy sized seeds and gave me some to plant up north. I now have fields of purple. I think of the incredible capacity of seeds to produce more seeds, enough, it would seem, to feed all our hunger. It is the "wonder" of which Thoreau speaks.

There are those, however, who try to control this "wonder" for their own ends. In *Biopiracy*, Vendana Shiva talks about the genetic manipulation of seeds and patents of ownership. Farmers who have, for centuries, saved seeds from their own crops, are now forced to buy the patented seed rather than be their own spreader of seed. A hundred and fifty years ago Thoreau noticed that same arrogance, the assumption that the source of life is one's brilliant new idea rather than nature's eternal way. In *Faith in the Seed*, Thoreau writes:

> *Thus much the English planters have discovered by patient experiment, and, for aught I know, they have taken out a patent for it; but they appear not to have discovered that it was discovered before, and that they are merely adopting the method of Nature, which she long ago made patent to all. She is all the while planting the oaks amid the pines without our knowledge, and at last, instead of government officers, we send a party of*

wood choppers to cut down the pines and so rescue an oak forest, at which we wonder, as if it had dropped from the skies. Nay, so far are the English from realizing that they are not the original inventors, in this case, but that their "art and design" are the same which are practiced by "unassisted nature," that they demean nature, insisting that it is only thru regulation and control that nature can reproduce, little knowing that 'art' of which they speak is the same which was practiced by the original inventor and planter of oak woods, so that theirs is at most only the rediscovery of a lost art.

So the white Europeans "discover" new lands and claim ownership for their "mother" country, sometimes battling another European nation for possession, never seeing their "object" of domination as subject, never recognizing the fullness and bounty of the lives that have lived there for eons of time, seeing only emptiness to be filled or enemies to be conquered. And men, throughout history, claim their semen as the source of creation, the woman's womb an empty vessel carrying male's potent force. Their idea, their discovery, their patent, their ownership. And in seeing "the other" as empty, we make the world sterile, our ignorant vision becoming the reality, "creating" sterile seeds unable to reproduce, packaged for purchase so that no one else can be a sower of seeds. But the seed, the seed … that is what this chapter is about.

I, like Thoreau, have great faith in seeds, in "unassisted" nature's seeds, in the inherent bounty within the earth and within each of us. My teaching rests on that belief and faith in the deep richness, the infinite and unknowable potential within all of us. And my experience has continually confirmed that faith in countless ways, countless like the seeds. But that faith is not in magic. A seed, like any being, cannot be separated from its context, its environment, its time and place. Seeds—both in nature and within us—land on specific ground, must be transported by wind or animal, must take root and grow.

While it is true that the acorn can only grow into an oak, not a maple or hemlock, it is not true that every acorn will grow at all. Some are eaten. Some are burnt in fires or never get sufficient water to grow. Some rest high on a mountain edge, shaped and buffeted by wind, by cold, by heat. There are oak trees in Greenland that grow to only a few inches, the maximum capacity that their environment of cold and snow will allow, doing all that they can in the two or three weeks when the land is green, fertile, warm and free of snow to be all of who they are. Some seemingly large and healthy trees in our Adirondack woods were uprooted and split with the strong winds of the recent hurricane. Other old beech and maple fall unexpectedly. I look at their soft centers, undetected when they stood vertical and strong against the sky. What in this Adirondack earth in which this seed took root created that weakness and susceptibility? Was it preventable or "natural"? Is it acid rain from the Midwest plants? Insects? Insects caused by global warming? By the destruction of the insects' predators? Is it vulnerability to insects and disease because of acid rain weakening roots? It is important to understand the complex layers of cause and effect.

In her *Silences,* Tillie Olsen talks about all that is in us that will never be brought to fruition because of external circumstances—economic class, gender, race. Virginia Woolf, in her *A Room of One's Own,* speaks of how genius is not disembodied, how it has a material base, how women need money and a room of their own for independence of mind, for the space which allows creativity to blossom. The milkweed does not float forever. It lands on some specific earth. Its flowers are the monarch butterfly's source for food, its leaves the nesting place for the Monarch's cocoon. Individuals are born within a family, in a certain time, place, culture, world. Everything shapes us. The question is not whether we are pine seeds or acorns, milkweed or burdock; that, really, is out of our control. The question is how who we are is shaped by different environments—which environments foster the individual's growth and which stunt, which allow for diversity and which insist on a monoculture of standardized forms and shapes.

I am "political" because I see the effects of institutions on individuals. While I do not believe there is a perfect society, I believe in the importance of trying to change institutions that constrict and damage our potential. I teach because it is one environment which I have some small power to shape. I think of teaching as gardening and can think of no work more life affirming: my hands in the earth, working with many different kinds of seeds, learning how to build good soil, experimenting, studying what conditions enable what kinds of growth, watching beings grow into their fullness, recognizing and respecting the mystery and power of the process. I know why my uncle plants vegetables and flowers.

I teach because, like Thoreau and like my uncle, I have deep faith in the seed and because I know the importance of the environment in which that seed lands. I teach with the belief that everyone yearns for, seeks, and loves to feel his or her own depth. But I also know, from experience, that most of us have been damaged and hurt in various ways and that that "depth" and yearning are often too vulnerable to be exposed. We are all deep wells covered over with heavy stones. The hardness that many teachers experience in the classroom is often a covering over the softness. It manifests as indifference, anger, boredom, cynicism, scorn, as if there were no clear and deep water, as if the stone were as deep as one could go.

In a later chapter, I will explore the difference between the inquiring mind, the doubting mind, the skeptical mind, and the cynical mind and how our culture promotes, in different ways, cynicism, teaching us to mock enthusiasm, curiosity, and deep inquiry. But here I want to talk about the necessity of faith, of believing that there is something below the stone, that there is pure water. To have that faith, however, one needs to understand and respect the courage required to trust in a possible opening, especially if one has been hurt deeply. As teachers, we cannot assume a student's open receptivity to us, to the material, or to themselves. Many forces out of our control have shaped and are shaping that seed.

One of the complexities and seeming contradictions that I needed to take in—with both my garden and the classroom—was that what I saw as a healthy soil was not necessarily one which enabled a plant to miraculously and immediately grow, or one that a student would welcome or consciously choose. Sometimes it was my ignorance and arrogance, my inability to really understand the complexity of cause and effect. Sometimes it was the very real difficulty of transplanting anything from its comfortable and familiar "home," even if the container were too small and confining, even if I were moving it from "bad" soil to "good." I didn't fully take in that the process of uprooting is not only painful but can feel life threatening, can feel like death, and that it requires patience and tenderness.

What strikes me, again and again, is how strong the inner voices are which yell all kinds of terrible things to people about who they are and aren't, about what they can and cannot do. Sometimes in class—whether in the prisons or in the college in which I now teach—I'll ask students to just write down what some of those voices are saying. The lists are often long: "Why are you in school anyway? You have nothing to say. You can't think. You're selfish. You're stupid. Everyone else knows much more. Who do you think you are anyway? You're not creative. You're too emotional. Everyone will find out how foolish you are. Keep quiet, you have nothing to say. No one will understand anything you say. No one cares about anything you say." What is amazing to me, given these internalized voices, is that a student is able to go to school at all, to write, to take any risks, to not be totally paralyzed by fear. What strikes me, again and again, is the great courage required to take the first step and to continue walking.

Pir Vilyat Khan, a Sufi master, talks about teachers providing students with a mirror and a window. I think of all those students who could not believe my honest feedback when I pointed out the power and depth of their writing, mirroring for them their own good words, students who began to cry, walk away, get angry, leave school, for awhile or forever. I think of the students who, after reading their papers aloud to a group, could not believe that others actually heard and understood their words, that they were able to communicate what was deep in their minds and hearts. I think of the surprised recognition: I can think clearly; I can understand this complex idea; I can write in a way that communicates; I can write in a way that moves others. Many of the students I teach have no idea of the depth of their well, the freshness and clarity of the water. It is, as one student saw so clearly, "the soft eyes of love watching" rather than the critical, judging, censoring or controlling eyes which make all the difference between speech and silence. We speak when we are listened to deeply; otherwise we are silent. It is that simple.

Besides mirrors, we also need, as Pir Vilyat says, windows—because we are all confined within our own small world. We need more air to breathe full life into us, need to know other possibilities, to read the words and ideas of others, to learn history and literature and science, to experience worlds beyond our own mind, to take our mind further then our own history so that we don't become the arrogant explorers who think we are discovering new lands because we have no knowledge of the natives and who see our individual "patents" as superior to nature's creative life force.

In prisons, where the mirrors are opaque or distorted, showing complex human beings as only numbers or evil monsters, and where, in that world of concrete and steel, the windows are tiny or not present at all, anyone providing a small clear mirror and a little air can do wonders. But whether we are actually inside a concrete prison or "free," we are all confined in our different ways, our seeds waiting for a little light and moisture in order to blossom. All of us yearn to grow, to become who we are, to be free. I live by and teach with that faith.

CHAPTER SEVEN:

MARVELOUS ERROR

Last Night as I was Sleeping

(Antonio Machado)

Last night, as I was sleeping,
I dreamt—marvelous error—
that a spring was breaking
out in my heart.
I said: Along which secret aqueduct,
water of a new life
that I have never drunk?

Last night, as I was sleeping I dreamt—marvelous error—
that I had a beehive
here inside my heart.
And the golden bees
were making white combs
and sweet honey
from my old failures.

Last night, as I was sleeping,
I dreamt—marvelous error—that a fiery sun was giving
light inside my heart.
It was fiery because I felt
warmth as from a hearth,
and sun because it gave light
and brought tears to my eyes.

Last night, as I was sleeping,
I dreamt—marvelous error!—that it was God I had
here inside my heart.

(in Robert Bly's *The Soul is Here for its Own Joy*)

And the golden bees were making white combs and sweet honey from my old failures—why does that bring such comfort, a tenderness close to tears? Why are we so hard on ourselves over our "failures"?

One of the strongest voices silencing students is the voice demanding perfection, that says, again and again while they are writing, "This is not right, not perfect." It is a voice that makes students constrict the movement of deep thought, a movement which is like a meandering river not quite knowing where it is going, into a fixed and narrow channel, safe and secure, established within someone else's lines of clear demarcation. It is the shift from exploration to certainty, from mystery to control, from excitement to obedience. It is the fear of being imperfect, as they were imperfect in elementary school, their papers filled with red marks showing all their mistakes. The red marks like wounds, like pain, like fear, now restricting the freedom of mind and pen. It is a hard lesson to unlearn since it is so engraved in the body, our learned instinct to protect ourselves from future attack by not making any mistakes, by being "perfect."

My Catholic partner attributes my not having any sense of perfection to my being Jewish. She notes, surprised, that I do not seem to whip myself with judgment, do not demand perfection, do not seem to have an ideal concept of how I should be. She's right—not necessarily about the Jewish source but about my having no sense of perfection, no sense of a perfect person, perfect action, perfect paper. What excites and compels me in both myself and others is watching something unknown unfold, grow into its life. With students' papers, I listen to their own coming to understanding. What is always true is that if they are thinking and feeling in the act of writing, than I, as reader, am thinking and feeling in the act of listening, following them in their journey. We are both attentive, engaged because we are both, as Krishnamurti says, "free from the known."

In his *Escape from Freedom*, Erich Fromm talks about "active thought." It is not, according to Fromm, that one all of a sudden thinks a totally new thought that has never been thought before. It is, rather, that through the process of writing and reflection, one comes to that thought as if for the first time. The small and exciting "aha," an organic process very different from repeating back to the teacher what one thinks s/he wants, trying to get "it" right and be perfect.

Today I picked up eggs from my neighbor down the road. The chickens greeted me as I put my two dollars in the can and took the eggs from the small cooler. When I opened the cardboard carton, I saw eggs ranging from light green to dark brown, speckled brown or black, small to very large, all different, all "perfect" in their own way, beautiful really, but none of them perfect in the sense of uniform, of being the same, of conforming to a certain standard set by another. I think of the apples growing in our old orchard year after year, wizened and strangely shaped, sweet and delicious. It's the same story really. Machines create uniform forms, but life, creating itself from the inside, is always unique. We create our faces, lines, bodies, beings. That is the essence of being alive. What strikes me as I watch people ignore the sweet apples on the trees and the very good apples fallen to the ground, going to the store to buy "perfect" apples wrapped in plastic bags, is how often we reject what is unique, rich, and full of its own being for something neat, wrapped, and costly, thinking the latter better, more beautiful. Instead of welcoming what is natural and organic, we take the chemically treated "food" that looks "perfect," those shiny red apples filled with poison. What is even more painful is when we do that to our own self, allowing our own bodies and minds to be shaped by others' notions of perfection, constricting our bodies and lives into tight and deadening forms, stopping our pen midair because what we are saying might not be right, crossing off what is true and substituting what seems better and nicer. My mind spins out with all the painful examples of these small and large self-inflicted mutilations and deaths.

Audre Lorde, a Black lesbian author, writes in *Sister Outsider* about the "illusion of safety" which controls our behavior: if only I do this or that, then I will be safe. An illusion because it is untrue, because there is no way to guarantee our safety. All that lives is fragile and vulnerable; all that lives will die, must die. But even if it were not an illusion, even if we could be "safe," the constriction of our actions to create that safety means we have already lost what is most precious: our own unfolding and expanding life. We wear corsets that constrict our internal organs; we seal a dead body in a vault with the illusion that it will not decay and that a "preserved body" is alive. We sell our souls for safety, and we do it again and again.

But it makes sense; it is our history that warns us, each time we take a step toward freedom, "Stop, you're going to be hurt." We all have our own stories. I remember one personal narrative in which a student wrote about a second grade art experience. Students were to draw snowmen. Usually shy and inhibited, for some inexplicable reason she allowed herself to become infected with joy and moved her pen in full and magnificent circles of imagination and fantasy. The snowman grew, wore a bright scarf, was almost dancing under her pen. Then the teacher came by, took the student's drawing, and pinned it on the board as an example of how not to paint a snowman, telling the other students that snowmen are made of three balls, not four or two, and that they do not look like the painting pinned to the board. As if the teacher knew, as if there were one real and perfect snowman, as if imagination and joy were not the art of painting. The student, now in her forties, concluded her paper by saying that she has not painted anything since that experience.

When I read her essay to students in my maximum security prison class, one of the students shook his head sadly and said that the teacher should be in prison because she had murdered her student, had killed her soul. He was right. But she remained unpunished, as do so many who misuse power out of the illusion they are doing good or out of need and desire to control what seems too unwieldy and full of life.

I think of my own second grade experience singing "In Dublin's fair city." My teacher, noticing that some of us were singing off key, had each of us sing alone until she could single out the offenders. I was one of the bad singers and was told to only mouth the words during our stage performance. I can still get back into my little body on the stage, the open mouth moving with no sound coming out, the embarrassment and shame, the silence as I "sang" about sweet Mollie Malone "crying cockles and mussels, alive, alive oh." Now, typing, I realize I know all the words to that song. There is an irony to "alive, alive oh." I think how, like my student and her painting, for years I did not sing, except by myself and to myself.

In my twenties, I asked a friend who was a very good singer to give me a voice lesson. We tried "Amazing Grace." I can still hear my tentative and fearful voice trying to sing about amazing grace. When I finished my friend said something about my being a natural soprano singing in a alto range and singing so softly that I would never be able to find my voice. Her words were, in a way, grace; they enabled me to "see as if for the first time" that the problem was not in my singing but in the constriction created by fear. What I needed to do, she said, was to sing in my high and strangely unfamiliar soprano voice as loudly as I could—in order to hear myself, to hear my own range, to shape my voice through my experience rather than through someone else's idea of perfection. One of my students many years later told me that jazz musicians, when they are improvising, do not stop if a note is "wrong"; instead they keep playing until that note is made "right." Exactly. To keep playing or singing or painting or writing until you make it "right." To hear yourself from the inside.

On our land, in the dark, around a campfire, I would have the illusion that no one could hear my singing, despite the reality that voice travels far through the silence of woods. It was a useful "illusion" enabling me to be the second grade student again, this time free to play with her own voice, to experiment with sound, to sing for its own joy, to sing loudly in my high soprano voice. I began, again, to love to sing and to do what I loved.

As a teacher, one of my functions is to try to create a "safe" space—like the Adirondack woodlands in the dark around the campfire—so that students can begin to hear their own voice, appreciate its unique resonance, play "it" until it becomes right to their own ears, ears that get more and more sensitive to sound as all the other critical voices cease to clamor. What I experience, again and again, is that the "problem" with many students' writings is not that they wander off too far but, rather, that they don't give themselves enough time and space to wander at all, to complete the journey they have begun, to gather together the threads that were real and significant, to see the larger patterns. Perhaps we all stop too soon, afraid we will get lost. We retreat back to the known, to the smaller forms that never really served our deeper minds, the safe patterns given to us by someone else. What we need, I believe, is a trust in the integrity and depth of our own mind and heart along with the courage that comes from that trust, a courage to go forward—with our painting, singing, writing—into the unknown, to see where our own feet take us, to make circles, to get lost, to make many mistakes, to find our way again, to see the larger circle, to keep going until we get to the heart, to our heart, to the center of the universe, to Jerusalem.

I think of the labyrinth, of how, if we only keep going, trusting the process, we will get to the center, to our center, to the heart. The momentary stopping is not the problem. What is a problem is the giving up, the loss of faith in our own ability to find our way, the trusting of another in authority to show us, the becoming dependent on the "expert" to tell us which way to go in order to arrive "home," not realizing that if they tell us, they are taking us to their house, not our home.

We have been told by those in power that the labyrinth is a maze and that, for safety's sake, we had better not begin our journey at all, had better stay within their circle of safety. And if we do begin and get scared or lost, as we will and must, we are not encouraged to continue but, rather, reprimanded, told that our mistake was setting off on our own, our questioning and our disobedience. And if we believe them, retreating and seeking safety in their directions, the weaker and more dependent we become on authority, on someone's telling us where to go, how to travel, the path to take.

It is true that the rut of a repeated movement can feel safe, especially at night, especially if we are told that dangers lurk everywhere in the dark woods. But I think of Thoreau, in *Walden*, talking about the value of being lost, about how it is only when we are lost that we begin to look around and really find ourselves:

> *In our most trivial walks, we are constantly, though unconsciously, steering like pilots by certain well-known beacons and headlands, and if we go beyond our usual course we still carry in our minds the bearing of some neighboring cape; and not till we are completely lost, or turned round— for a man needs only to be turned round once with his eyes shut in this world to be lost—do we appreciate the vastness and strangeness of Nature. Every man has to learn the points of compass again as often as he awakes, whether from sleep or any abstraction. Not till we are lost, in other words, not till we have lost the world, do we begin to find ourselves, and realize where we are and the infinite extent of our relations.*

Being lost can, clearly, be a way of being found, of bringing ourselves into awareness: we have to look around rather than move unconsciously and habitually on a path created by others or by our own repeated motion. In his poem "Lost," David Wagoner tells us to "stand still," to listen to the forest breathing, to the trees, to raven and wren: "The forest knows/Where you are." Even in my woods where I have walked for over twenty five years, I can, most fortunately, still get lost and be brought back to attention—can feel again the earth underfoot, recognize the shape of the mountain line, pay attention to the slant of light, be present. In my life and in my teaching, I see again and again the great value of being lost, of actually having to look around, and the grave danger of always knowing exactly where we are. And I also see how our failures, if treated with kindness and looked at with awareness, are part of a much larger and fuller journey to a much more spacious "home."

I think of all the classes in which I felt a loss of control, everything going in what seemed a very bad direction, I feeling the guilt of having done something terribly wrong. Why do I remember each of those much more clearly than the good classes that went "perfectly"? And in my life, too, those times when, to use Pema Chodron's terms, "things fell apart"—when I was most scared, fragile, and vulnerable—they, too, are etched in my memory, while the times everything went smoothly and I was in total control have all faded. These "marvelous errors" were the times of insight and understanding, of moving beyond the boundaries of the known. I think of the men I taught in prison who were great failures by every measure of societal success. Yet if I asked them—as I have—to trace the journey of their consciousness, to see where they have grown and deepened in their life, the line tracing growth often moves upward as the line of worldly success moves down.

I think of Tolstoy's "The Death of Ivan Ilych," where the lines of soul growth and worldly failure also seem to move in opposite directions. Ilych, a successful judge dying from some unknown disease, senses but cannot let in the terrible thought that perhaps he has lived his life all wrong, that his great "successes" were actually descents in terms of his soul and that his seeming failures were moments of passion and life. Ilych is lost, but it is too painful for him to look around to see where he really is.

I have given my students in prison some "death" haikus" written by monks in anticipation of and preparation for death ("Now that my storehouse/has burned down, nothing/conceals the moon" and "Moon in a barrel/you never know just when/the bottom will fall out") as well as the Thoreau quote and the Wagoner poem above and asked them to write a personal essay in response. For many, writing about their experience within this framework was a way of "making sweet honey," transforming bad fortune into good fortune through redefining "success" and through accepting and acknowledging their experience in prison as part of their labyrinth walk "home" to their deeper self.

I think of how teachers often do not allow students to walk their own long path home. It's not just stopping their painting of snowmen or silencing their singing of "In Dublin's Fair City," but something less conscious, less obvious, more subtle. It was one of my "failed" classes that enabled me to see this clearly.

I was teaching Children's Literature to a small class of future teachers, mainly women, mainly middle class. We had studied some of the history of children's literature and read many of the "classics." I then had them read a book of poems written by inner city children about home, neighborhood, family, seasons, life. When I walked into the classroom, I could feel tension and anger. Then one student said, "These are very depressing. Why are we reading these?" She pointed to one poem entitled "Spring" and said, "This isn't about spring; it's about garbage on a city street." And then others in the class joined in, criticizing the book. I remember being taken aback, confused, silent, guilty, thinking that perhaps I had done something wrong. And then in a quiet voice, one student said, "But this is their experience of spring. It is my experience, in my neighborhood, on my street." And it was as if, all of a sudden, everything became clear: how these other students as teachers would have, unconsciously, told the students that their words were not true, their drawings not accurate, their experiences not valid. That "this" was how a house should look, a neighborhood and a family should be, that this was how they really thought and felt, that this was a snow man, that "this" was reality, defined by the teacher from her/his experience. I could feel the ease of this process: The invalidation and silencing of the student's own reality, training them to lie, in time so separating them from their experience that they would not even know they were lying, that they were "truly lost." Education as a curse. And because, in that moment, I could see so clearly how I and we do that all the time—impose our reality on another, not really listening to their experience, assuming a universality of our experience, using our power to impose our vision—I could express that to the class, make conscious that process that is so harmful in the classroom and in life, my failed class leading us all to an understanding about control, fear, and power.

I think of other times when, as a teacher, I "failed" only to find that there were lessons much larger to be learned than I had originally conceived. One evening I opened my "Women in Literature" class discussion of Tillie Olsen's "Tell Me a Riddle" to relatives of my students. At the end of a very good discussion, one mother of a student raised her hand and said that the class was being too easy on Eva, the mother in Olsen's story, and too hard on David, the father. She accused us of distorting the text through our anti-male attitude. The bell rang, the students left, and I felt, as with the students who accused me of selecting depressing children's literature, on shaky ground. At our next session, I asked students about their reaction to the previous class. The daughter of that mother began to speak about how her mother was never able to express her own point of view, could only echo and support her husband, had no sense of self or of self-worth. She could not see Eva's point of view—or, even, David's ability, finally at the end, to stay with Eva through the pain, choosing love over escape—because she could not see or value her own point of view, her own life. As with Ivan Ilych, to question her chosen path was too painful.

I think of the time I was teaching an Autobiography Class in the prison and walked into yet another room filled with tension and anger. We had read Wright's *Black Boy*, Smedley's *Daughter of Earth*, and Kingston's *Woman Warrior* without there being any strong hostility. But with *Autobiography of a Yogi*, students were livid in way that totally surprised me. Again I was taken aback. And what I realize now, writing, is that being taken aback was exactly the motion necessary for me to see from a different point of view. And what I saw was how enraged we often get when someone presents a world view very different from our own. And the question: Why do we get so angry? What is so threatening? Who and what (and clearly it is different for each of us) are we not able to let into our world? And what would it mean to our sense of self and world to let in those very ideas and experiences that seem so threatening, to create a space for reflection rather than follow our familiar and habitual patterns of reaction?

I think of another prison class on "Social Problems in Literature," a class exploring Ellison's *Invisible Man*. Toward the end of one discussion, I felt the now familiar class anger. This time it was a student yelling that if you shatter someone's illusions you kill them, that we all need our illusions, and me, again being taken aback, forced to question what I had assumed. I remember the trip back from the prison, remember thinking: No, he's wrong; it is important to break through illusions. But I didn't know why or how, didn't know how to support what I felt to be true. That week I carried the question wherever I went, asking everyone. One friend distinguished illusions from visions, the latter coming, she believed, from within us, the former given to us by others. She was right; that was an essential difference. Then I asked women in my writing group to think about a belief they held which they later saw as illusion. I asked them to trace their journey—the cause of the shift, the effects. I can still feel the energy of a room full of people honestly trying to understand something complex by looking closely at their experience.

One woman started to talk about her illusion of safety, her belief that she would not, could not, be raped. In some subtle and only semiconscious way, she had believed that her looks, dress, neighborhood, age, strength, knowledge, and attitude would protect her. She was not actually raped, but when she joined a women's rape crisis center and began working with survivors, she realized that she, like them, could be raped, that her belief in her safety was an illusion; she was vulnerable. And then, slowly, aloud, she began to trace the effects of this "shattering of illusions" in a way that made me see "as if for the first time" why that shattering was so painful, like death, and so necessary, like life.

At first, she said, the effect was fear and tremendous vulnerability. She no longer walked the streets with total confidence. She felt anxious. It felt like a loss to not have the illusion, the "innocence." And I could understand the wish to go back to that innocence, could feel the loss, almost wished, myself, for the illusion which seemed to give strength. But she continued, reflecting slowly, tracing the effects, realizing that with the loss of the illusion, she felt much closer and more connected to other women, not only to the survivors with whom she worked but with all women, no longer seeing herself as, in some way, superior and separate. She became "one of them," feeling a sense of comradeship, compassion, and connection.

What was interesting to me was that at some point the knowledge of danger and of vulnerability actually strengthened rather than weakened her. Knowing she was vulnerable, she learned techniques of self defense, walked with others at night, was more aware of her surroundings. She knew that she, like all women, could be raped, but she empowered herself in whatever ways actually gave her some control.

I returned to the prison the following week with a much deeper understanding of why illusions are harmful: because they are fed to us by others, because they keep us within someone else's system and under someone else's power, because they separate us from others, because they necessitate our denying our reality, because that denial keeps us powerless, keeps us separate—from others, from our own experiences, from our own compassion, and from our own power. I could see how it is only when we break free of "their" illusions that we are able to create our own visions and bring those visions into manifested form, only then that we break out of prison into freedom. The shattering of the illusion was not death but, rather, the only way to a possible new birth. And of course it would be, like all births, accompanied by pain and joy.

I think of R, a blind student in my advisee group in Vermont College, describing to the group her struggle with college education: the audio tapes, the Braille books, the reader, the typing with a Braille typewriter, a woman who would retype ... While all students in the program work hard, and most are parents and work full time as well as being full time students, clearly R's struggles were different because she was blind. But the other students, trying to be empathetic and compassionate and to make a connection, began to say, much too quickly, that they understood her experience exactly, that they too took hours with their work. They were kind and meant well, but their response felt wrong, different from the woman who, in realizing that she too could be raped, connected to her "sisters." Here, it was clear that people who were not blind couldn't and didn't really know her experience; all we could do was listen and take in her feelings, which is, really, all she wanted: compassion through empathy and deep listening, awareness of the other as different from ourselves, not drawing the too easy and quick lines of connection which obliterate real and unique differences. Tasting the deliciousness of the unique apple.

R talked about her parents, how they wanted her to feel "normal," like everyone else, sending her to regular schools, acting as if she were not blind, she living out the family's illusion. And I could see, as she talked, the temptation of that seemingly loving, inclusive, liberal, and democratic illusion that I often hold—and how it operates in so many spheres. I could see the danger, perhaps for the first time. R talked about what happened when her illusion was shattered—the pain, the grief, and, then, the freedom that came as she reshaped her life based on her own actual experience rather than their idea of how she should be, redoing her home so that she could be more empowered rather than more dependent, restructuring her life so that she could be more free in her motion. Consciousness and acceptance allowed her to shape her own life, make manifest her own vision, the vision of a deeply intelligent, thoughtful, sensitive woman who is blind, following her own journey to her own center.

And how can I bring this chapter back around, full circle. I feel like a dog that keeps circling around some vague center, wondering if I am coming closer to that center or going too far out. But I tell my students to not fear wandering, to allow that process in their own mind, to trust its motion, gently following, tying one thread of thought to another, juxtaposing images and memories, seeing the patterns as they emerge rather than imposing them. I have been practicing what I preach, and this is what I see: how each mistake—in the classroom and in life—has taken me out of the rut of my assumptions and of my controlling and often arrogant ego and has enabled me to question, each question allowing me to see in a larger and more complex way. I see how control is not what is played up to be, nor perfection, nor safety, each keeping us within the small circle of the known. I see how, when our storehouse has burned, we can see the moon more clearly, and the stars. We can even realize that our true home may be somewhere else and that this seeming misfortune can be the fortune allowing us to move on, build anew, create a new home in a new place, make manifest our own vision, create our life, again and again. And we can see that what stops us from that act of re-creation are the illusions: of perfection—there is some perfect being we should be; of safety—that if we were that perfect being then we would be safe; of normality—that we all must conform to a specific form in order to be okay and that we must see someone as exactly like us in order for them (and us) to feel okay. All these illusions keep our large being in a small prison, afraid of making the very "mistakes" that could lead us to freedom. It is a question of choice: choosing the "safety" of control, of death, or choosing the mystery and energy of life, of growth.

In the Bible, God says, I give you the choice of life and death. Choose life. The desert fathers define sin as the refusal to grow. What I know from my experience is that the open space that failure and mistakes allow is the very place of growth and life. All that is required is tenderness, compassion, and awareness rather than critical judgment to make "sweet honey" from those old failures. As they say in meditation: It's simple but it is not easy.

CHAPTER EIGHT:

THE UNWANTED GUEST AND THE WELCOMING HOST

From Rumi's "The Guest House"

This being human is a guest house,
Every morning a new arrival.

A joy, a depression, a meanness
some momentary awareness comes
as an unexpected visitor.

Welcome and entertain them all!

(trans. Coleman Barks)

I'm having trouble writing this chapter. I think it is because of the contradiction between its content and my process. I am writing about unwelcomed visitors—the ones who come unbidden, whom we do not want and try to keep out, like those failures and mistakes in Chapter Seven. The problem with the chapter is that I know exactly what I want to say. It is a speech I have already given, a lesson I already know. There is no space or time for the unexpected visitor; in fact I probably would have "killed" him/her for interfering, so eagerly was I pursuing my goal, so clear was I in my destination, so confirmed and confined in my knowing.

It is a problem and a challenge: how to keep our focus by keeping out what interrupts and disrupts our mind and heart, and, at the same time, how to be open to the moment so we don't miss those unwelcomed "visitors" who, if they were included in the "discussion," could lead us to a deeper understanding and, in fact, might have the very "answers" to the questions we are asking, although they come in forms totally beyond our conscious wanting or knowing.

When I was growing up, neither the door to the small bedroom I shared with my sister nor the door to my parents' bedroom could be closed tightly. The doors hung vaguely closed, vaguely open. In my parents' eyes, our lives were totally interruptible; it was as if they could not see us as having separate lives around which our own worlds revolve. Given my history, it is no wonder that e-mail, call waiting, and cell phones not only have absolutely no appeal but are, in fact, like nightmare visions of my constantly interruptible childhood. No protected inviolable space, no sacred space. It's also no wonder that I am ever vigilant against interruption and am deeply moved when someone respects my space and that, when I am teaching, I insist students not interrupt or whisper when another is speaking, that they listen intently and allow each person his/her space and time. It is not surprising that I protect my space and time with a fierceness, sometimes even a rage, and that I protect another's time and space with the same intensity even when they do not feel the need or the violation.

My response to our society's insistence on immediate accessibility is, I think, a healthy response to a society that is geared to eliminate all the space in which deep reflection—or any reflection at all—can occur. I know the necessity of space and time for creativity, insight, imagination, for consciousness, choice, freedom. But like any of our childhood unmet needs, our later reactions can have, as discussed in Chapter Two, their slightly pathological side: our past need imprisoning our present ability to see clearly, to know when enough is enough. I am not only the child wanting to be free from that confined apartment in the Bronx but also the prison guard keeping out all unwanted visitors, all the "enemies" who seem to threaten my life by taking away my time and space. (It's interesting to think of the connection between prison guard and prisoner, of me as a guard. I hadn't seen that before; perhaps I am finally letting some unexpected visitors into this chapter.)

So, of course, Rumi's poem would speak to me, me standing guard at that door, allowing only certain guests to enter, feeling totally justified in my insistence on my space and time, not recognizing the suffocation in the air, the smallness of the space, the energy required for that vigilance, the danger of focusing on what I want to keep out. Not recognizing that I was not only creating a space for freedom but, also, imprisoning myself within it. And the reality is that those uninvited and unwanted visitors kept barging in anyway, even now that my mother has died, even now that I live in the wilderness with hardly any neighbors around. Few people but many animals—deer, raccoon, coyote, rabbits, porcupine, and cats, cats left on the road who come to our home, hungry and seeking shelter. And it is cats who I want, now, to write about: cats as unwanted visitors.

(I did not grow up with animals; the landlord of our apartment house did not allow them. I grew up afraid of the cats and dogs that wandered "wild" and "dangerous" in the neighborhood. Writing this now, I can see that "wild" and "dangerous" were, really, just hungry and trying to survive and that I was reacting to the external manifestation rather than recognizing a deeper cause. Even more, I can see that I was internalizing what my parents taught me, their fear of that wild hunger—in others, in themselves, in us. In some way, of course, my parents were right: Hunger that is not fed can lead to violence. Perhaps I and we need to be afraid. But perhaps, even more, we need, as individuals, as a society, and as a world, to recognize the reality and pain of hunger in order to find real ways to feed and be fed. But that is another chapter—one on violence, on Fromm, and Eva Hoffman, and the man, just two nights ago, who was cursing his kids in the hotel room next to mine. This chapter is about the unwelcomed guests and, particularly, those wild animals of my Bronx childhood who kept coming to my Adirondack doors wanting to get in. I need to stay focused, not dissipate energy by going in too many different directions. The question, again, of what to keep out and what to allow in. But because I can't totally let go of these thoughts, I have put have them within a parenthesis, a bit like a judge telling the jury to disregard the testimony they had just heard.)

I return to the unwanted guests who, in my case, took the form of animals: Margaret and her animals, her original four cats who became, with her generous spirit, seven, and her one dog, with her open love, becoming three. And all of them living in a small home that four of us built. Too many beings scattered around, barking and hissing, peeing and spraying, wet and smelly. I did not want them. I couldn't control them, despite my vigilance. How many days did I crawl on the ground, nose pressed to carpet, fuming, trying to find the urine smell? I had worked five years building a home and now I felt I could not live within it. There was no place for me to be. My childhood feelings were triggered and amplified.

It's a long story of how I got to love those beings I hated, how much their presence has added to my life, and how much larger my "room" had to become in order to include rather than exclude them. I think how much of our growth is about taking in what we have struggled to keep out, befriending all those "enemies," both within us and outside of us—the stretch required to be the welcoming host rather than the watchful guard. I think of what this receptivity and inclusion would mean for an individual, a group, a community, a nation, a world, and for all those beings throughout history continually cast out.

During one meditation retreat, a teacher spoke of watching our thoughts and feelings without judgment, being the welcoming host not just to those "guests" who are sweet, peaceful, and loving, but also to those rowdy and drunken bums who start demanding entry—anger, hatred, jealousy, boredom, fear …—those very beings whom many of us came to meditation to keep out. It was, clearly, a challenge to this particular gate keeper.

Pema Chodron talks about our desire to control our world. She uses an image of a room and our desire to control who enters and who leaves, the music played and not played, the temperature, the carpet on the floor and the paint on the walls, the amount of air let in and kept out. I cannot now separate her talk from where it led me, but I started to think about whom I would allow to enter my room. The admission might have to do with politics, values, ways of talking, ways of being. And I would keep out all those people who acted "inappropriately," said or felt the "wrong" things, made me feel things I didn't want to feel, stopped me from being peaceful and meditative. I thought of the energy required to keep others out; the smallness of the room because the thickness of the walls; the eventual suffocation because of too little air to breathe. I thought of my room in the Bronx and how little we sometimes "know" about what is really "good" for us and for the larger universe.

When I hear the weather forecast, I realize how good it is that I—or any one person—am not in control. If it has been dry and I feel the thirst of the garden, I want rain. The "very good forecast" of continual sun is not "good" if trees, vegetables, flowers are thirsty, if wells are running dry. And if I want to ski, it is not reassuring to know that there will be no snow in the future, although if I am traveling I do not want a snowstorm. My "good" is not only someone else's "bad," but even my own bad on a different day and in a different circumstance.

Yet still the understandable desire to control and the illusion that we really know what is best. Thus the story of Mudita, the cat that I wanted desperately to keep out of my home. It's a short story.

Two years ago it was a particularly cold February, with temperatures often going below zero. A huge black cat appeared, walking in front of our full length windows, meowing, peeing, spraying. In a very halfhearted gesture I would leave food for him outdoors because he was hungry, and I couldn't let him die. One very cold night my partner tried to bring him in. Not only did he fiercely attack our two other cats, both of them foundlings, both of them loved, but he also scratched my friend painfully on the back of her leg. Then our male cat, as a way of marking territory, began to spray all around the house, and I was plummeted back to the time of seven cats and three dogs, to the time of crawling on hands and knees focusing on all the smells that made my life miserable.

I had wanted a kitten for quite awhile. I loved their energy, playfulness, curiosity, their uncontrollable and mysterious spirit. I did not want a grown cat, particularly this one big cat. That's what I thought as I brought him to the vet to be fixed, holding the carrier as far from me as possible. That's what I thought when I saw two people with tiny kittens perched on lap and shoulder. That's what I thought when the vet said that he was an unneutered three year old male who probably would need to have two of his maimed and bloodied claws removed and that it would cost $150.00, the vet assuming that we would probably chose to have him "put to sleep." It was a clear choice: life or death. I didn't want him, but I could not choose death; there was no way to keep him out of our home.

What can I say? I love that cat now with the same fierceness that I felt when I tried to keep him out of my home. This welcoming house has, clearly, transformed him; his "hunger" was fed; he is very content. Almost a cross between a cat and a dog, he is devoted and loving. He follows us everywhere, "climbs every mountain," waits for us in the driveway when we are out, comes when he is called, sleeps with us. Right now he is stretched out on his chair, a beautiful velvet black form with small white cloud puffs under chin and on belly, his black expressive tail in the shape of a question mark. He is totally relaxed and trusting. He who attacked the other cats now wants to engage in play. I think how much less my life would be without him and how much I had tried to keep him out.

And I think of all the students I did not want in my group and how, almost always, they were the ones who taught me the most, although I was and still am a most unwilling learner. They are some of the "monsters" I talked about earlier, some of the experiences I want to explore more fully later. It's hard to tell which way this transformation process works, since the circle keeps turning. Were they transformed through my welcoming and accepting eyes or was I transformed through allowing them in, their actual and full being breaking through my narrow judging lens?

There is a story about Gurdjieff and his students. Apparently there was one student who drove everyone crazy with his obnoxious, combative spirit. When the student finally decided to leave, everyone was filled with the relief that comes when some difficult obstacle is finally removed. But immediately Gurdjieff told his students to find him and bring him back. How else to know our edges unless they are rubbed the wrong way? Pema Chodron talks about a monk who was going to Tibet. When told that all the people in Tibet were good and holy, he decided to bring his obnoxious Bengali tea man with him, needing this "enemy" to continually be reminded of parts of himself he would rather not know.

While the Lama chose to carry his Bengali tea man with him and Gurdjieff knew the value of the obnoxious student, most of us do not chose to have "the enemy" within our own home. The reality, however, is that whether we chose them or not, they will appear, again and again. The question becomes what to do with them when they appear: Do we pretend they are not there? Do we make our walls more impregnable, not just to them but to every being who tries to enter? Do we cast them beyond the pale or try to destroy them? Or do we become the welcoming host learning what they have to teach us—about ourselves, about them, about boundaries, and about a more spacious and possible world.

I think of all the students who have put their pen down in frustration saying, "I have nothing to say." As a teacher what is clear to me is that they have a great deal to say; ideas, feelings, thoughts are screaming to be heard. I can see and hear those very interesting and strange "guests" just waiting by the locked door. I shake my head. They, like all of us, welcome only a very select and limited number of "good" guests. I think how wrong our judgments often are in terms of who and what are good and bad.

As a teacher, I can try to train students to notice rather than ignore those "guests," to create a space for them, to listen to what they have to say. I think of Rilke's "Perhaps all our dragons of our lives are princesses just waiting to see us once, beautiful and brave. Perhaps everything terrible is in its deepest being something that needs our love." Anything seen with hate and judged with criticism constricts itself, often taking bizarre and strange forms. I think of my sweet soprano voice. I think of the men I taught in the prison. I think what it means to be seen with "the soft eyes of love," to be welcomed into the larger community rather than cast out, locked out, hated. I think of the transformation that can occur in both the viewer and that which is viewed. I think of our cat Mudita.

Chapter Nine:

Seeing and Not Seeing

In Lisel Mueller's poem, "Monet Refuses the Operation," Monet refuses the operation that will return him to world of edges, fixed lines, and separation, a "universe of objects that don't know each other." It has, as he says, taken him all his life "to arrive at the vision of gas lamps as angels" and to know that "the line I called the horizon does not exit." He will not return to the world of illusion from which he has finally freed himself.

These last six months I have gone to eye doctors complaining that the world is a blur. At night, the lights from oncoming cars are so bright I am blinded. I see only those pulsing haloes, do not know road from woods, feel insecure and vulnerable, lost and afraid. Coming home last night, I was on my familiar road, thinking I had almost made it, when I saw flashing lights, blues and greens and oranges, all spinning. It was the police and rescue squad, about ten cars lining the side of the road. I pulled over, felt helpless with no idea what was happening or where I was supposed to go. And that was with my contact lens, with the corrected vision. As for my close vision, I can no longer hold a book far enough to make the small lines form into intelligible letters. A large round magnifying glass sits on the table next to the phone book. Numbers are particularly confusing. The combination of bad memory and poor eyesight means that I often dial wrong numbers. The other day, I couldn't read the directions for my contact lens solution, or find the aisle I wanted in the grocery store, or read the street names unless I slowed the car down to an almost halt. The good news is that I move more slowly, am less arrogant and more humble, feel the compassion that comes from walking in someone else's shoes. But still if a doctor offered me clear eyesight, I probably would take it. I love to see clearly, to know where I am and where I am going.

And perhaps that is the problem, a variation on the issue raised in the preceding chapter. I tell my students that the "obstacle is the path" and that seeming obstacles often show us a more meaningful "way." I talk about "marvelous errors" and "uninvited guest," but still I want to see clearly. What I am now allowing in is that, perhaps, too clear vision can be a kind of blindness.

I've had inklings of this throughout my life, realizing that it is not just what is criticized in us that can harm but, also, what is affirmed. The ego has a way of latching onto praise and locking us into those traits which are affirmed by others. I remember looking at old photos of my sister and me, realizing how, at a very young age, she, the beautiful sister, began to pose for photographs, identifying with her looks and invested in the need for others to find her attractive. Now that she is getting older, she feels the fear that comes when we begin to lose those traits with which our ego identifies. Who would we be if we lost that which we ourselves and others affirm as essential to who we are, as the best of who we are?

This losing our concept of self is, perhaps, like getting lost: the first and necessary stage for finding our way by ourselves and to ourselves. But, still, it wasn't easy, there on that familiar road, to have no idea where I was going or how I would ever get home. I know I'm mixing metaphors—and that there is a vast difference between metaphor and literal reality—but I am trying to understand something about investment in certain seeming "strengths" and how that investment and identification imprison us. I'm the dog again, circling around, sniffing my way.

As a child and, now, as an adult, I have been invested in my ability to see and to think clearly, to make sharp distinctions between this and that, to follow arguments closely and logically, to see contradictions and inconsistencies. A very good trait, but also one that can make for a hardness of heart. The clear seeing like a knife that cuts through, but what if someone wants to spread butter rather than cut through, to use a knife to carve imaginative forms, to whittle into a different shape, to use as a palette knife to scoop out paint and mix colors?

All through my life I have had dreams which have told me that if I wanted to see more deeply I would have to see less clearly, to let go of my clear lines and distinctions, to not be so "hard lined." When I teach I can see the danger in student's writing of being "so clear" in their knowing that nothing new can enter the picture. The writing becomes dull, predictable. But when some strange figure enters, arousing unexpected feelings and honest questions, the writing becomes dynamic, the static world view now alive with unknown possibility. I ask students to think about what they have not said, who they have left out, and what it would mean to include the excluded. I ask them to bring in ideas and feelings that seem contradictory—to realize that you can both love and hate something or someone, can find something destructive and still grow from it—that most things are complex and partake of many colors.

I find that students—and, of course, everything I say about students also refers to regular people and, always, to me myself, how else would I know—often eliminate those very questions and ideas which would deepen their thought and their writing. They don't want to contradict their "thesis," want everything to be simple, do not want to blur any of the lines that have formed their clear concepts. They don't want the "creative chaos"; they want to be safe. If they do allow in other ideas, they often feel compelled to neutralize any strong statements, letting one idea moderate the other so that they (and the reader) never feel the dynamic dialogue and struggle between ideas. How to allow the real godwrestling, the process of coming to understanding, of stretching beyond the known and the clear so that we can comprehend larger and larger truths?

At some point in my life I became aware that I would feel slightly depressed if I were not able to "comprehend" something, if something were much larger than my ability to understand, my mind too small to put my actual and felt experience into intelligible form. In the next chapter I will talk about the violence—to others and to self—that comes when we have no way of giving form or voice to our vision. But here it is enough to say that I needed to find ways to be larger rather than to try to shrink my experience into a known form, to not only allow that "blurred" vision but to give praise and thanks for those haloes of light and my inability to distinguish sky and water, for that knowing that the room was too small and I needed to wander, seemingly lost, under a larger sky.

Yet even as I am writing, I feel the contradictions. I do still want clear thought and clear seeing. How could I not, in this world filled with prejudice, denial, assumptions, irrationality? The first exercise in English Composition, "Description," which I talk about in a later chapter, is geared to train students to look closely at details, to actually see the world outside of them—those lines, that color, the texture and contour—rather than unconsciously project their own ideas and concepts. I am terrified of the passion and destructiveness of prejudice—the unseeing, the false generalizations, the unclear thought. With the skill of analysis, I demand that students support their points, develop their ideas clearly, question. I am ruthless with fuzzy thinking and too quick generalizations. I want those clear lines. But I also know the confinement of those lines both for them and for myself, the too quick clarity often stopping a larger understanding and deeper questioning, often excluding the very real memories and experiences and ideas which seem to contradict. As a teacher, I want those contradictions included, want the struggle that leads us to a more comprehensive understanding. After the close observation and research, the reflection and the clear thought, I want the leaps of imagination of the artist and of the scientist, the understanding of the heart, the seeing towards which my dreams directed me. I understand Monet's not wanting to give up the vision it has taken him his whole life to see.

Tomorrow I go to the eye doctor again. My gas permeable hard lenses no longer allow me to see clearly, especially in the right eye where the astigmatism has made me unable to really focus. I look up astigmatism in the dictionary, using my handy magnifying glass: "A defect of an optical system in consequence of which rays from a point fail to meet in a focal point resulting in blurred and imperfect image." Exactly, exactly my condition. Or "distortive understanding suggestive of the blurred vision of an astigmatic person." And the definition of astigmatic: "Showing incapacity for observation or discrimination." And yet, and yet, Monet's vision was real, not distorted, not blurred.

My eye doctor recommends soft lenses to correct the astigmatism, but the right eye still cannot focus, the soft lens for some mysterious reason not shifting into its proper place, remaining 30% off the center of the eye. My left eye has been "corrected" so strongly with the soft lens that I can see sharply in the distance but see nothing close up. Playing the piano with sheet music, computer work, and reading are all blurred with the "corrective" lens. This business of seeing is, clearly, tricky. I am told that glasses might help. I have not worn glasses for thirty years, never liked how they felt on my nose, fogging in the cold, standing as an "obstacle" between me and the world. I know I don't want bifocals, don't want a clear and definite line between what is far and near; there are too many worlds in between.

I remember my first oil painting class. The teacher told us that we could not use store bought black paint; rather, we had to create the color black from mixing different complimentary colors. I remember how hard and frustrating it was to get the mixed colors to be deep black and my frustrated question, "why not just use 'black'"? But she knew and I learned that if we could create the black from ultramarine blue and burnt sienna, we would then begin to really see color, the range and subtle variation; we would have control, choice and power. Instead of black being flat and empty we would see it as vibrant with color and see our world with the same pulsing energy.

Instead of bifocals I have ordered the progressive lens which, hopefully, will allow me to see at different distances when I look through different parts of the lens. The eye doctor—and others—have said that it might take a while to get used to, that people are often dizzy at first. Something about the peripheral vision being distorted, something about looking through the wrong section of the glass. But I think of my dreams and the danger of seeing too clearly, think of the whirling dervishes and of getting lost, think that dizzy might be disorienting, might turn my world upside down, might make me feel the ground move under me, might be, in fact, a more accurate seeing of how this spinning world really is. I think about how we all need to keep different levels of vision at the same time, knowing that each level has its own truth, not letting the "doctor" correct our sight in ways that limit our deeper seeing.

CHAPTER TEN:

WHAT TO DO WITH ALL THIS ENERGY: EXPLOSION AND IMPLOSION

I had always seen myself as a shy and quiet introvert. My mother said that I barely talked for my first four years. I remember scarcely speaking for my first twenty. Yet if people met me now—or if I were to ask my students or my friends to describe me—they would see me as an enthusiast, as someone very much in the world. While still an introvert in the sense of loving quiet space, solitude, and inner reflection, I am also, clearly, an extrovert loving the energy of exchange with others and with the external world, loving the world of form and of the senses. It's been interesting to think of this seeming transformation and to question who is the "real me" and whether this "shift" is really a transformation of self or recognition of the self that always was.

I first realized the extent of the "transformation" when friends gave me an ennea-gram questionnaire. I usually approach a personality test with both skepticism and interest: skepticism because any classification always seems too simplified, without the complex shadings which register the multidimensional truths, like those bifocal glasses, like black and white vision; interesting because I like that focus of attention, whether astrological chart, Jungian personality type, handwriting analysis, palm line reading—that "tell me about me" excitement. So, I began to answer the 140 questions, each question asking me to choose between two alternatives, each of which seemed totally wrong, all the time proclaiming aloud the absurdity and impossibility of each choice I was offered, disliking this person whom, it seems, I was declaring I was with each check mark. What was amazing to me was the result—what happened when I read the thirty pages describing my particular personality. I was the enthusiast.

It's a long story, but the short version is that almost everything that was said about the enthusiast felt accurate to the way I perceive my world. What was strange to me was how deeply moved I was to be seen in terms of how I approach nature, people, politics, and spirituality, to have my energy named and described so accurately, and to realize that, for my first twenty years of life, that self that I was could not be welcomed into the earth that was my home. No wonder I did not speak, that I was so shy and introverted. Where could that enthusiast's energy go within that constricted home except deep inside the self?

Looking back, I see that decision was right—a clear perception of the environment in which my seed fell and how it/I could survive. As an almost silent introvert, I gained a detachment, an ability to reflect, a love of solitude, all clearly a part of who I was, of who I am, all clearly "good." But what I can also feel, now looking back, is the grief that comes with recognition of any loss, that sense of a certain potential of creativity and joy which might have been had these traits within me been welcomed and nurtured. What the enneagram enabled me to do—in a way that totally surprised me by its emotional depth—was to experience both the grief of loss and, at the same time, the joy of owning this other self which had been disowned, of welcoming myself home.

That self wasn't totally unfamiliar; I had come in contact with her on a few other homecomings. About twenty years before, some friends asked me if I would speak on a panel in a National Women's Studies Association conference on the connection between economic class and ethnicity. I was to speak about growing up Jewish in a lower middle class neighborhood, a neighborhood mainly of immigrants, uneducated beyond elementary school, speaking Yiddish, working in factories or having small businesses like my father's fruit and vegetable stand. It was interesting for me to think about it all and to try to come to some understanding of both my own personal psychology and, perhaps, something larger. I loved the writing, the energy of making connections. What I didn't feel confident about, however, was if anything I had written would mean anything to anyone else.

I still remember sitting in our tiny shack reading—with fear and deep insecurity—my speech to my partner and friend, reading very quickly and very quietly. My good friends listened so intently they could actually hear, and when I looked up, they were both crying. Their soft eyes of love and their welcoming of my words enabled me to actually think that perhaps what I had written might be of value.

I had never gone to a NWSA Conference. This one, at Spellman College, was focused on issues of class. I remember feeling the excitement of all the workshops, the energy of ideas, and the diversity of people. And then I remember the shock when I realized that I was one of the Plenary speakers, not a workshop leader, and that the Plenary was held in a huge auditorium and attended by everyone, thousands of people. I had never used a microphone, never spoken before more than twenty people.

There were to be seven speakers of different ethnicities. It turned out that all the speakers came from very poor backgrounds and were, clearly, much more "deprived"; I could feel my own guilt at not being poor enough, at being an imposter within this group. As each began to speak, I felt more and more incapable of giving voice to my own experience. Everything in me would have loved to have left that stage, to escape. In fact, if I were offered the option, I would have disappeared. Except I couldn't—and I could see my friends in the audience, waiting to hear my words.

When it was my turn, I read as quickly as I could and never looked up, quickness as a familiar way of not taking up space, of singing softly, of being close to invisible and almost inaudible, of not being heard. Except that in this case, I was heard. What I remember when I finally finished was long and loud applause and, later, many people coming up to tell me how moved they were by what I had said, how much they had identified with different points, and how my words had helped their understanding. And I remember the weeping, for days after the speech, that comes when a deep unknown wound has suddenly been both uncovered and healed: I had been heard and understood; people had actually welcomed my words.

When I came back to the Adirondacks, I remember pulling up to our shack and seeing a blue star from a box of Jean's potato chips nailed to the door and the words under it: "Our star is home." The wound was not only healed, but something now began sprouting actual joy. It was the beginning of the ability of this shy introvert to be present in the world, to allow her light to shine, to be a star.

Many years before, in Hunter College, I had taken a modern dance class in an attempt to free my body from some of its self-conscious inhibition, to be in my body rather than view my body through the judging eyes of others. I remember the teacher going to the center of the room, standing tall (although he was very short) and full bodied, moving his arms in a gesture that opened to and embraced the world, saying that in order to dance, one needed to be able to say "I am here," to take up one's space on the dance floor, to be present in one's body on this earth. I knew he was right, and I knew I couldn't do it. But that Plenary was the beginning of the trip back to the one whom, I realized later, I always was, the beginning of that journey from the shy introvert hiding her light to one who was more and more able to let it shine and who, in fact, began to love to be "a star." The enthusiast.

This is all apropos of what it means to have a way of expressing what is deep and fundamental within us, and what happens when those ways are stifled and blocked.

A week ago I was staying in a small, cheap hotel in Southern Maine, spending a few days by the ocean. One night I heard a lot of yelling from the room next door. The next morning, I heard the man cursing his children and his wife, every other word a "Fuck" or "fucken." When he finally slammed the door and left in his car, I felt a relief. But a few minutes later, the cursing began again, this time it was his two sons screaming at each other. They had learned their father's language, or, rather, lack of language.

I thought of Eva Hoffman's memoir, *Lost in Translation*. There is a section in her book where she writes about the street curses she hears under her window each night:

> *In my New York apartment, I listen almost nightly to fights that erupt like brushfire on the street below—and in their escalating fury of repetitious phrases ("Don't do this to me, man, you fucking bastard. I'll fucking kill you"), I hear not the pleasures of macho toughness but an infuriated beating against wordlessness, against the incapacity to make oneself understood, seen. Anger can be force—it can even be satisfying—if it can gather into words and explode in a storm, or a rapier-sharp attack. But without this means of ventilation, it only turns back inward, building and swirling like a head of stead—building to an impotent, murderous rage. If all therapy is speaking therapy—a talking cure—then perhaps all neurosis is a speech dis-ease.*

What I heard that night was that impotent murderous rage. That is what I hear a lot—in its many different forms—in our society and in our world. That is what our society is always trying to "analyze" in order to understand: why did this violence take place in a school in Columbine, Colorado, in a work place in Hawaii, in a small post office in the Midwest, on the highway between Washington D.C. and Baltimore, in the Middle East, in New York City, in the Sudan, and all over the world. For me, one answer has to do with "language," but language in a very broad sense, not as literal words but, rather, as vehicles for expression of self and for communication with others. We all, I believe, need a vehicle, a way of making manifest the energy within. If we have no form to express our life energy, then, it seems to me, we must destroy, either our-selves or others. The impotence of rage, and, also, the potency.

In his *Escape from Freedom*, published immediately after World War II, Erich Fromm, a social psychologist, explored the roots of violence in a way that still seems very helpful, simple, and revolutionary, whether analyzing the fascist violence of Nazi Germany or individual acts of violence to self or others:

> *It would seem that the amount of destructiveness to be found in individuals is proportionate to the amount to which expansiveness of life is curtailed. By this we do not refer to individual frustrations of this or that instinctive desire but to the thwarting of the whole of life, the blockage of spontaneity, of the growth and expression of man's sensuous, emotional, and intellectual capacities. Life has an inner dynamism of its own; it tends to grow, to be expressed, to be lived. It seems that if this tendency is thwarted the energy directed toward life undergoes a process of decomposition and change into energies directed toward destruction. In other words: the drive for life and the drive for destruction are not mutually independent factors but are in reversed interdependence. The more the drive toward life is thwarted, the more is the strength of destructiveness. Destructiveness is the outcome of unlived life. Those individual and social conditions that make for suppression of life produce the passion for destruction that forms, so to speak, the reservoir from which the particular hostile tendencies—either against others or against oneself—are nourished.*

I find Fromm's analysis very meaningful. Two images come to mind. The first, from my childhood, is an image of animals in a zoo: the powerful lions and tigers confined to tiny cages, walking back and forth in small, obsessive, angry circles or sitting passively, staring out vacantly; and the monkeys and chimps throwing feces through the bars at people watching them as they circle their cage. I lived only a few blocks from the Bronx Zoo. It was a time of cages and confined areas, before the zoological society was able to create larger environments for more "freedom." Many years later I saw a program analyzing the behavior described above in chimps, orangutans, and gorillas. What they, the experts, "discovered" was what I could feel in my own child's body watching those animals and remembering my own child's experience of confinement: the animals needed more space, were too confined, were bored, frustrated and angry.

What the "experts" realized was that the great apes had a curiosity, an intelligence, an emotional life. They needed not only space to move but also objects within that space to engage their minds and bodies, to allow them to explore, to figure out puzzles, to play, to create, to interrelate. The experts also came to that same realization when they analyzed depression and senility in older people: if people are not involved in activities that engage their minds and bodies, they lose those abilities, become sick and depressed, the imploded "expression" of impotent rage when we have no way to live our lives.

And the second image, connected to the first and, also, to the men within the caged prisons where I have taught, must have come from some television program I saw as a child and which haunted me for years after. It showed a "crazy person" using his feces to scribble unintelligible lines on a wall of a locked room. What I remember feeling was not a horror at the strange behavior, which I think the program was implying, as much as the desperate pain and struggle of someone trying to give form to his or her feelings with whatever limited tools were available. In a much smaller way, I must have identified with and known that pain.

Now, as an adult, I can articulate the questions that I felt as a child looking at that image: What was the person trying to say and why wasn't anyone listening? Why didn't someone give him something, some tool, a pen or paint or typewriter or clay or wood or drum, to help him express what he felt? There was only a dirty mattress in the room. The person was using the only means available to him or her, the only writing implement. Why were we blaming rather than giving the person what he or she needed? Why weren't those in authority listening more intently to what the person was trying so desperately to say in the only language he/she was able to speak? Why didn't we help them develop their language so that they could give voice to their experience and be heard?

Of course this is all relevant to the prison and to our world. In Great Meadows Correctional Institution, the cells were smaller than the cages in a zoo, the men often making the connection between their situation and that of the animals. In his poem "It Started," Jimmy Santiago Baca captures the cage, the movement behind bars, and the deep joy and power of coming into language.

> A little state-funded barrack
> in the desert, in a prison. A poetry workshop,
> an epicenter of originality, companionship,
> pain and openness,
> > For some,
> the first time in their life writing,
> for others the first time saying openly what they felt,
> the first time finding something in themselves,
> worthwhile, ugly and beautiful.
> > I think of you, and me. Last night I was
> thinking of you. I am your friend. I don't want you
> to think otherwise.
> > I was thinking, when we first wrote to each other.
> > I remember instances, of tremendous joy
> > when receiving your letters,
> > what cells I was in,
> > what emotional state, under
> > what circumstances.
> > Your letters always fell like meteorites
> > into my lap.
> > You were my first friendship
> > engendered in this state, perhaps,
> > all my past life.
> I showed you my first poem ever written,
> > "They Only came To See the Zoo"
> > But you didn't treat me like a wild ape,
> > or an elephant. You treated me like Jimmy.
>
> A mass of molten fury in this furnace of steel,
> > and yet, my thoughts became ladles, sifting carefully
> through my life, the pain and endurance,
> to the essence of my being,

> *I gently, into the long night, unmolding*
> *my shielded heart, the fierce figures*
> *of war and loss, I remolding them,*
> *my despair and anger into a cry and song,*
> *I took the path alone, nuded myself to my own caged animals,*
> *and learned their tongues and their spirits,*
> *and roamed the desert, went to my place of birth ...*
> > *Now tonight, I am a burning bush,*
> > *my bones a grill of fire,*
> > *I burn these words in praise,*
> > *of our meeting, our friendship.*

Our zoos are getting better because of a more enlightened attitude; we are learning that if we are going to take animals from their habitat and imprison them, we can at least try to provide a terrain that is somewhat familiar and meets some of their needs for companionship and contact, for exercise of body, mind, and spirit; that is, if we don't want passive, sick, unhealthy, depressed, or violent animals. In terms of incarcerated human beings, however, the prevailing attitude is that prisoners must suffer for their crime and that any program which allows them to feel the fullness of their own humanity and the possibility for their own lives is "soft on crime." It is the view that someone must be broken and dispirited in order to be saved. Clearly the effect we see follows from that point of view. What I knew as a child, I can now see even more clearly as an adult. We don't need experts to tell us what we can observe from our own experience.

My friend is an occupational therapist. The other day she was telling me that OT's are less in demand than physical therapists, the insurance companies more willing to pay for the medical model of the PT, for physical manipulation rather than the OT's less obvious work. She described her work as trying to see individuals within their environment: to see their specific abilities and to figure out how, given those abilities, one could create an environment enabling them to live their life most fully, with most independence.

It's the story of the acorn and where it lands again, of what is within us and how that can be nurtured. I think of all the institutions in our society and how that OT model could/should be used: zoos and mental hospitals, prisons and schools, factories and communities, homes and neighborhoods. The question is whether specific institutions enable people to feel their depth and fullness, their potential for growth and goodness, or whether they make people more passive, more dependent, easier to handle and to control. In old age homes an ambulatory person requires more labor than someone who cannot move. An object is easier to control than a free, engaged, independent, curious animal, child, old person, disabled person, student.

Whether in hospitals, schools, or in the larger society, the choice, again, of life or death, of keeping only the body alive or of nurturing that uncontrollable, unknowable and alive spirit.

What is so painful is to see how so many institutions, whether out of greed for profit, ignorance or fear, continually close potential doors and windows, giving people no way out, no vehicle for expression of self and, then, blaming those people for being tongue tied, inarticulate, stupid, for being angry and throwing their shit all over the place, for being evil. We call in experts to analyze the seemingly strange and bizarre behavior and build prisons to control what is wild and uncontrollable, both outside of us and within. I think of the truth of Barbara Demmings' powerful and simple quote: "We cannot live without our lives."

In his *Seeing Voices*, Dr. Oliver Sacks writes about deaf culture and deaf language. What struck me reading the book was how some "good people" (and I could have been one of them), wanting the deaf to fit into the major culture, forbid their speaking sign language, insisted they "speak" and lip read. The movement of "oralism" came, I think, from an impulse similar to R's mother acting as if R were not blind—from a kindness that wants another to fit in, to not feel the pain of being different, to feel "normal." But it is an inclusion based on the denial of who a person is. It is saying, you can be "part of us" but only if you are like us.

Sacks describes the energy and joy of people "speaking" sign. Even when forbidden, children would hide in the bathroom signing, risking punishment. I think of all the immigrants who are told not to speak in their own language or who are mocked for their accent, of Native Americans locked into boarding schools, forbidden to speak in their own tongue, harnessed into a strange and uncomfortable dress and culture, separated from their ancient and deep knowing. I think about the silence that comes when our language is mocked or forbidden, when we forget we even had a language, when we try to speak another and unfamiliar tongue and are then judged for being inarticulate, for stumbling over our own words, for not being cultured and civilized. The depression and despair, the rage and violence, the loss of so much vitality and the sterility when, finally, everyone speaks the same one language. And I think about what happens when we are finally "allowed" to speak in our own voice or when we finally rebel, feeling the power of our own voice singing in the dark woods.

Sacks talks about how deaf children born to deaf parents learn "language" and all subjects as easily as hearing children. But they can become bilingual only if they are first allowed to speak their natural tongue. And what is true for them is true for all of us: If what is natural is forbidden, if we must speak someone else's language first, we fall behind in school, do less well in all subjects, are seen as less intelligent, become less intelligent, never find our own voice. But if we can speak our "native tongue," get fluent in its sounds and gestures, then we can learn other tongues easily because we know the essence of language. And because we can speak our own language (language, again, in its broadest definition), we can hear others speak their language without feeling threatened, without feeling the need to make them speak like us in order to understand what they are saying.

Even as a hearing person, I could feel the aliveness of the gestures and expressions of people signing, loved what the signer added to a conference or a concert: a body that showed affect, showed enthusiasm. It felt like my language, the language of the enthusiast, but also the language of my own Jewish culture—the hand waving, strong and expressive gestures. Immigrant language, working class language, "uneducated" language. The "mother tongue," the language we hear as children, the language of our mothers sitting around the kitchen table, the poetic and rhythmic speech of Barbadian immigrants about whom Paule Marshall writes in essays and captures in her novels. The language that we are taught to restrict in order to be more civilized, more intellectual, more rational and more objective.

How, I wonder, did civilization become equated with suppression of and separation from the body?

In that same NWSA conference I went to a reading by Irena Klepfisz and Shay Youngblood. Irena's words were laced in Yiddish, deep in the Jewish culture and life of Poland and the immigrant and political culture of America. Shay Youngblood's *Big Mama Stories* were rich in Southern Black dialect and culture. The room was alive with the energy of different languages speaking their own knowing. Because each writer spoke so articulately and because we listened so intently, we, in the audience, understood everything, stories both familiar and unknown.

What became so clear that day was that we do not connect to others through the denial, suppression, or obscuring of our own distinct worlds but, rather, by going more deeply into them, tapping into the underground source that nourishes us all. What I felt in that NWSA room that day was the joy that comes from being able to put one's experience into words and to have those words speak to others. It was very different from what I heard and felt in that hotel room next to mine, the angry man cursing his wife and sons, the verbal assault feeling almost physical, hovering and threatening. The man was, it seems to me now, like the lion entrapped in the cage, entrapped in a pattern of behavior. He had no words to express, no space to reflect, no way to bring into awareness what was happening. His only "tool" was violence and, powerless as he felt, he was using it to hurt and destroy others, those less powerful than he.

I think of an essay I read a long time ago in which someone defined violence as "resourcelessness." The word is underlined on my computer, meaning that this word is not in the dictionary. Except I know exactly what it means: Resourceless because there are no resources within us and no resources outside of us. I look up the word "resource": "A source of supply or support, an available means, a natural source of wealth or revenue, a source of information or expertise, something in which one has recourse in difficulty, a possibility of relief or recovery, an ability to meet and handle a situation: resourcefulness."

Education, meditation, awareness are resources; they can give us that resourcefulness, can get us in touch with the natural sources within us. Sisyphus can be free even if condemned to continually take the huge stone up the mountain. A monk can be free in a cloister, a Yogi in a cave, and people within steel and concrete prisons. I know that is true.

There were prisoners who knew that internal freedom much more deeply than I. Part of why I taught in the prison was to learn from them their "practice" and their wisdom. But what is also clear to me is that there is an external world in which we all live, offering or denying us resources. To see each individual as the sole creator of his/her reality—to give a person that total responsibility and power—is to blind ourselves to political, social, environmental realities. It is to separate the individual from his/her world and to absolve ourselves from our responsibility to create a more just world, to create societal change by working to remove some of the external bars that limit the freedom and potential of so many people.

If we have very limited or no resources, if the door continually slams shut and there are no windows, if there is "no way out," then most of us, not just prisoners, will be in the revolving door of "recidivism." There might be a few extraordinary and enlightened individuals, but for most it's just too hard, too discouraging, no matter how strong we are, how aware. Most of us will feel the violence and despair of resourcelessness and will need to feel some power through destruction of self or other. Many of us will be, in different parts of our life, like the man cursing in the room next to me, hurting others, hurting self. I think of Langston Hughes' question: "What happens to a dream deferred?" in his "Harlem":

Does it dry up
like a raisin in the sun?
Or fester like a sore—
And then run?
does it stink like rotten meat?
Or crust and sugar over—
like a syrupy sweet?

Maybe it just sags
like a heavy load.

Or does it explode?

Clear, simple. Of course. No experts needed.

I think of how good it feels when I can express in words and actions what is in my heart and mind, how good it feels to do good work in the world, to feel the effects of my own action, to grow larger through struggle and effort. And I know how bad it feels when I am unable to bring anything into any form, when all my "gifts" lay blocked within me.

I teach believing that we all love to touch our own depth, that people are not only willing but actually like to struggle with what is difficult, to feel the sweat of good labor, to learn, to have their work come into fruition. Look at children learning to tie a shoelace, to dry dishes, to bake cookies, to dribble a basketball, to walk, to dance, to talk. Look at our own lives: the joy that comes when we feel our own power of mind, body, spirit. When people feel good about their lives, when they feel like they are doing good work and growing in heart, mind, and body, when they feel alive, they do not destroy others or themselves. It's as simple as that. The question, again, is how we, as individuals and as a society, either enable or disable ourselves and others.

Chapter Eleven:

More on violence and language. Or how, when everything is connected, there is no one beginning but only a circle turning

How can I not include these new thoughts that occur with each book I read, each jog, each discussion? Everything gets large. And always the question: Am I stretching something too far, tearing a fabric, or deepening and enriching it with color and pattern. It is a question for every writer, for every teacher reading a student's writing, for anyone wanting to communicate with another as well as follow the tendrils of her or his own mind. I have erred in each direction—stopping too soon, expanding too far.

But it is always so interesting—whether I am writing a speech, thinking about a question, reading a book—how everything does seem totally connected to everything else, new countries suddenly appearing on old maps, new stars in the winter sky. It's good—because with my memory and vision loss the old countries have disappeared and the familiar sky gets clouded over. I need the new material. But it is also hard, this evolving process and forever growing body. I keep having new beginnings to this book and, if I ever get to the end, I will probably have multiple endings, a continual "this too, and this...."

There are, however, resting places. The dog in me usually knows when it has circled around enough and needs to sleep in the center of the created space. But not yet, I say, feeling that energy and excitement of still to be discovered connections. I still have pieces of a puzzle spread before me, feeling intuitively that they are part of the same picture, that they belong here, at the end of this section, before I enter the classroom itself. I place one piece next to another to see if an image emerges, an image not quite created through my own hands but still something akin to that creative process. I am trying now to see why Abram's *Spell of the Sensuous*, Fouts' *Next of Kin*, Ursula LeGuin's speech on the mother tongue, Monty Roberts' *The Man Who Listened to Horses*, and Fromm's discussion on violence in his *Escape from Freedom* all feel part of this particular web of language and listening, violence and love, entrapment and freedom.

Let me start with a speech I heard this morning on Public Radio. It was by a doctor. In the beginning, I could feel his openness to both body and spirit. I loved when he talked about the trillions of cells being created every minute, the strands of DNA woven throughout our body, the trillions of dendrites not quite touching, the gap essential to the communication, the space necessary for energy to be sparked. I thought of poetry and the space of borders in Moslem tiles. I was interested when he talked of Chaos, how Eros converted chaos into cosmos. But having talked about the creation out of chaos, he then seemed to stop, pleased that he finally arrived at a fixed and certain place. He went on distinguishing "man" from animals, good from bad, monotheism from other religions. I could feel his love of order, his need to dichotomize, to judge and put into hierarchies, to draw boundaries. I could feel the fixedness of his created cosmos, his certainty restricting his ability to allow in other possibilities. Chaos became the enemy, no longer part of the continual dance of creation-preservation-destruction, the Hindu dance of Brahman-Vishnu-Shiva. I thought of Fritjof Capra and his "web of connections," of systems theory, chaos theory, the uncertainty principle; thought of our human grasping for certainty and how survival of our planet demands a living with complexity and mystery. And I thought of the book I was now reading, *Next of Kin*, by Roger Fouts, about the very clear connection between humans and chimpanzees and the question why we humans keep disconnecting ourselves from other forms, constructing hierarchies and binary opposition, seeing ourselves as separate and higher— whether it is humans superior to other animals, men superior to women, whites superior to people of color—and how that "seeing" prevents our connection to the actual world around us and within us.

In his *Spell of the Sensuous*, David Abram talks about our separation from the natural world as a very recent phenomenon in terms of human history. According to Abram, what now seems "supernatural" to many Westerners and "civilized people" is the not yet lost ability of many indigenous people to communicate with plants, herbs, flowers, trees, animals, mountains, to listen and hear. It's interesting and painful that not only have we lost our ability to hear, but we label those whose senses are still precisely attuned "crazy" and "primitive." It is an ironic reversal of Plato's shadows on the wall of the cave. Those of us in the cave not only do not believe those who have maintained their sensory awareness but pull them into our darkness, calling it the light of civilization and naming their deep knowing "ignorance."

In the academy this process of disconnection and amputation is often amplified. The voice of experience, the subjective I, the knowledge of the body and the senses, are seen as obstacles to objectivity and higher thought. We are asked to dismiss their messages in order to be impartial and scientific. It's the same old story: The objectivity of the scientist in a lab conducting animal experiments is called objective while the empathy of any scientist who feels the pain of "the other" is mocked as unscientific and subjective.

What strikes me in all its different manifestations is that those in power consciously and unconsciously continually assume that their language, their way of seeing and knowing, is the best way, the only way: this is how a snowman looks; this is what spring is like; this is thinking; this is the canon of good literature; this is the only God and the only religion. We insist that the "other" speak our language and then judge them for their imperfect accents. In North Africa, I met Arabs able to speak four or five languages fluently: Arabic, Berber, French, German, Italian . And I met French people, able to speak only French, who felt superior in their ability to speak eloquently in their own native tongue. I think of power, privilege, arrogance and ignorance, of who expects and assumes that another speak in and translate into his/her tongue.

In his *The Man Who Talked to Horses*, Monty Roberts talks about rounding up "wild horses" when he was thirteen or fourteen. He observes a young male horse being rambunctious and disruptive and how an older mare communicates to him that he must leave the connected circle. Roberts watches closely the subtle signs between the cast out teenager and the ruling mare, how the former eventually shows submission and how the mare indicates that he can now return within the circle. Curious and respectful, Roberts continues to closely observe, slowly and patiently learning the language of Equus and communicating to the horses in their tongue.

At one point Roberts tries to show his father how, through subtle and caring communication, he can more quickly and more thoroughly train horses. His father, who has used the tools of fear and control and of dominance and submission to break the will and spirit of both his horses and his children, not only is not pleased with his son's discovery but enraged. Despite the "proof" that is demonstrated in front of his eyes, Roberts' father insists that his old system of training is right. The sense that there might be another way is too threatening to his belief system and to his world view. Not only can't he hear the language of Equus, but he cannot hear his son or, probably, his own vulnerable child's voice before it was whipped into submission.

I think how once violence is used to control, it must continually intensify its grip in order to hold its power. More concrete enclosures of mind and heart, more prisons to keep others in line, more weapons and bombs. We can see the process on every level, both within our own internal worlds and the worlds outside of us.

In his *Next of Kin*, Fouts captures this dynamic of escalating violence:

> *This was my first lesson in the futility of getting into a battle of wills with a chimpanzee. Dominance that is based on physical power will almost always backfire. Human power leads to chimpanzee anger and aggression, which then leads to more human fear and violence. It is a cycle that can only escalate out of control. Lemmon's Institute was ample proof of that. First it was chains and leads. Then cattle prods. Then pellet guns. Later Lemmon wanted us to carry loaded pistols, even with the juveniles. It was hard to tell who was more scared of whom: Lemmon of the chimps or the chimps of Lemmon. When relationship is not built on mutual respect, the only way of maintaining control is through brutal force. On the other hand, when there is a respectful relationship between human and chimp, there is no fear and coercion is needed only on rare occasion.*

And what is true between humans and chimps is also true between humans and humans. It is simple. We see this cause and effect continually in terms of our world. Again, we don't need to call in the experts with their charts and statistics; rather, we need to look to our own experience; we need to be awake.

What I want to do in this book—and in my life—is attune my senses: train my ears—and eyes, and heart, and body—to pay close attention to the language of other beings in all their different forms. To be respectful. To not demand others speak my language, to not assume I know, to not react in fear, to catch myself when I do react in fear, to use fear as a companion in my further travels. I want to be the open eyed child, the curious, open and respectful stranger. And I want to give students tools for paying attention, for catching themselves in the act of inattention, dismissal, judgment, in the act of blocking out what goes contrary to a belief system, a value, a prejudice, an opinion. I want them to hear the language of equus and chimp and child so that they cannot separate out, believing animals do not feel pain when they are subjected to torturous experiments and held in tiny confinements, or that darker children from other cultures, imprisoned in factories working for 37 cents an hour, six days a week, do not feel the deprivation of their confinement. I want students—and of course myself—to listen closely to others and, also, to the others within ourselves, our own different voices. To listen, with curiosity, empathy, and love, to our own words flowing from our own pens. The host welcoming all to her/his guest house, treating all with respect.

CHAPTER TWELVE:

THE INQUIRING MIND, THE BELIEVING HEART, AND THE VOICE OF CYNICISM

Can one have both a deeply inquiring mind and a strong belief in one's own experience? In this chapter, I want to think more about why both believing and questioning are so essential to me—to my teaching and my life. Perhaps it is because I see both inquiry and belief as having the same "enemy": the voice of cynicism. Perhaps it is because, as a child, I had to fight that enemy in order to be able "to be." Perhaps I am still fighting that enemy—in my students and in myself. Perhaps now may be the time to unravel—or is it weave—some of these very tangled strands into some kind of understanding, to place these seeming contradictions within a larger whole.

I begin my exploration with a poem by Rumi, the 12th century Sufi mystic, on the openness of faith, and part of an essay by Loren Eiseley, the twentieth century American evolutionist, paleontologist, and essayist, on our human need to make meaning.

Love Dogs

One night a man was crying,
       Allah! Allah!
His lips grew sweet with the praising,
until a cynic said,
       "So, I have heard you
calling out, but have you ever
gotten any response?"

The man had no answer to that.
He quit praying and fell into a confused sleep.

He dreamed he saw Khidr,
the guide of souls,
in a thick, green foliage,
       "Why did you stop praising?"
"Because I've never heard anything back."
       "This longing
you express is the return message."

The grief you cry out from
draws you toward union.
Your pure sadness
that wants help
is the secret cup..

Listen to the moan of a dog for its master.
That whining is the connection.

There are love dogs
no one knows the names of.

Give your life
to be one of them.

(trans. Coleman Barks)

In "The Golden Alphabet," an essay in his *The Unexpected Universe*, Eiseley tells the following story:

> *Some months ago, walking along the shore of a desolate island off the Gulf Coast, I caught a glimpse of a beautiful shell, imprinted with what appeared to be strange writing, rolling in the breakers. Impelled by curiosity, I leaped into the surf and salvaged it. Golden characters like Chinese hieroglyphs ran in symmetrical lines around the cone of the shell. I lifted it up with the utmost excitement, as though a message had come to me from the green depths of the sea.*
>
> *Later I unwrapped the shell before a dealer in antiquities in the back streets of a seaport town.*
>
> *"Conus spurius atlanticus," he diagnosed for me with brisk efficiency, "otherwise known as the alphabet shell."*
>
> *But why spurious? I questioned inwardly as I left the grubby little shop. The shell, I was sure, contained a message. We live by messages—all true scientists, all lovers of the arts, indeed all true people of any stamp. Some of these messages cannot be read, but we will always try. We hunger for messages and when we cease to seek and interpret them we will no longer be human beings.*
>
> *The little cone lies now upon my desk, and I handle it as reverently as I would the tablets of a lost civilization.*
>
> *Each person deciphers from the ancient alphabets of nature only those secrets that his/her own deeps possess the power to endow with meaning ... The golden alphabet, in whatever shape it chooses to reveal itself, is never spurious. From its inscrutable lettering is created human beings and all the streaming cloudland of their dreams.*

The voice of the cynic stops our prayers and praising. The judgment of the expert stops our joy in discovery, our intuitive knowing of meaning and value. As a teacher, what strikes me, again and again, is how often we deny our own immediate, deep, and strong experiences giving power to the cynic, the judge, the expert. Eiseley, in another essay, talks about a deeply moving experience with birds, saying: "I knew I had seen a marvel, but the mind which was my human endowment was sure to question it and to be at me day by day with its heresies until I grew to doubt the meaning of what I had seen." The questioning and the doubt which undercut what we know through experience. As a teacher, an "expert," I myself have probably participated in that process, both consciously and unconsciously questioning a student's precious discovery. Yet still I feel and affirm the necessity of questioning as a most important tool for discovery and growth, for consciousness and freedom. What then to do with this seeming contradiction?

My car is filled with bumper stickers. I used to have a large "Question Authority." Pulling into the parking lot of Great Meadows Prison, however, the words seemed strangely inappropriate. Questioning authority, if one were inside those walls, could result in further imprisonment, solitary confinement, death. I changed the sticker to a seemingly more moderate but perhaps more inclusive "Question Assumptions." That felt essential—to question all assumptions in order to see what was true. Last winter, the "Assumptions" fell off and only "Question" remains. And thus it stays—question.

As a teacher, I feel the fundamental importance of questioning everything— standing apart, looking closely, examining and exploring rather than accepting the concepts, words, beliefs of others, or, even, of ourselves. I think how much of my teaching is consciously and unconsciously geared to train students to stop and question, to hold at bay the quick and easy claws of judgment and opinion, to look before they pounce. I see how, if our opinions enter the picture too soon, we are unable to really hear what an author or friend or enemy or child or animal or tree or painting is saying to us. The world becomes a mirror reflecting our own opinions, judgments, images, ideas—without windows and doors. Questioning lets in the fresh air. It has, for me, a wonderful energy. It is very much the quality of a child's curiosity, the sense of wonder, the explorer and adventurer moving into what is new with openness and excitement, the why, why, why.

I think about what happens to that fearless and eager questioning so connected to exploration and wonder. What makes the open door begin to feel like a closed, locked room with signs of danger and "do not enter"?

Some part of the change is perspective, the wisdom that comes from experience. As a small child, Richard Wright in *Black Boy* is intensely curious about the world. Some of that curiosity makes him take a match and light a fire, burning a curtain and his home. He is punished severely. We learn from experience; we gain perspective. And clearly the adult has what the child does not have: an ability to see cause and effect, to make connections. But what I am talking about is the silencing of the open questioning of the child, the killing of that curiosity pulsing with life energy.

Sometimes we silence the child because his/her questions—and, later, our adult questions—are too complex, too painful to think about and/or to answer. Growing up in Mississippi in the early twentieth century, Wright is continually trying to work out the illogic of black and white relationships in the Jim Crow South. His family's violent response to his questioning is an indication of their extraordinary fear, both conscious and unconscious, within a system of absolute power where questioning could result in death. And questions about death or pain, sadness or love, sexuality or violence are always difficult. Instead of an answer, the child is often met with silence or dismissal or a slap, or, more frequently, the busyness that has no time to respond and doesn't want to be bothered. The clear lesson we all receive is that we must stop asking questions or, at least, certain kinds of questions.

As children we begin to hear—and as adults begin to ask—questions very different from our open why, questions that are really judgments: Why did you pick up that dirty shell? Why are you staring into space? Why did you say that or do that or feel that? And who do you think you are anyway to question, feel, think, say, act …? So we learn to silence our questions because of "their" questions.

Schools, unfortunately, often continue and amplify the process. Questions come in the form of tests with right and wrong answers. We fail if we don't get the "right" answers, so we give them the answers we think "they" want. We lose touch with our own experience, our own knowing, our own ability to think and reason. Questions become weapons creating fear, and fear causes constriction, the opposite of openness and exploration. The door closes on the inquiring mind. And observing the effects of the closed minds, the "experts" try to "correct the problem" by administering more tests at lower grade levels to judge whether students are learning what we want them to know.

In his poem "Persimmons," Li Young Lee juxtaposes the lessons learned in school with the knowing felt deep within the body:

> *In sixth grade Mrs. Walker*
> *slapped the back of my head*
> *and made me stand in the corner*
> *for not knowing the difference*
> *between persimmon and precision.*
> *How to choose*

persimmons. This is precision.
Ripe ones are soft and brown-spotted.
Sniff the bottoms. The sweet one
will be fragrant. How to eat:
put the knife away, lay down newspaper.
> *Peel the skin tenderly, not to tear the meat.*
> *Chew the skin, suck it,*
and swallow. Now, eat
the meat of the fruit,
so sweet,
all of it, to the heart.

The poet then weaves the web of bodily knowing, the associations and connections precise and true but "wrong" in the classroom.

We all know the journey away from both heart and body as we go higher in academia and in our professional career, the insistence on the separation between mind and heart, on removing the body as part of knowing. Our feelings and our experiences become not only irrelevant but actual obstacles to understanding "objective truths." There is an insistence on the doubting, skeptical mind—as if that is the highest form of knowing, as if belief, passion, enthusiasm, connection, love, emotions and, even, meaning are immature and naive, unscientific and irrational, foolish and childish, something we need to grow beyond.

We are taught to become the "expert," the critic finding fault, dissecting another's words and experiences. The child's precious shell is labeled "spurious" with all kinds of facts supporting that judgment. And so the child hides the shell within her private self or leaves the shell along the path or, depending on how precious it was and how painful the experience of separation, throws the shell at some smaller child who stands open and excited, admiring a beautiful shell she has just found on the water's edge.

But now I stop and look around. How did I move, so quickly and unconsciously, from the inquiring mind to the believing mind? Why do I need to affirm both when most people would see the two in contradiction, the inquiring mind—necessary for critical thinking and for growing beyond the boundaries of irrationality and prejudice—as undercutting beliefs? And why do I see both belief and inquiry as being attacked by the same "enemy" which I name "separation," with cynicism one of separation's strongest allies?

I circle back to the earlier chapter on language, on being able to speak one's own language without being judged or mocked, without always needing to translate into a foreign and less fluent tongue. Ursula LeGuin, in her graduation speech to Bryn Mawr students, talks about how, in college, we are all taught to speak the "father tongue." It is not, according to LeGuin, the language of reason, although it poses itself as that, but of separation and distance. Instead of offering our experience as our truth and speaking in our "mother's tongue," we are told that our experience is irrelevant to objective knowing and are weaned from that close, intimate, and familiar way of knowing and expressing. Audre Lorde, in her essay "The Erotic as Power," writes about how we are also taught to distrust the power which rises from our body, our deepest embodied knowledge, because if we were to fully experience and trust our erotic knowing we would demand that energy in the rest of our lives. Knowing the possible joy and depth in work, art, love and life, we would not accept less, would not give up what is precious, would not allow ourselves to be controlled by another—by the judge, the politician, the media, the expert, the cynic.

I look up cynic in the dictionary and am surprised to read: "An adherent of an ancient Greek school of philosophers who held the view that virtue is the only good and that its essence lies in self-control and independence." How did that belief in virtue transform itself into "A faultfinding captious critic, especially one who believes that human conduct is motivated wholly by self-interest." Under "cynical," I find: "contemptuously distrustful of human nature and motives." How did the philosopher believing in the virtue of goodness become a voice undercutting belief in the possible goodness of individuals, the possible justness of a society, the possible good effect of our actions to create change in our world? How did it become the voice that stops us in our tracks, not so that we can look around and see where we are but, rather, so that we become hesitant and unsure, stuck in passivity and despair, without hope of creating change through consciousness and action? It is that voice that stops a man praying to Allah and that almost stops Eiseley's experience of the beauty and miracle of a shell. It is that voice that stops my students when they get excited about their ideas, discoveries, creativity, and political action, making them feel foolish, stupid, naive. It is that voice that undercuts enthusiasm, that stopped me in my tracks throughout much of my growing up. It is clear, given my innate enthusiasm, why cynicism would feel like such an enemy.

But, you ask (and I ask) shouldn't beliefs be questioned? Shouldn't we doubt? Isn't that the way to shatter illusions? Isn't that the way to dismantle prejudices and inherited beliefs? Isn't that the route to consciousness and freedom?

Isn't that what you are doing when you ask students where, in the poem or the essay or the book or their life, they saw what they believe they saw, and how they came to their understanding, what evidence led them to their conclusions, what logic they followed?

And I say, yes, yes, yes. These are the questions that both allow and force someone to pay closer attention (to both what is within them and outside of them), to look at and name their own actual experiences, to do research in order to ascertain the facts, to place facts within larger contexts, to move slowly rather than just react, to go more deeply in terms of understanding cause and effect, to come to their beliefs through the process of close and careful inquiry rather than through unconsciousness, habit, and obedience. I think of a recent talk by Sam Harris, author of the book *The End of Faith*. He speaks of the danger of religious doctrines that lead to immoral actions: the speaking against condoms in Africa where AIDS is an epidemic; the condemnation of embryonic stem cell research that could save the lives of millions; the belief of many that a mushroom cloud of a nuclear holocaust is a heavenly sign of Christ's second coming. Harris questions moderate religion's "tolerance." He wants us to question, to ask for evidence, to not tolerate opinions and concepts spouted by those in authority which lead to dangerous and even genocidal consequences. His work—and the work of others—makes me question the "goodness" of "tolerance," a value I always held dear. And I think: it is good to question. Questions do not undercut beliefs but, rather, make conscious what these beliefs really are, allowing us to disown those which, under close scrutiny, no longer feel true, and to strengthen other beliefs through that same process. There is no contradiction between belief and inquiry; they are, really, necessary and close friends, their relationship making each stronger and deeper.

Peter Elbow, in his *Writing With Power*, has as exercise which I have used with students: the believing and the doubting game. Students read an essay, break into small groups, and then relate to the essay using first one approach then the other. Interestingly, the last time I used the exercise was with Ursula LeGuin's graduation speech on the mother (and father) tongue. And this is what I saw: using the doubting lens, students could, easily, find fault, disagree, raise opposing arguments with LeGuin's ideas. But, I noticed, the discussions petered out in a very short time. With the believing approach, however, I could not stop the discussion. It was animated with personal experiences, connections, laughter, tears. Students kept referring to parts of the essay, kept making connections with what other students said, kept enlarging the dialogue.

I know there is a place for the doubting mind. I, like Harris, fear the dangerous doctrines of many so called fundamentalists (fascists and fanatics), the passionate and dangerous words of racism, the "proofs" that one group is superior to another, the arguments justifying sexism, heterosexism, the call for patriotism and for war. I want the doubting mind to question, to examine, to do research, to expose lies, to catch flaws in both its own arguments and the arguments of another. I want us all to question authority and assumptions, demand evidence, use logic, reason, and thoughtful analysis.

But what is clear in our fault finding society is that ferreting out small mistakes against which we can argue does not lead to deeper understanding. Often it obscures the real issues, resulting in a kind of gossip and sensationalism where all deeper meaning is lost. It is interesting that it is the believing game which often gets us closer to real inquiry, closer to the text and the reader of the text, to facts and evidence, to ourselves and our own experiences.

What I see about both the inquiring and the believing mind is that both require a certain approach to the world—an openness, like the child's, not yet closed by the voices of surety, prejudice, judgment and cynicism. It is what I see in the photo of me as a small child: those open eyes taking everything in, questioning everything.

One of my students spoke of her father's heavy cynicism as his lack of courage. If that is true, the question then is how we can befriend and transform fear rather than simply scream, judge, and argue against its manifestation as I am often prone to do. How can we begin, again, to trust, in order to both question and believe?

Chapter Thirteen:

A Stranger in a New Land: Some Guidelines

In the midst of a very meaningful study, a student said to me: "I feel like I am a stranger in a strange land." I thought that was accurate—and quite wonderful. She, on the other hand, thought it was terrible, a sign that she was stupid and incapable and that her study was going in the wrong direction; she was ready to return to a more familiar terrain.

Later I would ask different groups of students how one could approach "a strange and new land." Clearly different approaches were possible. One "way" would be the path of openness, the desire to experience the unknown: to listen and look, smell and taste, investigate and explore, question and experiment with no expectations or assumptions. This, of course, was the approach I hoped my student would take. What I hadn't seen clearly enough was the power of fear, the other possible and more common "approach."

For my student, the not knowing meant she was stupid, and that the complexity and ambiguity were too hard and she too limited. She got angry—at both herself and the study. And angry and frustrated, she retreated back to the old forms that never served her in the past and never would in the future.

In my own mind, I always respect students' boundaries and choices, not pushing them beyond where they want or where I feel they are able to go. But still I wonder if I do not pay enough attention to fear, don't notice its many guises, assume that joy, love, power, growth are the stronger pulls. I am continually surprised to see people returning to "the old ways," especially when there seemed so much joy and enthusiasm with the new discoveries. I am also surprised at how, in the larger society, a new way of seeing seems to pose a threat rather than an opportunity, how people continually return to the past even when the old ways were experienced as harsh, confining, restrictive, and filled with hypocrisy: "back to the basics," the 50's, the Family, the Patriarch, the one God; before the "turbulent 60's," before civil rights, feminism, gay rights began to split the old forms apart; back to the illusion of innocence and goodness, to a time before "the Fall," to patriotism and the old days. Clearly I don't pay enough heed to the difficulty many of us have with complexity, ambiguity, contradictions, relativity, process, and change, nor do I fully recognize the desire for what is fixed and absolute, unchanging and known, the need for control and order that Fromm sees as necrophily but which many people experience as security and safety. Now, after the attacks on September 11, 2001, the willingness to give up one's freedom for an illusionary security is even stronger and, for me, more frightening.

In his *The Web of Life*, Fritjof Capra explores the new paradigm which he sees replacing the old world view:

> *The new paradigm may be called a holistic worldview, seeing the world as an integrated whole rather than a dissociated collection of parts. It may also be called an ecological view, if the term ecological is used in a much broader and deeper sense than usual. Deep ecological awareness recognizes the fundamental interdependence of all phenomena and the fact that, as individuals and societies, we are all embedded in (and ultimately dependent on) the cyclical processes of nature.*

Capra explores this paradigm in its many different realms—psychology, science, spirituality, business. In all fields, there is a focus on process rather than product and a recognition of a complex network with shifting boundaries based on changing contexts. Heisenberg's uncertainty principle, Gestalt psychology, Systems' theory—the world is not fixed, boundaries are not clearly defined, what is observed cannot be separated from the observer, and the observer cannot be separated from his/her context for viewing. The universe is complex and mysterious, and we are part of that universe rather than apart from it.

Capra's capacity to show the weaving of this intricate web in all fields fed my love of process and spoke to my experience of interconnection. But it was a small paragraph early in the book that made me think more about fear:

> *In the Germany of the 1920's, the Weimar Republic, both organismic biology and Gestalt psychology were part of a larger intellectual trend that saw itself as a protest movement against the increasing fragmentation and alienation of human nature. The entire Weimar culture was characterized by an antimechanistic outlook, a "hunger for wholeness." Organismic biology, Gestalt psychology, ecology, and, later on, general systems theory holistic zeitgeist.*

Capra ends his paragraph here, but my mind continued—to the rise of Nazism and to the relationship between free, expansive thought and fascist control and power, to the fear triggered by a breaking of old forms, to the need for certainty, to the inability to abide chaos, groundlessness, relativity, process, multiplicity, to the need to know exactly what is, who one is, who others are, and how the world is constructed, to the Holocaust and the backlashes which often follow any significant change.

I don't remember much of Hardy's *Jude the Obscure* which I read in High School except being very moved by it, in particular moved by the character of the independent and free thinking Sue Bridehead. What I remember—and I probably need to reread it now from my forty years later perspective—was how her guilt at her children's death plummeted her back to the old, rigid ways of her early religious training, training she had rejected because of its narrow focus on sin and punishment. Pain and guilt made her return to the old world of asceticism and self-punishment rather than continue her journey into the unknown. I remember feeling the sadness that comes when you see someone go backwards. It is what I feel now when I see students retreat out of fear, or friends, or myself, or a whole society or a whole world. And fear, too, because a retreat based on fear threatens all those who have less power, all outsiders who seem "strange," all those who question those old ways and struggle for expansive change. Fear makes us grip tightly, and that death grip holds on and suffocates others as well as ourselves.

How then can we move more consciously and less reactively into what is unfamiliar and strange? In the essay "The Journey's End," in an anthology *Words from the Land*, edited by Stephen Trimbell, Wendell Berry helped me to see some of the implications and dangers of seeing "the other" as strange. He writes of first experiencing a place, the river gorge, as strange—a strange place, a place strange to him. He then writes:

> *The presumptuousness of that, it now occurs to me, is probably the key to the destructiveness that has characterized the whole history of the white man's relation to the American wilderness. For it is presumptuous to enter a place for the first time and pronounce it strange. Strange to whom? Certainly to its own creatures—to the birds and animals and insects and fish and snakes, to the human family I know that lives knowingly and lovingly there—it is not strange ... To call a place strange in the presence of its natives is bad manners at best. At worst, it partakes of the fateful arrogance of those explorers who familiarize the "strange" places they come to by planting in them the alien flag of the place they have left, and who have been followed, always, by the machinery of conquest and exploitation and destruction.*
>
> *The strangeness, as I recognized after a while, was all in me. And I believe that only in that realization lay the possibility that I would come to know the Red River Gorge even a little. If I had continued to look up on the place as strange, I would clearly have had only two choices: stay out of it altogether, or change it, destroy it as I found it and make it into something else. But once I learned to look upon myself as a stranger there, it became possible for me to return again and again without preaching to the natives or making treaties, or cutting down timber ... It became possible for me to leave the place as it is, to want it to be as it is, to be quiet in it, to learn about it and from it....*
>
> *Slowly, almost imperceptibly, the experience of strangeness was transformed into the experience of familiarity. The place did not become predictable; the more I learned of it, the less predictable it seemed. And its mysteries remained—for though we pretend otherwise, the unknown increases with the known. But mystery is not the same as strangeness.*

This passage feels very meaningful in its distinctions and implications. What would it mean to allow ourselves to be strangers rather than to label the "other"—person, place, culture, way of being, way of seeing—strange? How would individual and world dynamics shift if we were truly interested in and welcomed rather than judged and resisted another way of being? Children allow themselves to be strangers, do not assume that they should know. They walk with open eyes, learning from everything—until enough fear and pain teach them to stop their open journey. As adults, most of us are afraid: to walk around in the dark, to feel the texture of the earth with our bare feet, to not know where we are, who we are, where we are going. Afraid to be lost and vulnerable, we often cling to a fixed, known, and unchanging world. The theologian William Sloan Coffin speaks about rigid fundamentalists clinging to the bible as a drunkard clings to a lamplight, for security and not illumination. In our need for "security," we continue to lock not only ourselves but all others into roles, stereotypes, labels, and prisons, continue to imprison them and ourselves in fixed concepts of everyone's place in a fixed universe.

What I am now realizing is how much I have judged as "evil" those who have acted out of fear, my own reaction and my own fear mistaking effect for cause. The effects—control, tyranny, fascism, abusive power—do great harm to others. But, clearly, shouting my judgments about how terrible the people are who do such evil acts does nothing to change the situation.

I think of Thich Nhat Hanh, a Buddhist monk from Vietnam, who teaches mindfulness and meditation. He speaks of those parts within us that we want to cast out: rage, fear, hatred, jealousy, greed. In meditation they appear as Rumi's unwelcomed guests, the beings whom we would like keep out of our "guest house." And what Thich Nhat Hanh asks, simply and deeply, is what we would do if we heard a small child crying and screaming uncontrollably. Would we scream back, silencing the child with our own violence, or would we try to give some comfort, try to understand what the child was feeling? Wouldn't we try to find the source of the problem, even if the child couldn't, rather than just judge its manifestation?

I want to return to the cynic, my personal screaming child, in order to not just scream back. Perhaps the cynic, like the tyrant and rigid fundamentalist, is just fearful of the unknown, both within and outside the self. Perhaps the cynic is one who has been silenced so much s/he despairs about the possibility of faith, belief, values, investigation, inquiry, change. Perhaps s/he was mocked for praising Allah, showing her precious shell, refusing to eat another's unripe "persimmon," savoring her own sweet fruit. Perhaps the cynic was a love dog beaten at the gate. If the above is true, I need to do something other than shout and abuse the voice of cyncism, telling it how stupid and narrow it is. I need to find ways to make the cynic, the rigid fundamentalist, even the tyrant within us all a little less afraid, more willing to walk into what is strange and unfamiliar. And, at the same time, I need to create an atmosphere, within myself and within the classroom, where those fearful parts of us do not wield such power, either through their control or our lack of resistance. They need compassion and understanding; they do not, however, need obedience.

In many ways the second half of this book is about how to find ways to not give power to fear, to nurture the inquiring mind and open heart, to choose life over death—in both the classroom and in life.

I remember a talk I went to with Pir Vilyat Khan, a Sufi teacher and master. He was old, his voice low. In the room next to his talk, there was very loud construction. I could feel my anger and judgment at the noise, my frustration at not being able to hear someone I greatly respected. And then he said, as if reading my thoughts, "If you want to hear what I am saying, pay closer attention." He was exactly right: my anger had taken all my attention away. What I needed to do then—and what I need to do now in the classroom—is to make the inquiry more interesting, exciting, and powerful than the fear, to have students' attention so focused that fear, like pain, like confusion, like so much of life, ceases to pull our hearts and minds into their smaller tracks.

With Pir Vilyat Khan, and in much of life, it is possible, with awareness, to shift the focus of our attention. Since we give power—and often love—to whatever we pay attention to, it is important to be the one to choose, to have conscious intent. Because of his admonition, I could actually turn my attention to the words of Pir Vilyat Khan rather than to my anger at the noises of construction in the room next door and within my own head.

By not giving power to fear, we can actually use and transform fear's energy. I think of an Adirondack wilderness trip with Skidmore College's Freshman students which I co-led. The experience involved reading and discussing literature and, also, learning orienteering. As part of the experience, each student was to be alone for 24 hours. What I remember was that one young woman was very afraid. In her life she had hardly spent any time in the woods or alone. The combination of being alone in the wilderness in the dark was terrifying. For most of the others, particularly for one young man who had done a lot of mountain climbing, this was all very easy; child's stuff.

After twenty four hours, everyone returned. What I remember vividly was the joy and radiance in the face and body of the woman who had been so afraid. She had seen a fox, had marveled at the stars and the beauty of sunrise, had felt a deep connection to the wilderness both outside of herself and within. For those who had no fear, it was a nice experience going off into the woods, but is was nothing special. Not having to wrestle with any of their "demons," they had not grown much muscle. What became clear to me was the connection between fear and growth. When we do anything that we fear, our struggle with our own boundaries stretches us and makes us larger—whether it is going into the woods, being alone, changing a tire, building a shelter, going into therapy, writing, painting, speaking aloud, reading one's own work … Our growth is the movement between "here" and "there" and the courage required to traverse that space.

I think of those markings on the wall when we are children charting our physical growth. As adults we can also chart those movements. The deepest growth is often invisible to the eye of others, often discounted as "nothing" by the cynic. But we know. They are experiences that need to be recognized, honored, and affirmed—by us and by others. Our own charting and orienteering and compass readings show us the moments of real "success" and growth. Fear is not really the problem; in fact, it can be a catalyst that amplifies our life's meaning, a companion giving us energy rather than an enemy stopping us. But that is true only if we are conscious and aware, if we do not give fear the power to stop us.

Sometimes what is necessary within the classroom—and in life—is to name the fears so that they don't lurk in the shadows, vague, amorphous, and menacing. Often just the naming and saying them aloud lessens their power. The naming also makes for a connection between students, rather than an isolation in one's self judgment, and it gives recognition to the difficulty of the struggle—the fragility, courage, and triumph when we take even small steps into any feared terrain.

What's hard to describe is how moving it is to see the spirit struggle with what is hard, to witness the courage required to grow. Teaching one sees again and again how courage creates and inspires more courage, in the same way as allowing fear to rule strengthens its dominance in our lives. Once the process of courage gets ignited, the light spreads, illuminating almost everyone present. That is what can happen in the classroom and in our lives.

Yesterday I saw a PBS special on the Canyonlands. One of the sequences was on black crows nesting on a narrow edge on a high canyon wall, the parents conscientiously feeding their chicks day and night until it was time for the young to fly. The camera went back and forth between the parents and their little ones, the encouragement of the parents and the fear of those who had never flown. Protected in their little nest, the chicks hadn't ever tested their wings. Their nest was very high up, and it was a long way to the next resting place of possible safety. First one began to flutter his wings and tried to fly, then another. But the last bird was clearly terrified. The mother flew back and forth encouraging its flight, giving small rewards for each small attempt, and trying to inspire by catching the wind, soaring up and around so gracefully that even I might have tried had I been a chick in the nest. Finally the remaining little one, seeing its siblings and its mother, knowing it had to move, wanting to join the rest of the family, began to flutter its wings. It flew a bit and then plummeted to a lower rock where it sidled fearfully on its skinny legs until it began to experiment with its own wings, to feel them from the inside, to recognize this new tool within its own body that would enable it to explore both itself and its world. And then it flew, flew with its own power, as did my heart watching its flight.

And I thought of all of us as baby chicks in resting places, needing to grow beyond our small perch, fearing, needing the encouragement of parents and siblings, the guidance, the inspiration through example, needing to feel ourselves in our world—the wind under us and our wings within us—to feel our ability to fly through the act of our own wings learning the currents of the immense sky.

TRANSITION CHAPTER

What we call the beginning is often the end
and to make an end is to make a beginning
The end is where we start from.

(T.S. Eliot, *Little Gittings* in *Four Quartets*)

What has gone before was meant to be a short introduction, the bulk of the book focusing on specific lessons to help students break out of the prison of mind. The book was to be mainly examples of students' papers showing how that process worked, the depth and honesty of thought that can come from a simple English composition class within an enclosed prison system. But what I found was that my experiences—in life, in the classroom, through my readings, through my politics and spirituality—were what led me to my "practice," and that I could not give the practice without reflecting on my path there. It is important, I tell my students, to trace the path rather than just arrive at the "goal." The way there—the context, the journey, the process—is what is alive with the energy of discovery, with Fromm's "active thought."

As a student I always had trouble with outlines. I understand the necessity of organization, of having one idea lead to another, of having a beginning and middle and end, and of creating a whole that feels complete. And I understand that for some people and some students the outline is a way to bring order to chaos, to clarify the focus and the development of a central thesis. But the "I" and "II" and "a" and "b" always felt foreign to what I was doing. My "outline" was filled with arrows going in different directions and circles and dashes. At my best (or worst) I could sometimes create an outline after the fact, moving from the actual paper to its translation into outline form, but what I always felt was that the outline was not how my mind worked; it was a structured march while the movement of my mind was more fluid. Later I had the image of a spider's web, of weaving different strands. I wanted to spin webs, because the web was so beautiful in the light, so surprising, so strong and open. And so I have, now, spun many pages filled with tendrils of thoughts and experiences.

But there is another reason, I now realize, why what was to be the heart of the book and was the initial reason for writing at all—the writings of students, mostly from the prisons—is only now, finally and very slowly, entering the picture. When I finally took out the folder to read some of the papers I had saved—a very small remnant from those twelve years rich with possible papers—I realized this more unconscious reason.

I live very near Great Meadows Correctional Facility. It is large structure, flat and imposing, tiny windows in long horizontal lines, medieval towers flanking a shapeless monolith. At night it is aglow with a strange light—like in Reno and Las Vegas and other artificially constructed all night cities. There is no darkness, no natural light. Although inmates often talk of a great loneliness there is no solitude, no quiet. The first time I entered I was most struck by the heavy metal doors—being buzzed in, having a door electronically open, then close, then another door open, then close, and another. As an Aries, I always look for exits when I enter a room. What I felt in the prison was that there was no exit, no way out.

What I feel now, again, is the heaviness of those doors and the smallness of the windows. The tiny cages with their metal bars. Rereading some of the student papers, I feel, again, the fullness of the life pacing within that confinement. And I experience again the pain of seeing so many seeds unable to find any way to flower. I am not romanticizing all people in prison or, even, all the people that I taught or who attended the college program. They, like all of us, are a mixed lot of humanity. But I am feeling again the violence of imprisonment, the closed windows offering no fresh air of possibility. I am feeling deeply how the outside world has cast prisoners "beyond the pale," making them visible only as monsters, as evil. And I am feeling deeply the humanity of those students whom I did teach during all those years, some of whom have probably died and most of whom are still in prison and will be for a long time. It took me this long to open the folder and be with their papers because, I now see, one part of me did not want to feel the pain, frustration, and anger that come with awareness of another's pain and of one's own helplessness to create change.

Before teaching in Great Meadows and, later, Washington and Bedford Hills, I knew about the connection between racism and the prison system, the statistics on who is in prison and why. I knew about the prison-industrial complex and the role of prisons within our capitalist society. I knew how convenient it was to lock up poor people and people of color who could, potentially, rebel against economic injustices; to place prisons within rural areas so that locally depressed economies could have a "clean industry" for their unemployed white population; to attribute all societal problems to those people who are imprisoned, having them bear the burden while other criminals, those who profit from greed and exploitation, are free. I knew about the unfairness of prison terms where some serve very long sentences for minor crimes and others literally "get away with murder." I knew the whitewash: to create scapegoats, reinforce prejudice, give justification for racism, imprison those who might rebel, and make those in power seem like heroes rather than villains. It's an effective system and it seems to work, at least for those in power. But teaching in the prison, being with inmates and hearing their thoughts and ideas, made me feel my political outrage on a whole other level: in terms of human suffering.

Last week a friend who is an animal rights activist gave me Roger Fouts' *Next of Kin* about his work with chimpanzees, a book I refer to in an earlier chapter. For days I read about Washoe and other chimps, their emotions, their ability to connect and communicate, their curiosity, their need for social contact and affection. Then, the other night, I watched a PBS special on animals used in medical experiments. It showed chimps being clamped down to tables, injected with disease, shaved and electrocuted, imprisoned in tiny concrete blocks with almost no air to breath and no social contact. I had, theoretically, been against cruel experiments on animals, but this time I could not watch the torture without horror, could not maintain "objectivity," could only feel empathy, compassion, and rage. I had, through Fouts' writing, experienced the fullness of the chimps' being, their social interaction, their capacity for joy and pain. I could no longer see them as objects having no feelings.

Once beings become individual and unique subjects, it is not so easy to put them in concrete and windowless boxes. The issue is no longer theoretical or abstract; we are forced into empathy and consciousness, into responsibility. Taking living beings out of the boxes—both literally and within the conceptual bars of our own mind—we not only free "the other" but, also, ourselves, expanding our own humanity by enlarging our capacity to connect with another, to feel compassion.

That is what happened to me in the prison. That is why I wanted and needed to write this book. And that is why it has taken me so long to get here and why I am, finally, here at all.

What follows now is what was, originally, to be the beginning. The reader might want to begin here. Perhaps each chapter can be read separately, perhaps in any order. I don't know. What I do know is that my mind keeps circling around certain images, certain experiences, certain understanding, and that they keep appearing in different forms throughout this book. Is it repetition or just the integrity of a mind, of all our minds, that keeps posing the essential questions of our lives in new and different forms, that keeps seeking answers in different ways, that keeps us moving in a labyrinth closer and closer to our center?

Perhaps now I can actually have an "outline," the form finally emerging from all that circling. The form is, really, an English Composition course, English 101, the basic beginning Freshman course. How did it take me so long to get back here, to what is common to almost every book on rhetoric and on writing essays from personal experience?

I think of the story of the thousand fish. A wealthy man asks a famous Chinese artist to paint him a fish. He waits for days, weeks, months. Finally, in exasperation, he goes to the artist's door, demanding his fish. The artist takes out his brush and in one flowing stroke paints a graceful and lovely fish. It seems so easy and simple, the man questions why the artist had not painted the fish months earlier. The artist opens his closet and hundreds of paintings of fish come cascading down.

It has taken me this long to get to this "fish." And unlike the artist in the tale, I am not giving you only the one final painting but the thousand that got me here. As I say to my students all the time when I give feedback, take whatever is useful to you in your own journey. I say the same here, to the reader.

Chapter Fourteen:

The Journal

In the standard English Composition class, I usually ask students to keep a private journal. In the prison, the contradictions are immediately apparent. Nothing is private in the prison. Cells are totally open on one side, which means that inmates are totally visible at all times. At any minute a Correctional Officer can enter their cell, search everything, take away any books and papers, confiscate their journal. And while I tell them that their journal is theirs, I also say that writing in the journal is one of the requirements for the course and that I will be collecting their journal a few times during the semester. I tell them that I will not evaluate or grade or mark up any of their writing, that the grade will be based only on their doing the journal. I also tell them that if there is anything they do not want me to read, they can fold or tape papers together and I will not read them. But still there is an irony in the whole idea of a private personal journal within the prison and as a requirement for a course, an irony of which all the participants, including myself, are fully aware.

The amazing thing is that it still works despite all the contradictions, even under these circumstances, even in this context, even with resistance. In fact, the resistance itself can become part of the journey, can become "matter" for the journal—as long as one continues to write. And at some point the resistance drops. We forget that the assignment is imposed and that our journal can be stolen, and begin to follow our own minds and hearts, so interested in our own exploration the obstacles fall by the wayside. Perhaps it is a bit like role playing, or psychodrama, or creating situations within therapy that mirror actual experiences. We know that it is a constructed situation, not the "real thing," we are self-conscious at first and awkward, but in the act of doing we enter that other reality. Perhaps it is like Coleridge's "willing suspension of disbelief" that is required in order to immerse ourselves in literature. Perhaps, even more, it is our yearning to grow which allows us to enter the process, one part of us knowing something deeper and more honest is possible through this seeming pretense.

In a prison there is no inviolable space, no privacy. Journal writing gives inmates the power to self-create a sacred and safe space. Even if it is an illusion of safety—as with my singing aloud and strong in the dark of a campfire, as if no one could hear—we are still doing "it," being empowered through the act of doing. With journal writing as with meditation, what is necessary is the practice, the intent and the effort, the openness and the trust.

And of course it is not simple, not in the outside world but, particularly, not in the prison where everything seems to militate against vulnerability and trust. Why should inmates trust this white woman coming in from the outside, this stranger who couldn't possibly understand and who possibly could use their words against them. And in this environment where vulnerability can be seen as weakness, as danger, why should they make themselves open to their other classmates by actually reading their journal writings to the class? Besides, the whole idea of a private journal can seem very strange and foreign—an activity associated with women writing in their diaries, not macho violent men living in a maximum security prison.

And yet, and yet … the desire to communicate with the self through whatever means are available is real, as are the frustration and rage when there is no way and the joy when a way is discovered. Roger Fouts, in his *Next of Kin*, talks about his experience signing with chimpanzees and how it leads him to work with autistic children who are locked in their own worlds, unable to communicate except though seemingly obsessive, bizarre and sometimes violent behavior. When one young boy who had never communicated verbally with anyone starts leaping to the door, Fouts grabs his hand at the doorknob and teaches him the sign for "open." When the boy begins to run, he teaches him to sign "run." And with those two words a whole new world opens. Not only does the boy learn to sign, but he soon learns to speak. Behavior which had seemed so strange and destructive begins to disappear. Finding a way out of imprisonment, he no longer needs to batter head and body against real and imaginary walls.

The human need to dialogue is, clearly, not just with others but also with self—to chronicle events, to explore experiences, to express feelings, to think about life and meaning. I remember being surprised to read and hear of diary entries of slaves, of pioneer women on their journey west, of men in the civil war in the midst of battle, of explorers stranded in the North Pole. Even in dire circumstances people clearly feel the urgency and necessity to write in their journals, perhaps because those very situations need to be recorded, absorbed and processed through writing, whether or not the diaries are ever read by another. In fact, for many, in particular for women who have written in diaries for centuries, it is often the belief that their journals will never be read that provides the freedom to write what cannot be spoken. And for many that freedom comes to an abrupt end when their private journals or diaries are read or used by another, the betrayal by another often resulting in self-betrayal, the cutting off of a lifeline to heart and mind, the silencing, self destruction, and amputation that come when trust is broken. And the question how to get back what is life sustaining, to connect with self once again, to not give "them" the power to stop what gives us our deeper life.

Of course it is not only others who stop us but ourselves and our own fear. One student wrote about going through old journals she had kept for many years, observing their ebb and flow. What she noticed was that whenever she came close to a feeling or thought that was, in some way, threatening, she stopped writing, both consciously and unconsciously knowing that if she wrote the words she could no longer deny the reality of her experience and would have to make real changes in her life. The writing would forge the consciousness that would necessitate the change. And what she noticed was that for many years she "chose" unconsciousness in order to keep the status quo.

Many of us "choose" that path, choose not to write in a journal because we know, on some level, that the journey of the journal might lead us to places we are not yet ready or willing to go. I put "choose" in quotes because on some level we are totally unaware that we are choosing, fear taking on one of its many guises. For my student, it took a stepping back and observing to recognize what she had been doing during those years. She talked about what it would have meant to have had a circle of friends who, wanting our growth and recognizing our fear, agreed upon some signal, like gently touching our left shoulder, reminding us to pay attention, alerting us to the possibility of fear distorting reality, urging us to go on, to not stop. Since consciousness is not necessarily "good news," we often need these kinds of good friends, friends of the soul.

In Dorothy Bryant's novel *Ella Price's Journal*, Ella, an older woman returning to college, is assigned journal writing as part of her English Composition course. The novel consists of Ella's journal entrees. I could relate to both the teacher creating the assignment and the student resisting, for all kinds of reasonable reasons, for all kinds of unconscious reasons. In the first half of the novel, Ella's journals are all about the foolishness of the assignment, her anger at her professor, and her desire to not only stop writing in the journal but to withdraw from the class. But slowly—through the act of writing—ideas, thoughts, reflections, feelings, questions begin to emerge. The journal becomes a mirror allowing her to see her own life. And it becomes, also, a window, allowing her to begin to question, to make connections, to see other possibilities, and, eventually, to choose her own life. It's not a "happy forever after" story. Ella, as we all, makes unskillful choices. But she has a tool for learning from those mistakes. The journal is, for Ella, a beginning of the process of self expression and self reflection. It is the prying open of a previously unexamined package, a closed and confined life given to her by others, in order to observe the contents for the first time and begin the process of choosing her own life.

As a teacher, I don't assume that the journal people write in a composition class will transform their lives, but I do see it as a tool—like meditation—that will lead to consciousness. Within the prison, however, it is not a very accessible or immediately appealing tool. As with new and strange foods that do not look naturally enticing, it needs to be experienced in small ways in order to hook people in. It can even start simply with an in class writing, beginning with a simple "Recently I've been thinking … or questioning … or feeling …," having students write for ten minutes, telling them to continue writing even if they feel they have come to the end. After they stop, I might ask students to silently reread what they have written and underline a sentence or a few words that particularly touch them for some reason, making that a new beginning for a new journey. Then I ask students to volunteer to read their writings—and, amazingly, some do. I might, then, ask them to write what they felt in the writing, in the reading of their own words to themselves, in the reading aloud, in hearing other people read aloud. And the process goes on and on.

All our minds have been conditioned. What I try to do in the classroom is to create certain activities which necessitate certain actions, the actions creating new channels that widen with each subsequent action, making natural what at first seems strange and unnatural. In their study of the mind, Buddhists try to train the mind to pay attention, to be mindful, to observe how certain actions lead to certain effects. There is the awareness that we can recondition the mind to follow more skillful ways in order to bring less suffering and more freedom. In many ways the exercises I do as a teacher, all of them learned through my own attention to experience, are ways of reconditioning the mind from unconscious and habitual behavior into attention and consciousness. The act of writing in a journal, no matter what is written, becomes a way of reconditioning ourselves to follow the thoughts of our own mind. When we read our own words, we are able to observe where our mind has gone and to notice our emotional and mental responses to that mind's journey. And what is quite wonderful is that simply by doing, we grow—through practice, continual practice, even if it is "required" from a teacher, even if it is in the prison, even if there is resistance and anger.

When I went to my first meditation retreat, one of the teachers spoke of how we come to meditation for very different reasons, and that it doesn't matter how or why we came but, rather, that we are there. The act of sitting quietly and meditating—that simple and very difficult practice—will train the mind into awareness. And that, I believe, is true with journal writing also: the practice develops the skill. I say to my students what my teachers of meditation often say: "Don't believe me. Look to your own experience."

In his *In Over Our Heads*, Kegan writes about different levels of thinking and how we sometimes make demands of others in terms of their *actions* when we are really wanting them to be at a different level of consciousness. He does not talk about those different levels in terms of good or bad; rather, he speaks of what is needed within the individual and within the society at different time periods. He writes specifically about "the mental demands of modern life" and what is required so that we are not "in over our heads." What his book made very clear to me—in discussing, for example, why the fifth level of consciousness (which takes in the understanding of postmodernism) cannot be welcomed by people who have just grown into the fourth level (the renaming and redefining the world based on their experience)—is the importance of respecting where people are, welcoming where they have arrived, often through great struggle, rather than haranguing them for not moving more quickly.

What seems essential with all teaching is to not assume that a student is already where we want them to be and then blame and judge them for where they actually are, especially since they have often struggled with great courage and intelligence to get to that point. It is, rather, to give students the tools that will enable them to continually expand from wherever they are. I'm not talking about our obsession with quicker access to more and more information but, rather, about the slow growth of consciousness, of thinking about thinking, of seeing the larger patterns and getting free of the more subtle entrapments of mind, step by slow step. On a very minor—and major scale—that is exactly what a composition class does: train the mind to see in deeper and more complex ways. The journal—the idea and the reality—is an important beginning point. With a journal, everyone begins where they are. The journal is theirs to do with as they want. They can write anything, but they must write something.

To tell students, you can "write about anything" or "just write," however, is not particularly helpful. Students have been trained—as we all have—to answer the teachers' questions and write what they are asked to write. It's a little like pulling a child in a small rubber boat attached to your motor boat, he/she following your lead for many miles and then, suddenly, cutting them free in deep water, telling them they are now free to go anywhere they want. No oars, no maps, no sense of the water. What can one expect but frustration, anger, and fear.

How then to begin to be free? How to be a stranger in open waters or on new land? How to allow oneself to be a child, to have "beginner's mind"? How to feel the water, the current, to submerge one's foot and kick around, to play, experiment, explore? With writing, free writing, that's what one needs to do. It is a matter of immersing ourselves in the element, playing, with no expectations, getting ourselves used to different motions and currents within ourselves. It is a practice cultivating the natural curiosity and wonder which much of our education has squelched. It requires patience.

So we begin to write in class using different triggers. I give examples of journals and diaries: Thoreau, Emily Carr, Anne Frank, Virginia Woolf, May Sarton. I give them selections from Nina Holzer's *A Walk Between Heaven and Earth*, from Joanne Field's *A Life of One's Own*. I have them write about their experience. They talk about their process in writing. I ask for volunteers to read. I do more in class exercises whenever we meet. After a few weeks I ask them to reread all they have written—to step back and observe themselves. What can they learn about themselves by reading their own words? Do they notice any patterns? Are there repeated feelings, motifs, ways of seeing? Are there any changes in their entries, any shifts? This ability to step back and observe is, I believe, the beginning of critical thinking.

What is true is that some students never develop a hunger to write, always see it as an assignment imposed from without; they do the assignment but never really do the practice. Others never move beyond the simple chronicling of each day, reciting what they have done externally but never going beyond plot summary. But even the simple chronicling provides something useful: a sense of one's daily life in its repeated movements. And, usually, at some point, students themselves get bored and will begin to experiment, to explore on another level, to be inspired by the writings of other students or their readings, or by their own frustration and anger.

I remember one student saying that even if the guard took his journal, it didn't really matter; he was writing the journal now only for himself. Another student, K.J., in a paper trying to define the term "beautiful," saw his journal as one example of "beautiful" because it allowed him to voice his deeper feelings. That same student later wrote more directly about relationship with writing and, in particular, with his journal:

> As I'm coming to understand, writing for me is a form of release, an escape from all the pain, hurt and deprivation that is the lord and master of the existence which I'm currently living. I used to just think of writing as a form of communication between people, but now I view it as that and, also, my way of really releasing my inner self, a safety valve between myself and my sanity. This may sound insane, but I've come to grips with these things only recently.
>
> I will touch briefly on a very pressure packed incident that afforded me the chance to look at this. Not long ago, I called home (my mom's house) and after a series of evasive conversations with all of the people there, I found out that my mother had a tumor. Now imagine the utter helplessness that I felt if you can. After exploring every other avenue, I prayed to my maker and cried all over a piece of paper with my pen. Not that this changed anything, but when I finished I was emotionally drained. I once again felt that very serene state of being that only writing has been able to give me at this point in time. (To add a touch of goodness to the situation, my mom caught the tumor in time and is currently fine, which I took time out to write on also. This time a direct hot line to my lord and savior. Yes, that works too.)
>
> I believe that my relationship with writing has evolved to the state of utter dependence that it is now because of the situation that I currently live. So, in a sense, I thank the court system for inflicting this time upon me because through it, I feel that the most positive thing that has happened in my life has come to be. That is the finally being able to get in tune with myself through a medium that has always been open to me, but which I didn't have the insight to reach out and grab on to. Now that I have, the thirst in me to conquer it is insatiable, like a baby discovering

the wonder of the world around him for the first time. It is beyond my comprehension to explain my total relationship with writing, as it is with all of the things that I've come to covet and hold dear to me. I'm not sure that I'm giving it a very good effort now, perhaps because in doing that I might somehow upset the balance of something that has helped me so endure this very hostile, stifling existence. (KJ)

Another student, writing his journal within the class, wrote the following:

Incredibly enough, this is another first of sorts for this entry being that it is written during November 17th class. Forgive me for not paying closer attention to everyone but I'm really trying to expand on my uses of writing. It's quite possible that it could be the outlet I've always had but never used. I must say that writing is a lot safer and much more productive than doing drugs. Putting that aside for a moment, I feel unconnected by tonight's session. I think part of it has to do with the subject of the paper. Now I wish I had not wrote about it. Expressing my instant feelings of a certain moment on paper has made a permanent record of something I do not care to be reminded of. J's death was something that was never fully settled in my mind because I had gotten so involved with drugs during the years after. Not too many people were ever told about her and I don't feel like advertising the end of the life of someone who was so close to me. I am beginning to see the power of writing because like I said, I don't bring up that area of my past much. The writing seemed to take a form of control over me and that is a little frightening. I guess I should be careful with it. I have been upset with the reminder of what happened. I feel that when I gain a complete mastery and control over my writing, I will possess a useful and powerful tool to communicate with myself and others. I understand now that the other "side" of writing which I had not seen before a short time ago is as important as the side I have been good at (words, sentences, ideas). It might be that that is what this course is all about. It might also be that 3 months is only enough time to scratch the surface of what we've been talking about.

A journal entry from another student begins with a simple description of "Today I was ..." and then goes back to explore a relationship:

6/2/92: Today I was sitting on the steps in the small yard. I didn't have much on my mind. The sun was warm with a slight cool breeze now and then. I'm sitting there when pretty good size pigeon lands maybe 9 feet or so away from me. He was beautiful. He was predominantly gray with a green head and black lines along his wings. He was scrounging for food. He would peck here and there and look up at me. I enjoyed his company but he got too close and I scared him away. The reason I scared him away is cause I once had a pet pigeon. His name was Seamore, he was gray green and black, just like the one I saw today. Seamore was leery of me when I used to feed him. Eventually he let me touch him. That took about four months of cautious moves while throwing bread. I felt so good, getting a bird to trust me. The bird didn't care what color I was or what I'm in jail for. Seamore trusted me and he may have loved me. I know I grew very fond of him. I fed him and petted him everyday for three months. Seamore used to be sitting on the slate roof diagonally from the steps. All I had to do was throw a small ball of bread in the air and he came to eat it. Then he'd fly to me. I'd hold him in one hand while he ate out of my other hand. He communicated secretly. It was as if he'd move his head a certain way if I touched him in certain spots. I felt so peaceful when I shared moments with Seamore.

Seamore is dead now. It's my fault sort of. I gained his trust and confidence. He couldn't tell the difference between good and evil. Not unless you made your threat outright. The last time I saw him he was eating bread on the steps. An officer had to kill Seamore, cause only.... (and I could no longer read what followed in the journal). (RJ)

One student wrote voluminously in his journal, using it as a way to recollect and revisit his past as a country boy living on a swamp right outside of New Orleans, next to the Mississippi River, where he and his family moved when he was three. The following is only a small selection from his fifty pages of journal writing about his home:

Now upon my first moving on the swamp, although I'm a country boy I had a lot to learn about the swamp because my hearing and my sight were only accustomed to sounds and sights of my previous home of the forest and hills. Now that I lived on the swamp I heard and seen many sights and sounds that were not familiar to me. The very first thing that I became accustomed to was that very rich smell that only a swamp could produce. One evening as I sat on my porch eating friend catfish along with a few homemade biscuits, butter and corn syrup, the night air began to whisk by me. It brushed my skin and filled my nostrils. It was a very pleasant breeze and warm to the touch. With the rise of the breeze came the very refreshing scent of all the greenery—the trees and all wild plant life that the swamp produces. Even the very water of the swamp has its own unique smell and this alone fascinated me and was also what I had come to know first and from that moment on that I had fallen in love with the place. When I smelled the evening air, I smelled with it the strong aromous scent of the Weeping Willow, the Cypress, the Tupelo Gum and Water Oak trees along with the water lilies, the wild moss, and other aquatic plant life which contribute to the very beautiful, wild and unique smell of one of Louisiana's swamps, the one that I happened to live on.

My home on the swamp appeared to resemble any other residential home only it was surrounded by water. Now the way the house stayed atop the water without ever falling in is that it was held above water and supported by large oak pillars with solid steel poles driven through the center of each pillar supported by a strong, wedged footing driven deep into the swamp bottom. The house itself was constructed of white oak, pine and cherry wood. The three different types of wood helped to give the house a natural foresty scent ... Now the house was surrounded by a porch that was built right above the water, adjoined to the house, 4 feet in width and surrounding it 360 degrees. Now as for transportation each family had to have either narrow river boat or some other kind of boat ... if a guy has a girl he has to get to her house by water. The water was always pure and natural because it was kept free of pollutants and the sewer pipes led from each home to a reservoir about three miles away.

Once I became somewhat familiar with my surroundings in the swamp, I began to scout around more and more each day. Each time I set out to explore, I crossed the same paths but always found something new. There were many days where I would be completely at ease by just hopping in my boat and going out to the eastern part of the swamp and just remaining there all day. Sometimes I would take a book and sometimes I would take a radio or fishing rod or nothing at all. One of my favorite

trees was located in the eastern part of the swamp. It was a very beautiful
tree which offered plenty of shade and security. It was a Cypress tree.

He then writes of the dangers: the snakes that live on the swamp ("these snakes are beautiful creatures but most of them are dangerous to a person who doesn't know how to handle them or to someone who doesn't know the nature of them") and the alligators, and the encounters between the two. He writes about his family always having "an abundance of food" because "in the swamp there is more than enough food," naming the different fish and in what season each would be plentiful, about fishing and hunting only "out of necessity," and how he had learned to track at an early age. He continues:

I feel that I have been blessed to be of those who are in tune with nature,
to be able to understand it and become one with it, to know and appreci-
ate it. Many times I believe this has been instilled within my soul before
my physical birth. The reason I believe this is because I come from a rich
cultural background which thrived and existed with and upon nature for
a very long time. (JJ)

He writes of his mother, "directly of African descent, born and raised in Brazil, in Bahia, a township known for its strongly practiced African religious customs," a place where the slave traders transported slaves from the Yoruba tribe. He writes of his father, a Cajun or Creole, of African and North American Indian descent, a member of the Chitimacha tribe spread throughout Louisiana, Alabama, Mississippi, and Arkansas and how he believes that his deep connection to nature was created when he "was still in the fetus position within my mother's belly, because everything my ancestors did was based solely upon nature and the mysteries that it held and this was part of everyday life."

For this student the writing in his journal was a way of re-membering, of gaining his members back, of becoming whole. An editor would probably advise me to cut many of these journal entries in terms of this book, but for me, the fact that he wrote so diligently, richly, sensuously, knowingly, and beautifully speaks of the importance of the journal as a way to bring ourselves "home," to connect with body, heart, and spirit.

Reviewing his journal entries at the end of the semester, one student writes:

When I read my entries, I saw a young man who doesn't belong here. I do believe that I should be punished for my actions, but here is not the place for me. If anything it has been detrimental. Although I'm a pretty laid back person now, I can remember two years ago a boy on the peak of being a young man, very carefree and could get a few chuckles out of a stone. I've seen him try to hold on to those traits with all his might, but the environment he was in forced him to put his carefreeness and humor to sleep for an indefinite amount of time. But through the space of time everything balances out, so it was only right that my lost traits be replaced by new ones. I'm not happy with my new ones. My carefree style was replaced by shrewdness. But at least I still have my humor, but now there is often a sting behind it that it never had. And last but not least, I've found contempt. I've learned how to harbor it and nourish it. But maybe these changes were for the better. Because a man who gets respect gets more out of life than a man who is likeable. But I will say this. Every now and then when I'm alone or in the presence of someone I truly get along with, I wake up the little guy who is carefree and loves laughter, because the last thing in the world I would want is for him to die. (PG)

Me, too, the last thing I would want.

It makes me happy to see, again, how the journal provided a space for feelings and thoughts, how it helped to keep "the little guy" alive, to return to one's roots in nature, to connect to self, to past, to others, to God, how it provided a space to think about life and to feel the depth of one's own life. In the prison, where so much is geared to dehumanizing and disabling the spirit, the journal became a way to connect with that spirit. If that is all the journal did, it is good, very good; it is enough.

I've read some of these journal entries aloud to others, but typing them for the first time has had an effect even stronger than I anticipated. Writing their words, I picture their faces. I am touched again by their spirit—the openness, honesty, depth. I wonder where they are now, after so many years. I have a strong desire to reconnect with them, to find out how they are, to remind them of their words, to thank them for their words. Perhaps, as one of the students said earlier in his entry, that reconnection with them is what this book is all about.

CHAPTER FIFTEEN:

THE DIFFICULTY OF LOOKING AT WHAT IS RIGHT IN FRONT OF US

I know that on one level—whether I am looking from the lens of physics or systems theory or postmodernism or spirituality—there is no objective reality "out there," apart from the viewer, apart from context and relationships; that everything is impermanent, always changing, and, in some way, an "illusion." On the other hand, much of my teaching is geared, especially in the beginning, to get students to look at the "reality" outside of themselves, to see "it" before imposing their concept or judgment or idea of "it." To stand back long enough to actually hear and see another before reacting, projecting, anticipating, assuming, presuming, judging, silencing, defending. The child's open eyes looking as if for the first time, the stranger in a new land—I want them to see and describe "it" with as many sensory and specific details as possible, holding off generalizations, abstractions, thoughts, and feelings about "it." It is not an easy task.

In one prison composition class, I asked students to look closely at their non-dominant hand and then to describe what they observed with as many details as possible. A few minutes into the exercise I noticed that about half of them were no longer looking at anything. They were busily writing about their hand, but the hand was somewhere out of sight. For some reason the idea of just observing was difficult, made them uncomfortable; it was easier to write their ideas about how a hand looked than to look at their actual hand. I had to keep reminding them to actually observe the hand they were describing.

In a woman's writing class, I did the same exercise. There, too, I noticed that many women stopped looking, and some started laughing nervously. When I asked why, it became clear that their judgments were so strong they could not see; it was too painful. All they saw was ugly, old, wrinkled, distorted, misshapen. They, too, could not look at their own hand.

Simple observation is, clearly, not so simple. How to train the mind to pay attention, to observe with precision, care, and slowness, when all of our societal and media training has us speed through life, not present in our bodies or our environments, blurring the complex and intricate edges of our world and seeing only general forms.

Even here, in the Adirondack woodlands, I need to remind myself to slow down in order to be more present. Meditating and writing in a journal are ways of consciously stopping myself in my tracks. But every spring I want to slow myself even more, so rich is each day's new blossoming. My spring sketch book becomes a tool for paying attention, each morning allowing me to be present with just one emerging form: leaf, blossom, flower. I can't describe the joy of sitting on the earth and bending close to the fern still tight in its spiral circle, seeing and drawing the delicate and precise pattern. Or looking closely at the helibore as it moves from tight spear to spiral dance, one leaf emerging from another, large crenellated leaves catching sunlight in their folds, impossible to capture as contour drawing or sketch, but incredibly exciting to really see in its intricate motion. And every year I see again the dandelions—their spurts of golden cylinders radiating from a center and, later, their diaphanous puffs, the dark seed at the end of the invisible thread only visible as I begin to draw. My sketch journal becomes a kind of magnifying glass enlarging everything through slowing everything down, enabling me to see and chronicle the ancient and ever changing procession: spring beauty, trout lily, wild leeks, bloodroot, trillium, starflower, Canada mayflower; beech leaf emerging from brown shiny cusp, soft white hair over silky lime green; bright red spurting from the green-white sheath of poppy, the crimson flaring, the flowing skirt of a dancer, sunlight shining through paper thin petal; apple blossoms and clusters of hanging locust flowers, and daisies and queen anne's lace, the procession going on and on and I recording it all, learning name and form, observing growth pattern and seed dispersal. Georgia O'Keefe, in answer to the question why she painted her flowers so large, said: "Still, in a way, nobody sees a flower—really—it is so small—we haven't time. If I could paint the flower exactly as I see it no one would see what I see because I would paint it small like a flower is small. So I said to myself—I'll paint what I see—what the flower is to me—but I'll paint it big and they will be surprised into taking time to look at it."

That is what my slowing down does: it makes everything large. And miraculous. I think of Willa Cather's "Miracles rest not so much upon faces or voices or healing powers coming to us from afar off but on our perceptions being made finer, so that for a moment our eyes can see and our ears can hear what there is about us always." I know that whatever I look at with that kind of attention I begin to connect to and love, to honor and respect, whether it is the daisy or day lily or my own hand or face.

In many ways, this close attention transforms every object into a subject, infusing it with life. Paul Tillich defines "sin" as separation. For him all cruelty stems from this separation, both from self and from the other. Looking closely becomes, then, the opposing principle: a way of connecting, enabling us to see another in terms of its unique flowering life, as subject not object. From that perspective, the teaching of seeing is very important.

In his essay "Marrakech," George Orwell talks about the invisibility of dark skinned people to the white colonialists:

> But what I strange about these people is their invisibility. For several weeks, always at about the same time of the day, the file of old women had hobbled past the house with their firewood, and though they had registered themselves on my eyeballs, I cannot truly say that I saw them. Firewood was passing—that was how I saw it. It was only that one day, I happened to be walking behind them, and the curious up-and-down motion of a load of wood drew my attention to the human being beneath it. Then for the first time I noticed the poor old earth-colored bodies, bodies reduced to bones and leathery skin, bent double under the crushing weight.

In another part of his essay, Orwell writes about the Jewish ghettoes, crowded and windowless: "An old man sits at a lathe, his left leg is warped out of shape … his grandson, aged six, already starting the simpler part of the job." He continues:

As the Jews live in self-contained communities they follow the same trades as the Arabs, except for agriculture. Fruit-sellers, potters, silversmiths, blacksmiths, butchers, leatherworkers, tailors, water-carriers, beggars, porters—whichever way you look you see nothing but Jews. As a matter of fact there are thirteen thousand of them, all living in the space of a few acres. A good job Hitler wasn't here. Perhaps he was on his way, however. You hear the usual dark rumors about the Jews, not only from the Arabs but from the poorer Europeans. "Yes, mon vieux, they took my job away from me and gave it to a Jew. The Jews! They're the real rulers of this country, you know. They've got all the money. They control the banks, finance—everything. "But," I said, "Isn't it a fact that the average Jew is a laborer working for about a penny an hour?" "Ah, that's only for show! They're all money lenders really. They're cunning, the Jews." In just the same way, a couple of hundred years ago, poor old women used to be burned for witchcraft when they could not even work enough magic to get themselves a square meal.

Even when something is right before our eyes, it is, clearly, difficult to see "it" when we already have a belief or concept or prejudice that renders the reality invisible, our idea, even our "knowledge," more present than our actual experience. How important it is, then, to train the eye to stop and actually look— whether at the hand or the flower or the old dark skinned woman or the Jews. In one of his journal entrees, collected by Shepard in his *The Heart of Thoreau's Journals*, Thoreau speaks about what we need to forget in order to really see:

It is only when we forget all our learning that we begin to know. I do not get nearer by a hair's breadth to any natural object so long as I presume that I have an introduction to it from some learned man. To conceive of it with a total apprehension I must for the thousandth time approach it as something totally strange. If you would make acquaintance with the ferns you must forget your botany. You must get rid of what is commonly called knowledge of them. Not a single scientific term or distinction is the least to the purpose, for you would fain perceive something, and you must approach the object totally unprejudiced. You must be aware that no thing is what you have taken it to be. In what book is this world and its beauty described? Who has plotted the steps toward the discovery of beauty? You have

got to be in a different state from common. Your greatest success will
be simply to perceive that such things are.

To recondition the mind to that different state of close attention, I sometimes use the following exercise on contour drawing from Frederick Franck's *Zen and Seeing* with my students. I often use the hand, because, like the breath in meditation, it is our constant companion, but sometimes I have them choose an object from nature. Sometimes I have them draw the face of one who is sitting next to them.

Look it in the eye until you feel it looking back at you. Feel that you
are alone with it, that it is the most important thing in the universe,
that it contains all the riddles of life and death. It does! You are no
longer looking; you are seeing. Now take your pencil loosely in your
hand and while you keep your eyes focused allow the pencil to fol-
low on the paper what the eye perceives. Feel as if with the point of
the pencil you are caressing the contours, the whole circumference.
Just let your hand move. Don't check what gets on the paper; it does
not matter at all. Only don't let your mind wander from what it is
seeing, and don't lift your pencil from your paper. And, above all,
don't try too hard, don't "think" about what you are drawing, just
let the hand follow what the eye sees. We are conducting an experi-
ment in seeing, in undivided attention. The experiment is successful
if you succeed in feeling that you have become that object regardless
of what appears on the paper.

In the classroom, I again often experience the nervous laughing, the inability to move slowly, the judgment, all of which are now compounded by the fear of drawing: that it won't look right, be accurate, be "perfect." All that self-judgment and fear despite Franck's words, despite my saying it does not matter what it looks like, despite the "purpose" being "seeing" and "undivided attention" rather than drawing accurately or well, despite the fact that they are not to look at their drawing but only at the object being drawn. Here, too, I see students place the hand they are to observe out of sight, preferring to draw *a general hand* from memory rather than their actual hand from observation. I see them move quickly rather than slowly. I feel their fear of not doing something right and their judgment at their final drawing. But often there is also a wonderful and freeing laughter at the actual "picture" of the hand, the shell, the leaf, the face of their companion as we talk about the process.

I think of an experience with my then seven year old nephew when he visited our land. We had been using crayons and drawing and I thought it might be fun to do a contour drawing of each other's face. I described Franck's exercise: not lifting the pen from the paper, not looking at the paper, looking only at the other person, not being concerned with what our drawing looked like. When we each finished our drawing, David looked embarrassed to show me his picture, as if I would be insulted by the large and angular nose, the strange and intense eye, the lines not meeting, the proportions off. But I loved the portrait; the lines captured something essential about my face. He, on the other hand, wanted to try again. This time, without looking at my face at all, he quickly began to draw one of those "traditional" faces with the almond shaped eyes and the straight nondescript nose. He held it up proudly, clearly preferring the stereo-typical features over the true and real and animated lines, even when I showed him how "true" and interesting his first lines were and how I could actually see myself in them. For him, the second picture looked prettier, was better. At the age of seven he had already been conditioned to prefer the false, seemingly nicer image, to the true, like those uniform and "perfect" store bought apples over the ones growing in the fields.

How do we retrain ourselves to prefer truth over niceness, the real over the sen-timental, the wrinkles rather than the facelift, the angles and texture of a real hand (or real face) of a living person rather than a seemingly "perfect" hand (or face) of a model or manikin? And clearly this question pertains not only to writing and art but to all of life: how do we honor real life rather than fantasy, struggle rather than denial, honesty rather than glibness, truth rather than sen-timentality and romanticism, complexity rather than superficiality? How do we keep our eye trained to see rather than to gloss over and deny? And the par-allel questions: How can we break through prejudice, assumptions, illusions? How can we begin to question what we have been taught to believe? To me, the questions are essential, and the most immediate and accessible "answer" is to practice the simple and difficult art of paying attention. It is the skill of "description," the very beginning of a College Composition class.

In her *Drawing on the Right Side of the Brain*, Betty Edwards has various "tricks" to enable students to see lines and patterns rather than concepts and ideas. One of her exercises involves sketching a painting upside down, forcing the left side of the brain into silence so that the right side can focus on lines and spatial rela-tionships without being taken over by ideas about how something should look.

As a way of upping the ante or, rather, lessening the expectations, I often ask students not only to draw a hand or object without looking at the paper but, also, to use their nondominant hand—their unskilled and untrained hand, the one that doesn't "know."

What I have found both in my own sketches and in life is that whenever I hand the field over to the one who doesn't know and cannot do, there is a humbleness and vulnerability allowing a different kind of honesty and truth. Drawing with my nondominant left hand, I feel like a small child. I become all focused and concentrated, become even more open to and present with daffodil or cat or mountain line, with whatever it is I am drawing. Many of the lines are a little shaky. Nothing looks fabricated or perfect because I have, in reality, very little control. But the lines have the same truth as my nephew David's contour drawing of my nose and eyes.

I have kept many of my own contour drawings because they still touch me: the index finger pointing, the curled in fist, the outstretched open palm, the round cupped openness, the creases at the joints, the scars, the way each finger bends, the knuckles now much larger, the lines more pronounced, the nails bitten and vulnerable. My own hand. The pine cone or nautilus shell or banana peel. The curves and edges.

After the drawing, I ask students to write about the whole process still using their nondominant hand. One student observed that her tongue was out, in the corner of her mouth, while she drew, as it had been when she used to write in elementary school—until she was scolded by a nun and told to put her tongue where it belonged. Other students describe the nervousness and awkwardness and fear, the difficulty of not looking at their paper, but also the feeling of concentration, really seeing their "object," seeing as if for the first time. Some students who had been told that they couldn't draw—as I had been told I couldn't sing—actually found that they loved their lines as well as the process, and began to keep a sketch journal, to draw, to paint.

What is interesting to me is how looking closely at the "outside world" often enables us to be more fully "inside" our own body, to be embodied, to feel our own hand moving slowly across the page. And, also, how that slow observation of a concrete object, the exact and precise details, forces us into an honesty. In his "Politics and the English Language," George Orwell describes how language, particularly political language, is filled with abstractions used to deceive and manipulate. When we describe with concrete details what is directly in front of us, however, we do not lie:

What is above all needed is to let the meaning choose the word, and not the other way about. In prose, the worst thing one can do with words is to surrender to them. When you think of a concrete object, you think wordlessly, and then, if you want to describe the thing you have been visualizing you probably hunt about till you find the exact words that seem to fit. When you think of something abstract you are more inclined to use words from the start, and unless you make a conscious effort to prevent it, the existing dialect will come rushing in and do the job for you, at the expense of blurring or even changing your meaning.

It's true; once we start to generalize, the words come pouring out. We spout concepts and ideas we have been taught (by the media, our parents, our religion, our conditioning), thinking these ideas are ours and that our words are spontaneous. But many of our ideas and even cherished beliefs have not been examined or explored, have not come to us through our actual experiences, are not really embodied in reality. What I keep trying to do—in whatever way is possible—is to get myself and my students to stop and really look at the concrete object so that we don't "lie" to ourselves or others.

I remember the first time I took a drawing class. The teacher asked us to bring in a natural object. I had a branch with one leaf still attached. She asked us to draw our object, and I did, in a few minutes. I felt finished. She then told us that we would spend the next hour on that same branch. Years later I read in Assagioli's *The Act of Will*, a story from Ramacharaka's *Raja Yoga* about the naturalist Agassiz and his method of training students. One student, the story goes, was told by Agassiz to observe carefully a fish he had taken from a jar: "In a half hour (the student) felt certain that he had observed all about the fish that there was to be perceived. But the naturalist remained away." The student returned to

gaze again at that wearisome fish ... felt disgusted and discouraged and wished he had never come to Agassiz, who, it seemed, was a stupid old man ... Then, in order to kill time, he began to count the scales. This completed he counted the spines of the fins. Then he began to draw a picture of the fish. In drawing the picture, he noticed that the fish had no dyends. He thus made the discovery that as his teacher had expressed often in lectures, "a pencil is the best of eyes." Shortly after the teacher returned and after ascertaining what the youth had observed, he left rather disappointed, telling the boy to keep on looking and maybe he would see something. This put the boy on his mettle, and he began to work with his pencil, putting down little details that had escaped him before but which now seemed very plain to him. He began to catch the secret of observation. Little by little he brought to light new objects of interest about the fish. But this did not suffice his teacher who kept him at work on the same fish for three whole days. At the end of that time the student really knew something about the fish and, better than all, and acquired the "knack" and habit of careful observation and perception in detail.

That is the training we all need. What is interesting to me, however, is that Agassiz himself, someone so aware of the necessity of close observation, limited his own vision in areas which threatened his religious concepts. Believing in creationism, he could not allow in the possibility of evolution, could not follow his own lesson of close observation and openness to experience. For all of us, clearly, there is always something "beyond the pale," something that consciously and/or unconsciously we cannot or do not want to see. The training in close observation, however, gives us a tool to continually expand our world, to lessen those areas of blindness and ignorance, and, sometimes, to catch ourselves in the act of denial.

Within the prison composition class, the first description I ask students to do is of their cell. And of course there is resistance: "I hate the cell, why would I write about it?" "I'm there all day, why do I need to think about it when I'm not there." And, always, the feeling that what they experience could never be communicated, that someone in the outside world could never understand what it was like to be in prison or really care. I tell them I start with the cell, as I start with their hand, as insight meditation starts with the breath, because it is there, in front of them, because they can actually observe the details. And what I don't say but I feel is that the process of writing might enable them to more deeply connect to themselves, their feelings, their reality and, even, to their cell.

With all of us, I think, there is a tendency to state our feelings and our judgments as if we were describing, repeating the same abstract words over and over as if to amplify meaning. It is a bit like screaming more loudly to a deaf person in order to be heard: "I feel very lonely here." "I hate the ugliness of the cell." It's not that the feeling or judgment is unimportant or not true, but, as we've been told by countless books and teachers, we need to show—to give the specific details—not tell, if we want others to feel the experience themselves, to feel the ugliness or the loneliness. And it is not just for "the other," the reader, but, rather, for ourselves, the writer. By starting with the details rather than the generalization, the observer/writer is able to touch into feelings and thoughts that might lie under the surface, still untapped by the conscious mind. Through the process of writing, through looking closely at hand or cell, the writer might actually discover what s/he does not yet know.

I wish I had some of those early papers. One that I remember focused very specifically on the water stains on the concrete walls and the patterns they made and on the dust within the cell. What became very strong in this student's paper was the opposition between water and earth—two of life's elements—and the atmosphere of death and decay within the cell. At the end of his description, he talked directly about the cell as death, but it was the close looking—at the dust and the water stains—that brought both him and the reader to that powerful realization. Another student began by listing the exact measurements of floor space, bars, windows, bed. Then he measured himself and how many paces he could take within the cell. Reading his description, I could feel the cramped confinement: no room to be. Another student looked around the cell and mentioned all that he had put there, describing in detail the specific photographs, the calendar, the poster, the bedcovering—capturing his attempt to create a home through small gestures of warmth and color. Another student just named the books piled up by his bed in a way that conveyed his ability to remove himself from that cell and journey into other realms. Another began to list all that was not in the cell, capturing his loneliness by naming the absence of all he loved.

In class we discuss the difference between a topic and a thesis and between concrete details and abstract generalizations, and we talk about the conscious selection and ordering of details rather than just an unconnected listing. But, really, what I mainly want is for them to see how the journey itself can reveal something they might not have known, how they can come to their thesis rather than begin with it. I want them to use their own eyes and their other senses—their own writing of the specific details—to get to that central feeling or idea or image. When they realize their "thesis," they might go back: selecting out some details that now seem superfluous or repetitive, adding others that now seem important, relevant, and real; they might rearrange and reorder the different details, extending and developing certain ones. At this later stage, they consciously control and shape their paper. But the beginning must come from another place, less known to the ego and the conscious mind, must come out of themselves—like a spider spinning its web from its own gut—if they are to build something real and meaningful. By looking closely at the outside world, they will actually start to see something about their inside world, their paper slowly tracing the sometimes circuitous, sometimes contradictory, often complex journey "home."

When someone follows that process, what I experience in the writing is close to what I felt with David's contour drawing: the honesty of the lines, the power that resides in what is true … even in the writing of a brief description of a hand or of a cell. What we are doing, as Agassiz did, is teaching the skill of observation, of stopping long enough to actually see. It is the groundwork for all that follows.

CHAPTER SIXTEEN:

LOOKING OUT, LOOKING IN, THE SAME PROCESS

Robert Bly, in his introduction to his *Selected Poems of Rainer Maria Rilke*, writes of Rilke feeling that some of his earlier poems were "vague, poetic, and talky" and that he needed to look more closely and listen more intently to the outside world. As Rodin's secretary, Rilke learned much from the sculptor about form. According to Bly, "When Rilke confided one day that he hadn't been writing lately, Rodin … suggested that Rilke go to the zoo … and look at an animal until (he saw it). Two of three weeks might not be too long." It was a bit like Agassiz' advise to his student to look at the fish to try to see "the thing itself." Interesting that for his first "seeing poem," Rilke chose to observe a panther. What he saw were bars and confinement, the prison that is the focus of this book:

From seeing the bars, his seeing is so exhausted
that it no longer holds anything anymore.
To him the world is bars, a hundred thousand
bars, and behind the bars, nothing.

The lithe swinging of that rhythmical easy stride
which circles down to the tiniest hub

is like a dance of energy around a point

in which a great will stands stunned and numb.

Only at times the curtains of the pupil rise
without a sound ... then a shape enters,
slips through the tightened silence of the shoulders,
reaches the heart, and dies.

Looking at the outside world so intently, Rilke captures something deep about the interior world and the essence of confinement and imprisonment; he is able to see "the great will" which "stands stunned and numb."

Bly writes about this process of "seeing" in Rilke and other poets:

> *Goethe observed plants meticulously with scientific method, and this labor seemed to feed his oceanic, passionate poems, to fill them with inward intensity. Goethe respected the discipline of seeing. Novalis, slightly younger than Goethe, wrote an aphorism in 1800 and declared that there are two natural stages in an artist's life. During the first stage the artist goes inward, to Innigkeit, exclusive contemplation of the self, a stage that may last years. But if an artist stays there, he or she has gone only halfway, because the second stage, according to Novalis, involves 'a sober and spontaneous' observation of the outer world. Putting "sober" and "spontaneous" next to each other is wonderful. Both adjectives are apt for Durer's crab or his clump of marsh grass or his rabbit; both apply to the meticulous detail Chinese artists influenced by Buddhism brought into their paintings. It's as if there was some spiritual force that leaves our body through the eyes, spontaneously pulled out, and this force or being gets stronger precisely by being out there, seeing what is not us. Walter Spink has called attention to the old Chinese statement "When a question is posed ceremoniously, the universe responds."*

Bly then talks about Francis Ponge, "the living master of the 'seeing' poem," quoting from Ponge about "'the primacy accorded to matter, to the object, to the unbelievable qualities that emerge from it ... Nothing can prevent the meanings which have been locked into the simplest object or person from always striking the hours.... In these terms one will surely understand what I consider to be the function of poetry. It is to nourish the spirit of man by giving him the cosmos to suckle.'"

The "meanings which have been locked into the simplest object"—I have experienced that throughout my life, when I have been open enough and looked and listened long enough at what is not me, whether the tall grass blowing in a wide field, the sound of ocean water receding over rounded stones, my cat lapping water at the stream, the wet and soft beech leaf in Spring breaking through its brown husk, the poppy emerging bright red out of its mint green nestpod—the beginning ruffle at the base, the long dress unfurling suddenly—or my own hand moving in the air. The close observation of the "object" seems to lead, quite naturally and unexpectedly, to a deeper seeing and understanding of "life."

In "A Green Crab's Shell," Mark Doty captures this movement (in and out) beautifully:

> *Not, exactly, green:*
> *closer to bronze*
> *preserved in kind brine,*
>
> *something retrieved*
> *from a Greco-Roman wreck,*
> *patinated and oddly*
>
> *muscular. We cannot*
> *know what his fantastic*
> *legs were like—*
>
> *though evidence*
> *suggests eight*
> *complexly folded*
>
> *scuttling works*
> *of armaments, crowned*
> *by the foreclaws'*
>
> *gesture of menace*
> *and power. A gull's*
> *gobbled the center,*
>
> *leaving this chamber*
> *—size of a demitasse—*

open to reveal

a shocking, Giotto blue.
Though it smells
Of seaweed and ruin,

This little traveling case
comes with such lavish lining!
Imagine breathing

Surrounded by
The brilliant rinse
Of summer's firmament.

What color is
The underside of skin?
Not so bad, to die,

If we could be opened
Into this—
if the smallest chambers

of ourselves,
similarly,
revealed some sky.

Through this concentrated focus on "the other," some subtle "trickery" seems to occur. Somehow the ego is no longer the one defining the world through its perspective, insisting on its concepts, ideas, values, judgments. It is as if the ego has disappeared from the scene, been lulled to sleep, or is just standing on the side, silent, humble, one of many participants. We are able to be with what is—in front of us and in the universe. As with Franck's exercise in seeing, we become one with the object we observe. And, according to Ponge, in seeing the very specific, concrete object, we are given the "cosmos."

When I look at my teaching, I see, again and again, how much I try to trick those various gatekeepers who keep under lock and key all that could inform and deepen our seeing and understanding. This book, in many ways, is my book of sorcery revealing those slights of hands—drawing with the nondominant hand, writing in a journal, singing around the campfire in the dark as if no one can hear—anything that will allow the prisoners to escape from the guards who reside both within and outside of the self. Paying close attention to external details is one way. A quick and spontaneous listing of those specific facts and details is another.

Usually when students come to a weekend at the college where I now teach, they are either exhausted or speeding, very rarely centered and relaxed. In that atmosphere, if I just asked "how are you," some students would give plot summaries, others might give nondescript generalizations like good or lousy, others might start to complain, others might go off on tangents, giving every detail of a very long story, and others might sit silently. I often begin groups with writing rather than speaking not as a way to silence feelings but as a way for students to come more deeply into those feelings, to reside more fully in their body that has been rushing from one place to another. To be here. It is a good way to get centered—for myself as well as them—even if no writing comes into the silence of that space. But almost always writing does come.

Students have been apart from each other for one month; clearly much has transpired. Sometimes I ask students to just list some of what they have seen, heard, smelled, eaten, thought, dreamed, a simple list of specific details. What's interesting is how much is revealed by those small details, the immediacy and honesty of external facts giving a sense of what touches our lives, allowing us to see the waves and changes. It's like meditation where we watch the mind and consciously note its travels. Instead of generalizing too soon that our month or life has been depressing and empty or wonderful and perfect, we learn about the always changing terrain.

Writing in group becomes a way that each person can tap into his/her own thoughts and feelings before those ideas are lost or moderated or silenced, and it is a way that people can connect to each other on a deeper and more intimate level. Although anyone can choose to pass and not read, most people do not. Even with quivering voice and with apologies, most read and all are heard. When students comment, at the end of the semester, about the depth of sharing within the group, I reveal the simple path to this real "magic." The beginning writing and listening create a channel for what is usually more real and honest than our usual social talk. We connect on a deeper level, becoming more intimate with self and other.

The list is, in a way, similar to story, but with many short plots and no central theme. Along with the list, I also work with images. I ask students to close their eyes and image an animal or an instrument or a vegetable that in some way captures some of what they are feeling now (or what they have been experiencing during the month). It's another one of those "silly" exercises that, somehow and quite miraculously, works. I see students go inside themselves. I hear the silence and feel the concentration as they begin to write. When they finish, or think they have finished, I ask them to write more. And they will—about brussel sprouts growing in late Autumn or a porcupine or squirrel or jelly fish or a violin that is out of tune—in a way that is clearly true, the specific external details revealing something about one's emotional and psychological state: the violin with a broken string; the mariachi band missing two lead musicians; the water drum; the wooden flute in a quiet woods; the pepper planted too close to other peppers, its inside all pulpy; the red cabbage with its intricate lines running through it; the still green tomato fearful of the coming frost. I remember one student reading her image: "a dishrag," used by everyone, cleaning up messes, worn out, largely ignored, just lying around. The image shocked her, saddened her, and made her change her study and, eventually, her life. She knew the image was true.

What is constantly amazing is the power of the simple image to capture a complex emotion, the image, like the specific details, forcing an honesty that allows us to see and reveal what might otherwise stay hidden. Images are a bit like a knife; they cut through denser matter with a sharpness, clarity, and truth that can be surprising and, to the ego, threatening. In "Poetry is not a Luxury," an essay in her *Sister Outsider*, Audre Lorde says, "I could name at least ten ideas I would have found intolerable or incomprehensible and frightening, except as they came after dreams and poems." The image finds a way to sneak through the censoring mind and the watchful ego.

Our outside world is filled with forms and images; our inside world has that same wealth. We go in and out between the two realms, the images echoing and amplifying. Images appear continuously on the periphery of our mind and in our dreams, informing us about our feelings, thoughts, perceptions. The problem is that often we pay them no attention, no matter how persistent or powerful they are, not noticing them, thinking them foolish or irrelevant to our lives, not wanting to see or hear what an image might reveal.

What I try to do in class is create exercises which call our mind into attention and create a space to see and welcome the "unexpected visitors" rather than have them standing ignored at the gate. Exercises which let in ideas which would have been "intolerable or incomprehensible and frightening"—letting them in before the gates lock and doors close. We might still reject those images, but we are no longer unconscious; they have already entered our psyche and we then have choice.

I know that I, myself, have trouble with guided visualizations in which I am told where I am and what I am feeling. I feel controlled and I rebel; it's natural for someone who wants to be free from any prison. But I love when I close my eyes and someone allows me to journey where I already am, imaging concrete details of an imagined terrain in order to understand something existing within me on a less conscious level. One exercise I sometimes do towards the end of the semester in the college in which I teach, where students have created and shaped their studies around specific questions they want to explore, is to ask students to visualize their study as a landscape. I then give them time to look around the landscape they have created—to listen, smell, touch. At a certain point I ask them to visualize some obstacle which is blocking their way and to examine it closely. I ask them to look around and notice any object or being which, in some way, might give them a clue about how to move through that obstacle. At the end of the visualization, I ask them to write about their experience.

For some students, the vision becomes the seed for a long essay. Almost all students are informed by their own vision: whether seeing a turtle telling them that it is okay to protect themselves inside their shell, or a rabbit telling them that vulnerability and softness are "the way," or a snake showing them the beauty of what had been seen as ugly. Or, in an arid desert, a landscape of death, suddenly finding a source for water by noticing the prints of animals.

In one exercise, I remember asking students who they would want to keep out of their landscape. One student wrote of dogs, because their energy would disturb the quiet of the wilderness. The more she wrote, the more she began to understand about those she didn't want and why: the dog as an energy of connection, devotion, love, an energy that would disturb her solitude. And when she read her visualization, she began to weep, to see the possibility of including that "love dog" within her environment rather than excluding it as a threat to her being.

It is quite amazing this language of image and where it leads us when we give it space. It is simple in its concreteness and complex in its meaning. Image, like story, is spoken in the mother tongue, accessible to all of us, if we allow ourselves to be simple, to let in the visitors standing outside our door, to invite them to sit around the kitchen table and to speak in their native tongue.

CHAPTER SEVENTEEN:

NARRATION, TELLING THE STORIES OF OUR LIVES

When I was young, sitting around our Bronx kitchen table, I wanted more nourishment than my mother's quite wonderful cooking. Then, and really all through our lives, my sister and I would try to engage our parents in telling stories of their lives. It was not easy. Although someone looking from the outside might see their lives as rich, neither felt they had anything interesting to say.

My father came from a small village, Piaterer, outside of Kiev, a Jewish shtetl. He and his father were peddlers, driving the wagon from Piaterer to other towns. My father did well in the cheder, the Jewish school, and would have been allowed to continue schooling in Kiev if he had found a Jewish family with whom to live. But it felt too lonely in Kiev, he said, and so he stopped the education which he loved. When he was thirteen he decided to leave Russia and come to America with his uncle and aunt, pretending he was their son. They stayed in Rumania for three years, on a waiting list, and finally arrived in New York City when my father was sixteen. My father lived as a boarder, worked two jobs, one at night baking bread. He attended school to learn English but would, he said, fall asleep in class. At some point he had saved enough money to send for his parents and siblings. When they arrived, they all settled in the Southeast Bronx, an apartment in which my grandparents lived until they died and which we visited every Sunday of my childhood, my father's one day off. My grandparents and uncle and aunt all worked in a fruit and vegetable store which they owned. My father chose to work alone, selling wholesale tomatoes and bananas which he picked up at the Hunts Street market, ripened in his cellar, and sold to stores in the Bronx. He also had a very small fruit stand right beside his cellar. He lived with his parents and siblings until he was thirty seven when he met and married my mother. They moved further north, to the then almost rural section of Pelham Parkway in the Bronx, to an apartment house in which they lived until their death and in which I grew up. He continued his same work at his same stand until he retired at seventy, my mother helping him at the stand on the busy days—Thursday, Friday, and Saturday—after my sister and I had completed elementary school. And thus goes the external details of his life.

I can only imagine the shifts of worlds, from the small shtetl to the large city, from a horse drawn wagon to airplanes, from 1904 when he was born to 1984 when he died. I think about the fear of the Jews living in the Ukraine, the history of pogroms and anti-Semitic violence, the beginning of the Russian Revolution, the coming to this land. I wanted to hear those stories, not just the external facts. When he and we were older, my sister and I would come with pencil and paper asking him about certain parts of his life, wanting those details about the village and the way of life there, what it was like being "a stranger in a new land," what he knew about the condition of the Jews during WWII, what happened when he spoke up against the exploitative policies of United Fruit ... But while my father loved to argue politics and to talk philosophy, knew history, was able to name all the anti-Semites in America, storytelling was clearly not his language. Perhaps he felt that English, as opposed to Yiddish, was not really his mother tongue. I know he was afraid. And ashamed.

My father was always ashamed of his accent and hardly ever wrote a letter in English because of his insecurity about spelling, grammar and vocabulary. When I read a book with selections from *Daily Forward's* "Bintel Brief" (letters written by immigrant Jews to the Yiddish daily newspaper), my father dismissed the questions and concerns voiced as coming from "ignorant greenhorns," feeling shame rather than interest, memory, or pride. When I was in elementary school and we were all required to say what our fathers (and it was fathers) did for a living, I remember my father telling me to say that "my father sells wholesale and retail fruits and vegetables," not that he sold tomatoes and bananas from a small stand underneath the elevator trains, he and all the other small merchants paying off the cops in order to stay there, the women squeezing the fruit, he having a big box of soft tomatoes that he would give to poor families at the end of every day, not that every morning at 6 a.m. he would go up and down the cellar steps bringing up the ripened fruit, that it got harder to carry such weight and he became more afraid as he got older and the neighborhood tougher, not the details of the changing ethnic groups and the food that was most important for each group, not the details that would make a good story but, rather, the description that would be more acceptable to the conventional world. The "revised" drawing of my nephew who took out all the specific and real details that gave life to the portrait.

With my mother, it was the same story, or lack of story. I did hear about her father—for some reason she liked to tell of his being the first Jewish immigrant to Quincy, Massachusetts, his passport getting threadbare from his using it so often to sponsor each new Jewish immigrant; about his being so generous that he gave everyone credit in his small grocery store until he had to close the store because of debt. She also told of her mother, but only how she came to America five years after her husband had left, never wanting to leave her parents and the old country, how her boat began to sink just a short distance out of Ellis Island, she and the others coming to the new country with only the clothes they were wearing. My mother spoke of how her mother kept the old ways, never "adjusted" to the new country, and died in the influenza epidemic when she, my mother, was only nine.

When my mother was in her eighties, I came to visit with my new video camera, hoping, once again, to record stories of her life—not just the often repeated "stories" of her visit to the various doctors, about the different bills she was charged, about Mrs. B or Mrs. K and their daughters and grandchildren's marriage or Bar Mitzvah. I wanted to hear about her childhood, about what it felt like growing up without a mother, about leaving all her family in Quincy and coming to the Bronx with a mother-in-law who clearly never welcomed or loved her, about working at the fruit stand with my father, about living with and then without my father, about getting older and being alone. But what she would say, and what I captured on the video, is her sitting at the table, a sweet smile on her face, saying: "Bernice, what can I say, I have no stories to tell." Never having completed junior high school, believing herself stupid and her life uninteresting, my mother, too, would not tell her own stories, never draw the actual lines of her life, but instead speak about other people's children, the crimes in the area, the high prices of goods.

To tell or write stories we must, on some level, feel that we have stories worth telling, ones that others might want to hear, that our lives are, in some way, interesting or meaningful. It is a version of my modern dance teacher's "I am here," a necessary declaration of one's right to one's place in the universe. I do not think my parents felt that right and thus did not tell their stories, a loss for both them and me. But many people are natural storytellers. And the narrative essay is probably the easiest "form" to teach because stories are usually accessible, on the tips of our tongues, around the campfires, around the tables, on the streets, in the bedrooms. All indigenous cultures, all people close to the earth, all peoples tell stories, either orally or in written form. It is, clearly, in our blood.

What is interesting is which stories we tell and which we do not. There are stories we have repeated so many times that they have lost any dynamic life; they are like a rut in which our tongues are stuck, repeating over and over a deadened litany. And there are the stories that have never been told, their silence another form of death and burial. I have sometimes started a class with the first sentence of Maxine Kingston's *Woman Warrior*, "Don't tell anyone what I am about to tell you," as an impetus for writing. What is amazing is that people actually write what they have never spoken, bringing into the light what had been in darkness. In one memoir class, as one student after another read her untold story, it was almost as if there were a video screen behind each speaker capturing the event being described, the reality finally breaking through the veil of family secrecy, everyone now, finally, present to witness that past.

Within the prison class, I do not ask people to go into the forbidden and secret; there is already too much darkness, fear, and vulnerability. Usually I just ask students to re-member one story from their childhood, stressing that it does it does not have to be large or dramatic in terms of the outside world but only an event that, for some reason, has remained sculpted in their mind. I ask them to go back, remembering all they can about the external surroundings, all the sensory details, using all the skills that they have begun to hone in their earlier descriptive writing. To get back into their child's body and re-member—that is, to get their "members" back through the act of memory. And they often do, allowing themselves an almost innocence as they speak from that small body.

Some students, however, do not go back to childhood; they are compelled to write of the more recent past, particularly of their crime and the trial. Needing to tell that story again and again—and I can understand that compulsion—they often get bogged down with the specific facts and chronological sequence, giving a thousand details chronicling their crime, the trial, and their imprisonment. It's interesting to think of the distinction between the reciting of chronological facts and the telling of a story, between external events and reflection on one's experience; that, in itself, becomes a rich focus for discussion within the class.

In Washington Correctional Facility most of the students were young, in their early twenties. Because of their age, I found their level of reflection generally less deep than the reflection of the older students in Great Meadows. I remember once asking those younger students, when we began the study of analysis, to define and/or analyze "analysis." One student's honest response was: "Analysis is something I have never done." He was the same student who, in his first narration, wrote about his gang bringing guns and knives to high school in order to get back at another gang who had done something to their gang member the day before. He gave many details: the entry into school, the placement of various weapons in the lockers, the exact chronology of events, the specificity of the violence ... But something clearly was missing. After he had read his paper, one student looked at him and asked: "Is that it? Is that the end of the story?" And what he was really asking, although he didn't use these words, was: What is the story you are telling and why? The student had told a sequence of events but how not framed those events into an experience. It was not yet a story.

It was that student—who had never analyzed and who recited sequential events rather than reflecting on experience—who taught me the possibility of teaching "thinking," a process which began for him with the realization that he had not yet shaped a story through conscious reflection and that he had never learned to analyze. Analysis was, as he said later, a muscle that had never been used. A sense of "story" was there, within him, but it needed to be developed through "exercise."

I wish I had that student's papers from the beginning of the semester to the end. They would have shown the incredible growth of both mind and heart, the transformation of external event into internal experience, the development of consciousness. When I saw and spoke to the student years later, he seemed, I told him, "like a man, not a boy." He was very mature, very thoughtful. He talked about his changes and his growth. Still in prison, never having graduated because the college program was stopped, he nevertheless continued learning; he read voluminously and was, in fact, a scholar. Perhaps the narrative essay was the beginning of his intellectual journey.

For their narration, I usually ask students to first capture the experience itself as vividly as they can and, then, to stand back and reflect on its meaning. As examples, I distribute narrative essays—Orwell's personal essay on bedwetting in boarding school, his shame and the brutality of the punishment, in his *Such, Such Were the Joys* and/or Audre Lorde's vivid snapshots of experiences of racism and sexism in her "Eye to Eye" in *Sister Outsider*, her book of essays.

At the end of his essay, after vividly capturing his actual experience, Orwell reflects on memory:

> *In general one's memories of any period must necessarily weaken as one moves away from it. One is constantly learning new facts, and old ones have to drop out to make way for them. At twenty I could have written the history of my schooldays with an accuracy which would be quite impossible now. But it can also happen that one's memories grow sharper after a long lapse of time, because one can look at the past with fresh eyes and can isolate and, as it were, notice facts which previously existed undifferentiated among a number of others. Here are two things which in a sense I remembered which did not strike me as strange or interesting until quite recently. One is that the second beating seemed to me a just and reasonable punishment. To get one beating, and then to get another and fiercer one on top of it, for being so unwise as to show that the first had not hurt—that was quite natural. The gods are jealous, and when you have good fortune you should conceal it. The other is that I accepted the broken riding crop as my own crime. I can still recall my feeling as I saw the handle lying on the carpet—the feeling of having done an ill-bred clumsy thing, and ruined an expensive object. I had broken it: so Sambo told me, and so I believed. This acceptance of guilt lay unnoticed in my memory for twenty or thirty years.*

Through the act of writing, Orwell is able to resee his past through adult's eyes and, thus, free himself from the guilt he had unconsciously internalized as a child.

In her essay "Eye to Eye" Lorde explores the question why black women seem to have such anger at other black women. To understand, she looks closely at her early experiences where she feels the eye of hatred cast upon her. She begins her essay with the following reflection:

> *When I started to write about the intensity of the angers between Black women, I found I had only begun to touch one tip of a three pronged iceberg, the deepest understructure of which was Hatred, that societal deathwish directed against us from the moment we were born Black and female in America. From that moment on we have been steeped in hatred—for*

our color, for our sex, for our effrontery in daring to presume we had any right to live. As children we absorbed that hatred, passed it through our-selves, and for the most part, we still live our lives outside of the recogni-tion of what that hatred really is and how it functions. Echoes of it return as cruelty and anger in our dealings with each other....

Children know only themselves as reasons for the happenings in their lives. So of course as a child I decided there must be something terribly wrong with me that inspired such contempt. The bus driver didn't look at other people like that. All the things my mother had warned me not to do and be that I had gone right ahead and done must be to blame.

To search for power within myself means I must be willing to move through being afraid to whatever lies beyond. If I look at my most vulner-able places and acknowledge the pain I have felt, I can remove the source of that pain from my enemies' arsenals. My history cannot be used to feather my enemies' arrows then, and that lessens their power over me. Nothing I accept about myself can be used against me to diminish me ...

America's measurement of me has lain like a barrier across the real-ization of my own powers. It was a barrier which I had to examine and dismantle, piece by painful piece, in order to use my energies fully and creatively. It is easier to deal with the external manifestations of racism and sexism than it is to deal with the results of those distortions internal-ized within our consciousness of ourselves and one another.

Both Orwell and Lorde capture their childhood experiences vividly. Both use writing as a way to resee their experiences: to examine, reflect, question, and break free from unconscious, internalized, and habitual responses. While most students at this stage do not usually incorporate those complex layerings within their writing, it feels important to provide examples that show possibilities, to fill reservoirs for future use. What they do write is the story itself. And that is a very good beginning.

The following narrative by J.M. is one that I thought to Xerox; there were many, many others that I could have included had I saved them. It is not from child-hood nor does it really "reflect," but it is very rich:

I carefully scraped together the last remnants of thick lumpy sauce to the corner of my plate, positioning it so that it could be scooped up easily onto the chunk of fresh warm Italian bread waiting patiently in my other hand. When they were finally joined and devoured, I turned to compliment him on the meal, only to find him looking at me, quite sullen, with a pain in his eyes that I wished I could have removed but knew that to be impossible because it was me that put it there. I could not hold eye contact with him long; my shame would not allow me. He knew it too and to make me more comfortable he turned and fussed with the espresso pot by the stove, measuring carefully the dark almost black coffee grinds and adding precisely the amount of water to be used. The anisette and lemon peel were already on the table, along with the small fine crystal coffee cups that momma brought to this country from Bori. He only used them for special occasions and I didn't understand why they were out now. I felt self conscious and honored at the same time.

He turned from the stove with the smoking pot and placed it in the center of the table. He glanced at his loving wife who was just finishing the dishes and as if on cue she shut the water off, dried her hands on a dish towel and started to leave the room. Before exiting she stopped behind me, placed her hands lovingly on my shoulders and kissed the back of my head. She then did what she had done so many times before when her husband wished to speak to someone alone. She left the room and occupied herself in another part of the house.

He looked at me again, but this time the pain and sullenness were gone from his eyes and in their place was a look somewhat resembling a judge about to pass a harsh sentence on someone. He pulled the chair out and started to sit. My mind raced with thoughts that swept through it. I knew it was coming then, the speech, the lecture of how I was told a million times and how he should have beaten it into my head, about what a stupid little jerk off kid I was, who did nothing but hang out with a bunch of punks who thought they were tough guys and how he told me that the little slut I was running around with would get me into big trouble one of these days and that this is it, this is the last time he was going to help me out of a jam, that from here on in I was on my own.

He nestled himself into the chair and poured us each a cup of coffee. I sat there stirring it with my spoon, blending the clear licorice liqueur with the coffee, watching the lemon peel twirl in the liquid for what seemed an eternity, waiting, bracing myself for the verbal onslaught that did not come.

He was looking directly at me, the judge in him now gone. His eyes and mine locked and in that moment his eyes told me how much he loved me, of how he had raised me since birth and tried to be the father I never had.

Of how he had done his best to teach me about honor and respect and that all the punishments he administered throughout the years were for my own good and how he planned on me having a better life than he did and how he was going to miss me dearly.

My humble eyes did not know what to say to him.

He pushed a brown bag across the table in front of me and finally spoke. "Everything you need is in the bag ... Dey will be lookin for you here soon, you betta get goin ... Take care of yourself kid."

I stuffed the bag into my belt and under my shirt. In it was a new set of identification, a one way ticket to San Francisco, and $5000 in small used bills.

We both stood at the same time and embraced. I kissed him on his cheek. He let me go and waved his hand toward the door. I was leaving.

As I reached the door a deja-vu type feeling overcame me. Lost memories came back like ghosts to crowd my mind, of a child growing up in hell's kitchen, of being approached by the authorities as I trotted home from school asking me questions about where my brother was, and how they were friends of his. But also of being taught that I never knew where he was even when I did.

With a sad smile of sweet recollections on my face, I turned at the door to say goodbye and caught my brother, the alleged murderer of many, gambling kingpin and known organized crime figure, dabbing at his eyes with his hanky. It was at that instant I came to understand and realize that though we were from different generations, we were exactly alike and that my life was somehow, someway, a carbon of his.

Time was pressing and I had to go. Besides my eyes were ready and I had no hanky.

In class, I often ask students to write about what happened during the writing of the essay—and to include that as a kind of postscript to their essay. Although they never think to include that process as part of their actual paper, for me it is, often, a possible conclusion to the paper: a stepping back in order to see, a way of moving from event into experience, a strengthening of the muscle.

After JM read his paper, there was an animated discussion. It seems that many in the class—including me—were from the same neighborhood in the Bronx, Tremont Avenue, a place of intersection of Black, Italian, Hispanic, and Jewish. There was a wonderful energy and, even, joy. When I asked, "What did you feel in the process of writing this paper," JM wrote that he felt a deep love for his brother and gratitude. He had not spoken to his brother for ten years; after writing his paper, he called him to express his love.

One could say he never moved from narration to reflection, but, clearly, the narration took his mind and heart to a deep place. It showed the ability of writing to connect us to ourselves, to another, to our heart. Even if this were all, it is enough.

Between Seventeen
and Eighteen:

How to get from
there to here

How to move from a simple narrative to more complex thought? To not stop with the one experience, singular and unconnected? And how, later, to not forget the story, the experience, that led to the knowing? Often people stay with one "language," one way of "thinking": they tell personal stories rich in specific details but cannot move out to a larger understanding; or they discourse about ideas, stay with abstract concepts, but never bring the abstract into the concrete with specific examples. Clearly there is a danger of each approach: the first can keep us locked in a small and personal world, not able to understand larger implications of a wider world; the danger of egotism, narcissism, self-centeredness. The second, the academic voice which Ursula LeGuin names the "father tongue," can keep us separate from both heart and earth, from what we have touched with our own hands and know through our own experience; caught up in our ideas, we are capable of dangerous and cruel acts, whether it is dropping an atom bomb or experimenting on animals. In both cases, there is the danger of not seeing, of separation and disconnection. The challenge—in teaching and in life—is to keep making bridges between the two paths—thinking/feeling with both mind and heart. Much of my teaching is the process of building that bridge and conditioning the mind to travel that bridge in both directions.

In my teaching of composition, I find it useful, natural, and less dangerous to begin with the direct, concrete description and experience and to use the process of writing as a way to come to the broader understanding—inductive reasoning rather than deductive. For me personally, beginning with an outline and a thesis puts the process in reverse, since it is through the writing that I come to understand and name my thesis, allowing it to evolve. Through writing, I learn what I really want to say. I remember one student asking what happens when we get to the end of a paper and find that we no longer believe our original thesis. His question captured precisely the problem if the thesis is the beginning point rather than the end, especially if we are unwilling to let go of our original "idea." But if we are willing to let go, the "problem" becomes a point of true learning, the sense of "contradiction" and confusion a sign of "active thought," the breakup, in small and large ways, of the world as we have known it. The new understanding has come unbeknownst and unplanned, has broken through previously held concepts, expanded the student's seeing and knowing.

 How wonderful. Eureka! And with writing or with research or in life, we have the choice of either letting in the new insight, revising and/or expanding our thesis, or holding steadfast to our concept, keeping out all that might threaten its notion of "truth."

In my classes I often use the term "creative chaos" to capture this insecure, exciting learning space, the place where the old forms are breaking down, where we have to think in more expansive and complex ways in order to really understand. Once we come to our new understanding, we can name what we have discovered, can call it "thesis," can make an outline consciously organizing the movement from one point to another. To answer the student's question: We can begin a new paper, now knowing our thesis, or, and I think this can be more meaningful, make our original paper the beginning section of a more extended essay.

What is important is to include in our writing the path to our understanding; the journey needs to be traced in order for the essay to touch and move a reader. Few of the abstract truths we come to are really new. It is our path there that is uniquely ours; that is what we can give to another. It's interesting to me how often I need to remind students that the final insight is not the "point." Students can feel where the power is when they hear another's writing, but they seem to forget when they are writing their own papers. Because it doesn't seem totally natural to trace our journey, we need to recondition ourselves. I think, again, of Alice Walker's "I can never condemn the bridge that got me where I am." I think of all the harm that comes when we don't remember the source of our knowing. In college we talk about plagiarism, about not crediting the source of our information. But there is another way of not "crediting": when we omit the "source," deny what has passed through our own hands and body.

What I know is that a lot of my teaching asks students to get back to their actual experience, to look at it closely, to move slowly and carefully from that point. We can then move from the narrative essay to an essay on definition, from story to meaning.

CHAPTER EIGHTEEN:

IN BETWEEN NARRATION AND DEFINITION ...

The next rhetorical skill in many composition classes is "Definition." For me it follows organically from narration. It asks students to choose an abstract word that they want to explore and understand more deeply: to look closely at their experiences involving that word (using the skills of description and narration) and then to evolve their own definition. The definition is their thesis; it comes as an end result of the process of reflection, not as the beginning point. While it is one of my favorite assignments, it is often the least favorite paper for students. As opposed to argumentative and persuasive prose where one knows one's position in the beginning and tries to support and defend that position, a definition paper, in the way I define it, starts with not knowing. It requires careful and close thought, an ability to ask oneself questions, and patience in ferreting out meaning. It is slow, like the contour drawing, the following of each line carefully to see how one line connects with another. Often when I teach definition, I can actually hear minds thinking (and resisting). It is that rigorous and slow; it demands that honesty. Because the "Definition" paper is difficult, I sometimes provide a stepping stone.

In Bedford Hills Women's prison where I taught for only one semester, I asked students to think of some opinion or idea they had held which shifted or expanded or changed through their actual experiences. A bit like my earlier discussion on recognizing a firmly held belief as an illusion, or, as in Orwell's

"Marrakech," of seeing what had been invisible. For the paper, I ask students to trace that process of coming to a new awareness.

What is always miraculous and inspiring is that students are willing to read words that are so personal and vulnerable. The first student who volunteered prefaced her reading by saying that others in the class might object or feel uncomfortable with her paper. As she read, I could feel the discomfort, both in the room and within me.

I wish I had a copy of her paper, but I do not. I do remember it well, however. T. began by talking about all her earlier ideas on homosexuality, particularly on lesbianism: that it was unnatural and disgusting, that women who related to women were masculine and ugly, that if a woman were really a woman she would only relate to men. She then began talking about an experience she had with another woman, the growing closeness and friendship evolving naturally into physical contact and sexuality. She started to talk about the difference between her sexual relations with men and those with this woman. She raised questions in terms of her sexual orientation, about whether the past history and present context shaped her sexuality, whether sexuality was fluid or fixed, whether she would return to relations with men in the outside world. What she knew for sure was that her earlier ideas about homosexuality had been contradicted by her experience. Her paper was very thoughtful, very well written. When she finished, the atmosphere was charged.

What I remember clearly was the sequence of my own feelings as she read. I had not come out as a lesbian in that class or, really, in any of the prison classes. In class, as in the larger society, I fear lesbian stereotypes, as I do anti-Semitic or sexist or racist stereotypes. Within class and in student papers, I walk an edge: trying not to use my authority to silence anyone's ideas but, at the same time, challenging students to examine their too easy stereotypes and glib generalizations, getting students to stop and look closely at their opinions and belief system, to catch themselves in prejudgment. In my own mind, I see a clear difference between someone talking about their experience—something which cannot and shouldn't be questioned—and the generalizations which, in their mind, follow from those experiences. It is those leaps and generalizations which, I believe, can and must be questioned. We can ask students—as we must ask ourselves—to move more slowly, carefully, and logically from cause to effect. We can ask them for support or evidence or facts. I think, again, of Orwell's "Marrakech" essay and our human ability to not see what is right in front of our eyes, to have the generalization override the actual experience because our concept is so strong.

When T. began to read I felt fear, anticipating the stereotypes and the hatred. But the more she read, the happier I felt, almost elated that she could answer the earlier prejudice with such intelligent, thoughtful, honest, and sensitive awareness. The discussion that followed felt rich and deep and complex, showed people really thinking, opening up their blinders, willing to let in other possibilities. It is true that in this particular case I had a vested interest in the more open attitude, but I had that same joy with almost all of the papers that were written for that assignment. Many wrote about their own attitude toward prisoners before they came to prison and how the experience with other women in Bedford Hills shattered those stereotypes. Some talked about a shattering in terms of their own self-concept—how they had seen themselves as somehow superior and better. Some spoke of how they had seen themselves as worse, as inferior. Some talked about racism, about motherhood, about economic class … All showed the widening of a world view through the conscious recognition, acknowledgment, and naming of experience.

I think of the women's consciousness raising groups in the early seventies. A group of women would get together and speak of their experiences: early gender socialization, beginning menstruation, messages received in school about how girls or women should act or be, feelings around sex or sexuality or their body or motherhood. One after another, a woman would speak, not interrupted or questioned or judged, but, rather, heard and received, her experience recognized as her experience. The listening and acceptance allowed the speaking, and the speaking allowed the experience to be brought into fuller recognition: to be named, perhaps for the first time. This feminist process is very close to what I am talking about in terms of writing—journal writing, observation, narration, and, now, definition. It is the coming into consciousness through the process of speaking or writing. It is the working from actual experience rather than from concept or theory, particularly when those concepts have been shaped by patriarchal beliefs and myths used to maintain and justify domination.

And what was true for us within those early women's groups, is also true for any group that speaks its experiential truths: certain patterns start emerging and certain societal myths begin to shatter. That is what I think was meant by "the personal is political": the shattering of those myths and illusions which keep us imprisoned in someone else's definitions, concepts, and frameworks—whether it is the myth of the happy family of the 50's or of Columbus discovering America or of a level playing field with equal opportunity for all or of men or whites or Europeans as superior to women and dark skinned people. Freedom comes from this shattering of illusions as does the possibility of change—in self and in society. People begin to question, rather than obey, those in power as well as their own internalized myths. For me, the definition paper is a way of defining not just a word but our world; it shows us a way to rename our world through our own eyes and our own experience. It feels very important, essential. But it is not an accessible or easy process. In fact, all our training works against us.

Chapter Nineteen:

Redefining the Word and the World

In *The Arts of the Possible*, Adrienne Rich writes, "Revision, the art of looking back, of seeing with fresh eyes, of entering an old text from a new critical direction, is for women more than a chapter in cultural history: It is an act of survival." As a woman, a lesbian, a Jew, I know my survival depends on my continually redefining the world according to my experience rather than another's definition of who I am, who I should be, what is good or bad, ugly or beautiful, right or wrong. Otherwise, through the media, the culture, those in power, I would see myself as inferior, perverse, evil, feel hatred for who I am, be powerless. This need to redefine is especially important for all who are in a subordinate position, the dominant group always having the power to name and define. But it is also necessary for anyone who wants to live an authentic and real life. Since all of us were children, we have all had the experience of being powerless and having another define our world. We have all been socialized. Part of maturing—whether as individuals or as a group or a society—involves the questioning of what we have been taught, the questioning of those in authority.

I think of my friend who describes the conflict she felt at the age of thirteen between the words she heard from the church—that the love she felt for another girl/woman was a sin and that she was condemning to hell both her self and the friend she most loved—and her own experience of love, care, tenderness and joy. Not just a difference but an opposite reality: heaven or hell, love or hate. Her choice was to either accept the judgment of the church and the larger society—becoming who others wanted her to be and internalizing a hated self image—or trust her own experience, seeing her love as good. The choice: to believe "them" or to believe her own experience.

It is clearly not an easy choice since not believing "them" means leaving the familial shore, the familiar and known world. It often means isolation and, sometimes, danger. And it is also not easy to really know what is *our own experience*, since we experience through eyes, minds, and hearts socialized to see and feel a certain way. Often it is difficult to distinguish our actual experience from our concepts and beliefs about that experience.

Nadine Gordimer, in an interview, talked about growing up as a white person in South Africa believing that apartheid was natural, like the sun coming up and going down. She spoke of the incredible leap required to question the world she was born into, to question what she had learned since birth, to see that apartheid was not "natural" but an institution established to keep a certain group in privilege and power. (And as I write, I think of a student who, hearing me speak of Gordimer and the sun, pointed out that the sun going up and down was not "natural" but, rather, based on the belief that our earth was the center of the universe.) And of course this would be true growing up with any set of beliefs: always the difficulty of seeing beyond the blinders of any one world view; the "heresy" and "blasphemy" of seeing something other than what we have been taught; the threat to those in power; the threat of violence when that power is questioned; and the real courage required to question and resist.

For those who have had the power to define, the first challenge is to recognize that there is an "other" with a different point of view, that there are other possible ways of experiencing something, other realities. Privilege can be particularly blinding to sight. Usually we need something to stop us in our tracks: getting lost, getting sick, being unsuccessful, going to prison. For those who are not and have never been on the success track, the process of questioning is, in many ways, easier and more "natural."

The possible "gift" of being an outsider is that one cannot as easily be unconscious, cannot just slide into the definitions and roles created by those in power. As a lesbian, I did not have ready made categories and roles telling me how I should act as girl, woman, wife. While I'm sure I was and am stuck in some of my own personal psychological patterns, there were no gender role expectations or assumptions of who should do what, both within and outside the home. My partner and I could consciously choose: who cooked, cleaned, led in dancing, fixed the car, paid for what, how we pooled money, spent time, lived our lives.

Nothing was fixed; all was negotiable. Two individuals creating their lives without following (or even rebelling against) established guidelines set by others.

Because the outsider stands apart from his/her major culture, s/he can often see more clearly the established "norms" of society, the prescribed patterns and behaviors less visible to those who follow the established way. If one is not allowed on the tracks, it is easier to observe those tracks and question some of the destinations.

But along with this gift of perspective and choice, there is the challenge of not internalizing the judgments of those in authority. We are all socialized to believe the words of those in power, the "truths" we are given, even when they seem absurd and illogical and contradict our own experience. George Orwell, in his memory of being beaten for bedwetting, remembers believing the words of the headmaster that he, Orwell, was to blame for breaking the riding crop used to beat him: "I accepted the broken riding-crop as my own crime. I can still recall my feeling as I saw the handle lying on the carpet—the feeling of having done an ill-bred clumsy thing, and ruined an expensive object. I had broken it: so Sambo told me, and so I believed." And in her essay "Eye to Eye" in *Sister Outsider*, Audre Lorde says, "Children know only themselves as reasons for the happenings in their lives" and speaks of the necessity "to examine and dismantle piece by painful piece" America's sexist and racist 'measurement' of her being."

There is an incredible freedom and power when we begin to question, to break out of a prison constructed by another, to "dismantle piece by painful piece," brick by brick, their imprisoning words and concepts, rebuilding a world/our world based on our continually evolving experience, knowledge and reflection.

The first and most revolutionary step, and, for me, the most exhilarating, is to actually take in that what seemed universal and objective is, really, subjective and partial. I think of an interview in which Toni Morrison spoke to Bill Moyers about the white literary canon, calling it "the master's narrative." Moyers, in his open innocence, says something like, "you mean the history of literature," and Morrison repeats, "No, the master's narrative," the narrative of white men (mostly wealthy, heterosexual, Christian white men). What I felt then is what I always feel when, to use the poet Muriel Rukeyser's words, the "world splits open." All of a sudden there is space and air. I am no longer entrapped in another's definition of reality. It is a moment of incredible excitement for those imprisoned, as we all are, to see a way out. And it is a time of great threat for their gatekeepers who do not want to relinquish their power or privilege.

These moments of awakenings occur throughout our lives, in small and large ways. They are always exciting, clarifying, deepening. I remember feeling that opening in terms of religious beliefs when I read the following passage from Judith Plaskow's *Standing Again At Sinai*:

> *These problems with traditional images of God generate a need for new language that can better express the meaning of God for a pluralistic and responsible community. But the move to new images, as well as feminist criticisms of traditional God-language, presuppose an understanding of what images of God are about that needs to be made explicit before we can turn to construction. Criticism of received images of God is not, of course, criticism of God. It is criticism of ways of speaking about a reality that, in its full reality, is finally unknowable. Taking seriously the established Jewish suspicion of anthropomorphisms—without for that reason ceasing to use them—feminists insist that our language about God is constructive and metaphorical. Everything we say about God represents our human efforts to create, recapture, and evoke experiences of God sustained within linguistic and cultural frameworks that already color our experience and interpretation. All our images have an "as if" or "as it were" in front of them that reminds us they are to be taken neither literally nor as final, but as part of an ongoing quest for language that can provide a framework for meaningful living and give expression to our experience.*

Of course, and yet I had forgotten, because those in power kept naming as "blasphemy" a different experience of the unknowable. "Criticism of received images of God is not, of course, criticism of God." Yes.

And I had that same joy reading Elizabeth Minnich's distinction between excellence and exclusivity in her *Transforming Knowledge*:

> *Calls for a new inclusiveness on any grounds, particularly when they are couched in terms of equity, are heard as threatening to excellence itself, although, of course, such calls are in no way aimed at attacking excellence, any more than new laws, rules, and regulations necessarily threaten the overarching notion of justice that particular laws and codes are meant to serve. What is put in question by proposals to make the curriculum more inclusive is, quite simply, exclusivity. What is revealed by claims that these*

efforts are an attack on excellence is the lack of any idea of excellence that does not conflate it with exclusivity.

Of course, again.

But it is not always easy to see what is so simple. Because Minnich's reasoning is so clear and direct, I will quote her a bit more:

> *Some country clubs and private men's clubs are exclusive, but that by no means makes them excellent. It simply means they refuse membership to some categories of people, and although doing so may make members feel special, it doesn't make them better. If we wish to make institutions as central to democracy and government itself, less like the old white male clubs, we have to be very careful about the exclusions that take place as by-products of choices made, requirements established, practices followed. One sure test for the confusion of excellence with exclusivity is in consequences. A set of tests established to sort out who is and who is not prepared to work on the 'higher' levels at which excellence is approached that is consistently failed by more women than men, more Black people than white reveals itself to be a protection of the old exclusivities, not a neutral, and certainly not a disinterested test of abilities.... We are not asking (institutions) to lower their standards when we suggest that an exclusive tradition needs, at the very least, augmenting. We are asking them not to apply particular standards as if they were universal, and to take the time to learn something about new materials before they rush to judge them by old, inappropriate standards.*

I think of Gerda Lerner and her work in women's history, of Gilligan and her work with young girls, of Belenky, etal, and their work in *Women's Ways of Knowing*, of Morrison and Walker, Plaskow and Daly and Spretnak, of Frantz Fanon, Albert Memmi, Paolo Freire, James Baldwin, and of the hundreds and thousands of people who have split my small world so that I could see something larger, more inclusive, more "true." I think how they all informed my teaching, and how the process of redefining is so essential to that breaking up of an old world view.

Minnich introduces her distinction between excellent and exclusive with the following:

What is important to me is to make the very familiar begin to seem strange and worthy of a great deal more serious thought and conversation and reading, and to inspire searches for further source materials. The words, the concepts we are about to consider tend to be mind-numbing either because they are worn smoothly into platitudes (as in the pious invocations of 'excellence') or because they are fraught with emotion and/ or taboo and confusion (sex, war). I want us to think about them for precisely those reasons; platitudes and taboos are two sides of the same coin.

Yes, that is what I want: to get students to *think about mind numbing words and concepts*, the very things we are trained not to think about. To use writing as a way of stopping, questioning, and coming to our own understanding. To use, in particular, the definition paper as a way of "requiring" close observation and the rigor of careful and clear logic in the movement from the particular example to the larger understanding.

Because I feel the power of words—to express, communicate, and touch, as well as to manipulate and dominate—I sometimes begin this "lesson" by examining what I call "trigger" words, words that have power, that cause immediate and strong and often unconscious reactions, words that sometimes lead to violence. I ask students to list some personal trigger words. Usually there are personal adjectives internalized from childhood and, often, re-enforced in later relationships: bad, stupid, selfish, crazy. Or labels used to put down groups of people, racial or sexist slurs like nigger, bitch, queer, fag, white trash. I ask students to think about actual experiences in which those words have been used, either by them or towards them, to describe those experiences in writing and, then, to step back and reflect: Who was using the word and how and why? What was the effect on both the speaker and the receiver? What do you feel now, reflecting on the word? My hope is to have students "dismantle" the power of the word through close examination.

PG wrote about the word "Izzy," a word that carried great emotional weight for him as a child: "The word Izzy is probably not a word that affects most people. When I was younger that word spoken towards me was a sure way to make me hostile."

He writes of having a childhood crush on a young girl who, at one point, asks him, "What are you?": "I was about to tell her why I am considered black when I heard one of the school bullies who happened to be near us say, "He's an Izzy.""

I am an insecure person now and I was even more so then. At that time in life, if someone referred to me as something I had never heard of, I automatically got defensive. If someone would have told me I had charisma back then I would have thought it was a mental disorder. So when Nick, the bully, said that I was an Izzy my muscles tightened. Then Janice asked, "What are you talking about Nick? What's an Izzy?" Nick said, with a malicious grin on his face, "Izzy he white or Izzy black." My voice cracked on me as I told him to repeat what he said. I had a vague idea of what he was talking about, but I was hoping that I misinterpreted it. Nick said, "Izzy white or Izzy black...."

P talks about fighting, getting beaten up, and finding himself crying "because of the frustration and embarrassment, also the anger at Nick and the rest of the world for being so cruel. Anger at god for making me the way I was and making people like Nick."

I did a lot of crying that day. My father tried to make things better, like he always did, but my adoptive father, who is white, just couldn't say the right things. He couldn't understand what it was like for me not to really be able to belong to either racial group. Back then and even now when a white man is mad at me, I'm a nigger. When a black man is mad, I'm a honky.

Then and now I have qualities of both races, although socially I am considered black.

What made the word "Izzy" so powerful is it actually makes people ask, "just what is he?" I was so confused myself that the last thing I wanted were inquiries about my racial background. I just couldn't understand why I couldn't fit in.

At present if the term "Izzy" was used I probably would laugh at the user. On what level of mind would a grown man be on to say something that stupid? I could even pity him. To this day I still get asked, "What are you" often. I sometimes wonder why it matters to people. Why couldn't I just be PG? That's what I am. But for some reason it does matter.

When I think about it, it's a shame. When I was younger I was probably one of the few people that was absolutely racially unbiased. But over the years I have picked up my share of racial bias and it is not altogether directed towards one race.

I think of the openness and honesty of this paper and how courageous it is to write and speak about what is vulnerable. This openness and trust were present in many students' writings throughout my years teaching. Within the class itself, however, I often begin with an abstract word that is less personal, less charged, in order to illustrate the process of coming to one's own personal definition: beautiful, successful ... I ask students to think of three actual and concrete experiences of the word/concept, to just list those examples. When they have finished their short list, I ask them to write a little more about each example, to go into more detail. If someone chose the word beautiful, for example, they might, as one student actually did, list the following "beautiful" experiences: my daughter being born, a sunset, freedom. And I would say, as I always do, write a little more about each, about how and why each is beautiful.

I know that the situation is artificial, that asking for three examples is too prescriptive and structured. But my experience is that students *know*, in a relatively unconscious but very real way, that these situations *are* beautiful to them. What they are less able to do is figure out why they are beautiful and, even more, to figure out how these very disparate and seemingly unconnected examples are connected to each other, and how, through reflective process, they can actually come to an awareness of their own personal definition of "beautiful."

It is not an easy process, not an easy paper. What is "easy" is to just give synonyms or repeat the adjective before various nouns: beautiful is lovely, graceful, harmonious, is a beautiful sunset, a beautiful woman. This is something we all do, bringing nothing new into consciousness. But how to bring together the birth of your child, a sunset, and freedom from imprisonment—that requires struggle and patience.

In class I'll ask for a student to read his list. I'll put his words on the board and keep asking questions: why is the birth of your child beautiful, what is so beautiful about freedom, what about the sunset is beautiful? When other students try to help him, I silence them. This is a definition particular to that person; to have other people say how freedom is beautiful to them does not allow the process of the mind coming to its own meaning.

Sometimes I feel like I am harassing a student, his response a frustrated "because it is beautiful" or "you know" or "I don't know really know but...." But they do know—that is the point. In all my experience, *we all know* on a deep and unconscious level. The challenge is to bring what we know into our consciousness. And that is, also, the joy, the joy that comes through struggle.

In both class and in papers, I have found that students can usually think of specific experiences and can describe those experiences with details. What is more difficult, however, is to see the connecting links between their examples, to come to a clear thesis/definition. In their papers, their conclusion (which is both their thesis and their definition) is sometimes totally unrelated to what has preceded it. Sometimes they end with Webster's definition or some glib (even if truthful) "beauty is in the eyes of the beholder." Sometimes they just give up, having no concluding paragraph or ending their paper with "There is no way to define this term." The problem, it seems to me, is not just one of writing but one of thinking: how do we make our generalizations follow from the concrete experiences of our own life. Why is there often such a gap?

In class, when I struggle with students and their examples, I feel like a coach forcing them to do strenuous mind exercises in order to build up the mind's muscles. In many ways we are all reluctant to struggle with what is hard and complex; we get tired, lazy, fearful. I push, however, because I believe, as I probably have said too many times in this book, that we all love our own depth, even when we struggle against it. A good teacher pushes edges to enable another's growth, even when there is resistance.

I think of all the times I have asked students to revise what I know was already a difficult paper, when I insist that they develop and expand their ideas knowing how much work they still need to do and how hard their life already is. Yet students continually thank me, for almost always those were points of greatest blocks and, therefore, most growth. I remind myself to remember these experiences in order to push my own edge with what is personally difficult—to demand more of someone.

I think of the often repeated story of a woman (or sometimes man) who sees a butterfly struggling to emerge from a cocoon. In her concern and compassion, she tries to assist by blowing warm air into the cocoon and gently enlarging the hole. The butterfly comes out, but then staggers on the ground, unable to open the wings clasped closely to its body, unable to fly. What she hadn't known was that the slow struggle to emerge from the cocoon developed the muscles necessary for winged flight. Her compassion was not informed by knowledge; her "help" kept the other "weak." We develop muscles through our own hard work, not by being "saved" or protected by another.

But still another can, sometimes, help us see what we cannot see, has the distance and detachment we lack. In the classroom, when I have listed the specific examples on the board, including the student's descriptive expansion, I open the discussion: what does everyone see as that student's definition. That, in itself, feels important: the ability to distinguish between another's definition and one's own, to look at another's thoughts and experiences, to know that there are other points of view in our universe, and, then, to mirror back to another what he or she might not be able to see.

For me, both the in-class discussions and the papers are exciting in terms of process and in terms of the final definition. I remember within one class trying to come to a group definition of pacification. The examples given during the brainstorming were interesting, each new example making the definition more meaningful and complex: a baby's pacifier, giving a child a cookie when they are hungry, giving the prisoners more television time, telling a girlfriend that you will take her out soon, giving someone something, giving them something but not what they really want or need, giving it to them so that they will be quiet, will not threaten, quieting someone's real hunger by giving them an illusionary substitute in order to keep the status quo ...

I remember the student's definition of compassion that I quoted earlier: "Compassion comes from the consciousness of one's own ability to do malevolent acts," a definition that has stayed with me for many years, helping me to expand my understanding of both compassion and arrogance and to think more deeply about what it means to allow in one's shadow or to deny that shadow, to recognize one's own capacity to do evil or to see all evil outside of oneself, to see those in prisons as like you or to see yourself as totally separate and they as totally foreign. And I think, again, of those students in Bedford Hills who, having come to prison, recognized their former judgments of "the other" as an illusory concept, who grew in compassion through their experience of their own ability to do malevolent acts.

I can see in my own life how definitions of others have enabled me to see in more expansive ways: Tillich's defining sin as separation; the desert father's defining sin as the refusal to grow; Jews defining sin as missing the mark; Jo Vellacott's defining violence as powerlessness; Joanna Macy's definition of power as "process, a verb, something that happens through us" rather than being "synonomous with domination"; Carolyn Heilbrun defining power as the ability to "take one's place in whatever discourse is essential to action and the right to have one's part matter." I remember the light that came when I read Erich Fromm's essay distinguishing selfishness from self-love: self-love as the source for our love of others rather than its opposing principle; self-denial not "good" but, rather, coming out of the hatred of self. And I could go on and on, as we all could.

It is not that I accept all these new definitions as mine or as "true"; rather, each allows me to see in new and more expansive ways, splits apart an old world and allows me to question what had been unquestioned. The redefinitions of sin, selfishness, compassion liberated me from confinements of mind of which I, myself, was unaware, belief systems which had functioned unbeknownst to my conscious mind. Each new definition widened the channel in my own mind and helped develop the "muscle" for continually redefining the word and the world. Each reminded me to continually ask: Whose definition is this, what is my actual experience, what is the experience of others, who has been left out of this definition, what research do I need to do in order to know more, who profits from this definition and at whose cost? To question the master's definition and to try to recreate my own based on my own experiences, inquiry, research, logic, and understanding.

The following are a few of the papers that I saved from those many years. All of them taught me about both the process of definition and the actual possibilities contained within different abstract words.

Love

Love was Jerry and Jerry was love. From the first time we met to the last time I saw her, there was a love that we both knew was there.

We met on a warm April evening in 1973. I was five years old at the time and I was just recovering from the chicken pox. I heard my father come home from work but made no attempt to leave the comfort of my warm bed nor my entertainment, namely my T.V. Not that it mattered much, my father would never walk by my room without stopping to see me. As I heard him close and lock the door, I waited to hear the familiar sound of his coming footsteps. But the sound that I heard was no footsteps at all. It sounded like a baby crying. Or better yet, it sounded like me right before I stopped crying. I jumped out of bed and immediately attended to my ritual which consisted of putting on my high-top house shoes, strapping on my sword, which was plastic, and last but not least the putting on of my pirate's scarf.

I ran from my root to the kitchen where my mother and father were both bent over a cardboard box which emitted that whimpering sound I'd heard before.

"What's that, mommy?"

"Come and see for yourself."

I walked over to them not really knowing what to expect, certainly not what I found. There in that cardboard box looking frightened and confused was a little bitty puppy. When I saw little I mean little.

"Where did you get him from, pop?" I said.

"Him is a her and I got her from a friend."

Can I hold her?"

"Sure, son. Let me get her out of this box for you."

With that he bent down to pick up the dog and she seemed to scream like a child.

"Dad, you're scaring her," I said. I went over to him and took the puppy out of his hands and I held her like a mother would hold a baby. I don't know what made me act this way nor did any one else considering the way that my family was looking at me. My two brothers and two sisters had come into the kitchen to witness this little miracle. And a miracle it was because as soon as I had the puppy in my arms, she immediately stopped crying and gave a sigh that told me that she finally felt safe. This made me hug her even tighter."

"Careful, Troy, she's only a baby."

"What's her name, pop?" I said.

"She doesn't have one yet. Why don't you give her a name now?"

"Well, why don't we call her Love?"

Come on, son. It's a dog. You have to give it a dog's name like Queenie, Lady, or something like that."

"But she doesn't look like a Queenie, dad. She looks like a Love."

You don't even know what a love looks like, stupid!" yelled my oldest brother.

"Why don't you mind your business and let him name the stupid dog, stupid," said my oldest sister Michelle.

"She's not stupid," I started but was cut off by my father's booming voice that seemed to rock the whole house.

"Cut the shit, NOW!!! I'll name the dog." My father got down on his knees and looked at the puppy and said, "From now on you are to be known as Geraldine." Everyone groaned, even the owner of the new name, but my father continued, "But to the family you may be called Jerry for short."

An argument quickly followed my father's words, but we all knew that his word was law and that he wasn't likely to change his mind over a decision that he made.

I looked down at the bundle of fur that was in my arms and noticed that she was licking my fingers, which I took that she was hungry.

"They may call you Jerry, but to me you're Love."

(AM)

It is true that this student never came to a definition of love, nor did he really reflect, but it was such a clear, honest, open, well written and moving narrative, that was enough. I felt "love"—and innocence and sweetness—when I read it and, now, many years later, as I type it. And sadness, a wanting to connect with the author to tell him the power of his words, to find out where he is and ask how he is. At the end of his paper, in response to my asking what happened in the process, he wrote: "When I was writing this paper all sorts of thoughts ran through my head. I wanted to write all day on my 'Love.' Maybe I will write the whole story in my journal." And I wrote, in response to those words, "Good, I would like that very much." And I would.

Another student, in a less heartfelt but very real way, carefully followed my prescribed method, using four very different examples of beautiful. He had no introduction and no conclusion and never did come to a definition, but his process was right and I thought his examples excellent in terms of where he took both his mind and mine:

Yesterday I saw the sun setting over Lake Catherine. The violet sky with crimson clouds formed an umbrella above the Prussian blue water. At the most distant point from view, they seemed to come together in a kiss. There the sky exploded like an ember of coal in a dark furnace. I lingered on the ridge inhaling the smell of orchids that floated in the damp air as I watched the earth slowly swallow the illuminated heavens.

We sat at a crowded table in a crowded bar, but to me we were wonderfully alone. The smoke from the many cigarettes formed a halo over your head. The sound of the musicians became isolated and distant like sounds from heaven when I gazed at you. Neither the smell of spilled beer or wine nor the bodies feverishly dancing could offend this moment. Everything contributed to make this the most beautiful time of my life.

I had heard many tales about tornadoes though I had never seen one until that day on my summer vacation in the Midwest. We had all taken shelter in the basement after making sure the house was secured extra tight. The fact that we, with our advanced technology, could not prevent or adequately protect ourselves from this phenomenon fascinated me. I was determined to get my first look at this marvelous event. As the tornado approached, I left the safety of the cellar and ventured upstairs to the small window in the bathroom. I fixed my eyes out toward the plains and there it came. It was vividly dark and moved with the swirling motion of a spinning top, with an awkward symmetrical movement. It reminded me of a black ice cream cone running through the dust. I stared in awe of this magnificently beautiful sight.

She was a very obese woman with a forlorn expression; my friends called her fat and ugly. I was in the military stationed in California. We met at a small supper club where my buddies and I frequented. In spite of their obvious disfavor for her appearance, we became intimate friends and developed a sexual relationship. I still remember our first affair in detail, especially the drama of her undressing in the moonlight from the window. As she slipped out of her gown, I saw her rounded shoulders, strong and straight, that supported her breasts, which were plump. Little blue veins made their way across her chest and led to her pink teats that stood erect. Her navel seemed so endlessly deep in the protruding flesh around her stomach that I dreamed of exploring it fully. Her thighs were strong like the horses and cows on uncle's farm. The hair on her body was contrastingly different from her head to her armpits to the nest between those enormous thighs. She appeared to me as a large sculptured mass decorated with godly ornaments. I knew nothing could compare to this discovery nor could any be as beautiful as she was then. (LL)

That was the end of his paper. In class he wrote: "I really felt inadequate in expressing my meaningful feeling of this word. This makes me unhappy." He then tried a definition: "Beautiful—everything is beautiful when looked at from its inherent nature or characteristics."

I loved his examples. What I wrote at the end, and what I feel even more now typing his words, was: "Your four images are excellent in their diversity, in the power of your description, in their ability to clarify beauty for you (and to break through traditional, stereotyped notions of beauty). Your eye for details, your creation of images, your use of words, your selection of examples are very, very good." I remember asking him to read his paper in class and having the class talk about his examples—if the ordering of the examples felt right, whether he needed any transition between the paragraphs or if the abrupt juxtapositions were more effective. And then we all, as a class, developed his definition of beauty evolving from his examples, his own thoughtful "looked at from its inherent nature" a very good beginning. I remember the excitement with the evolving definition, watching it take shape into something like the following: "Everything is—or can be—beautiful when looked at in terms of its own inherent nature. What is necessary is that the viewer be totally present in a situation, in a vivid sensory world, undistracted by possible disturbances. The viewer feels the quality of light, awe, power. He or she has the sense that this experience is unique and that external judgments are irrelevant. One enters into a total world: of senses, images, presence, power."

What is interesting to me is that I often do not remember names or faces, even though when I teach a class I assume I will remember each student for the rest of my life. But I do remember these papers that I am retyping and many more that exist now only in my mind, and I remember class discussions when students read their papers. I remember exact quotes, when words struck me with the sharpness and depth of truth, and class dynamics, when the room was filled with energy, surprise, fear, and love. I feel, again, the gifts that teachers receive in the classroom. Perhaps I would give as one example of "beautiful" to me some of those vital classroom dynamics where one feels the energy of focused attention.

Earlier, I quoted a student's words from his journal about the importance of writing. In his paper on "beautiful," the student spoke more fully about the power of writing, seeing writing as a strong example of "beautiful." He, like the preceding student, juxtaposed his different examples without any transitions. He also could not really move from specific examples to a clear definition. But he, like the earlier student, was clearly involved in active search and in very honest and thoughtful writing:

> *Beautiful to me is the gorgeous sunrise in a nature setting. The way the world seems to be awakening anew. The birds as they come alive to meet the challenges of day to day life in song. The smell for me is one of freshness, vitality, euphoria. It exudes strength and power to me that goes beyond the confines of definition. The adventurous nature that engulfs my entire being as I meet these exhilarating things is all encompassing, the feeling that no obstacle is too large to surmount. As I go forth on my countless journeys into nature, the virginal existence of the wildlife I encounter puts me in the frame of mind that god must have been in while creating these things.*
>
> *The feelings I get as a result of being able to express myself are also beautiful in that I feel a great release at being able to relay my ideas to another. Also through expression I come together as one with myself to allay all my fears and resultant feelings of inadequacies. When I express myself, I'm at one with the world. I feel in control of my destiny because I can make my point understood and, therefore, tear down any barriers of communication that might have been prevalent before. I feel good about this because there was once a time when I would, no couldn't, express myself, and I felt like a time bomb ready to explode at any given time. My thoughts, feelings and emotions were so bottled up it was stifling and the opening of that bottle was like a euphoria, the magnitude of which I have never experienced before in this lifetime and probably will never experience again. If I do, I fear I will have to exact some sort of new vocabulary to explain the feelings.*

> *Women in general are very beautiful to me also in that they exude a feline grace about them that I relate to a fine work of art. I'm very envious of my woman in particular, the way that she totally gives herself to me as far as feelings are concerned. I mean the confidence she shows in my judgment and the way that she totally puts herself in my hands is a very wonderful thing. I'm envious because the way society deems or perceives that a man should be strictly prohibits my total emotional release to anyone in such a simple basic way. I love her madly for this. Through these acts, I draw strength from her daily. Her submissive behavior towards me gives me a sense of purpose unequaled by anything to date and gives me the power of serenity within myself that I need in order to make it. A very beautiful thing.* (KJ)

In class, reflecting on his process, the student wrote: "In writing this paper and in the final analysis, beautiful means to me a sense of strength and power, exuded or received. What I do know is that the writing of it was a very pleasurable experience for me. I felt a free flowing easiness." Yes, I felt that too, someone really opening himself up to receive what was real, looking closely at his experiences, flowing with his words, learning as he wrote, coming to understanding. It's true that the part about her "submissive behavior" did not make me happy as a woman and a feminist, but the issue is not, ever, what makes me happy or whether I like or agree with a person's ideas but, rather, whether s/he is struggling to come to understanding. And he, clearly, was.

The others in the class helped him with the transition from examples to generalization: "The 'beautiful' in some way releases something within us, creates a certain euphoria, a feeling that cannot be expressed in words but is connected to awakening and creation. One feels one's own power, almost a godlike power, within oneself, feels that no obstacle is too large. Beautiful is a feeling of deep connection to another and to self giving one a sense of both control and total openness."

With a little more practice, both the above students would have been led to very meaningful, complex, and deep definitions. Each had a very clear sense of what was beautiful to them; they just needed to consciously name what they, unconsciously, already knew.

When I recently read these papers to a friend, I could tell that they were not particularly interesting to her. She, a teacher herself, had such student papers; she thought I could and should omit them. To her, they weren't really revolutionary or transformative in terms of shifting the axis of the student's world or the world of the reader. Perhaps she is right. But what I felt was the extraordinary nature of these ordinary papers. The "revolutionary" nature of even thinking that we can try to define our world for ourselves and see through our own eyes, the knowing that we all have a deep understanding of beauty and love and god, and that we can question the definitions of others. I think now of what the second student began to say about "everything being beautiful when looked at from its inherent nature." Perhaps it is because I was so present to their words and their process that I could see the beauty, that I defined them as beautiful (and essential for this chapter).

This next paper is from Bedford Hill Women's Prison. The author clearly understood the process, let go of my prescribed three examples, and used writing to understand and name courage for herself in a very meaningful way:

> *I believe that to possess courage you must also possess inner peace. To some that may be a contradiction when you think of the definition of the word courage. You may think of a soldier ready to do battle or of a person taking a stand on their political beliefs, but in each of these circumstances you must have focus, strong will, and a solid sense of inner peace.*
>
> *I've always been shy and quiet while at the same time drawn to people who were loud and strong. Growing up, I didn't feel any courage. My younger brother and sister were always beating me up. I had to find someone to be courageous for me. That meant I would let people speak for me and defend me when I needed it, even make decisions for me. I looked for people who were bigger than me physically too. I would be protected. I became dependent, in a sense, on those I deemed as my heroes.*
>
> *I admired those who weren't afraid to skip class or talk back to any authority while I meekly did everything I was supposed to do.*
>
> *I think that's why I always liked loud metal music; it exudes such power and energy, you can lose yourself in it. You need good self esteem for courage to happen. Confidence and courage go hand in hand. The singers and musicians in the bands I liked weren't afraid to be in front of people—be themselves. Their self esteem bordered on arrogance, but I loved them. They had what I felt I lacked. For a long while courage was defined to me as being something I felt I wasn't capable of.*
>
> *In my house I didn't dare talk back to my father, although I had plenty to say under my breath. I always wished just once I would have the guts to speak up and be heard. My sister and brother had no problem with it. Why couldn't I?*

I never liked how I looked growing up, which meant I never wanted to be the center of attention—ever. But when my first baby was born, I felt a total re-birth within myself. I had finally accomplished something which required me to act upon my own strength—my courage. When Ashley was born I found my inner peace. This time I liked not only being the center of attention, but I liked sharing it with my daughter. The discovery of this peace, this self-esteem, this well sought after courage changed me. Although I had been happy to learn I was pregnant, I was still scared. Who could do this for me? Where were my heroes, my defenders, my speakers? While I planned my nursery, bought my maternity clothes and went to Lamaze, I was outwardly floating with joy. Inside, however, I was wondering if I could do it.

My fear was brought to my attention, to the surface, one day while watching a video which showed actual births. It was loud and in full color. I would do this? Panic set in. No air was coming in. The realization came that I would have to do this. Who made up those ridiculous fairy tales of babies coming from the stork or the cabbage patch? I was convinced I was a coward; I couldn't stop crying.

Eventually the day came and it was time to face the music. I'd been well educated and prepared, I tried to be brave. My labor progressed and a feeling of sudden calm settled over me. I knew what I had to do and I knew I could do it. I was a soldier ready to do battle.

Having that surge of courage gave me strength. I wasn't afraid anymore— I wanted to meet my baby. My daughter was delivered a few hours later and to my amazement the courage stayed with me.

I feel like I've come a long way from the shy kid I once was. I now feel my strong will, my focus on life, and my inner peace. (DS)

In class, the student wrote: "I noticed when I was writing this I repeated a lot of things I wrote in other papers in my rough drafts. I took them out, but I feel like I'm becoming aware of parts of myself I didn't realize were there." Yes, the awareness coming through the writing, through the seeing and naming. And what is interesting is that in reading her paper I felt her courage; in reading the two preceding papers, I felt their beauty; and in the first paper I felt love. On a whole other level, each writer conveyed something essential about their word and their world, the "definition" embodied in a way that moved beyond the specifics about which they wrote.

Now, many years later, I want to speak to the student who wrote about courage. In her narrative paper, she wrote of her own experience going to kindergarten, her fear and tears when her mother left her. She contrasted her trauma with her daughter's seeming ease and excitement on her first day. I think of her and all the mothers in prison separated from the children they love. Seventy-five percent of those in Bedford Hills are mothers. I think of the love, and the courage, the pain and the sadness. Writing may be one way out of a prison, but it, clearly is not enough when those prison bars separate us from those we love. While there is a real joy when we can put our feelings, thoughts, and experiences into written form, the awareness that comes through writing can also touch feelings we might otherwise try to suppress: pain, guilt, sadness. Consciousness does not mean happiness. It is always a choice. Some students resist writing for many reasons; others continue to chose awareness.

The following are a few excerpted passages from a much longer essay tracing a student's changing awareness and understanding of oppression:

> *I started using drugs at the early age of 14. At that time I didn't know that drug use was the shape oppression would take to keep me down and hinder me from realizing my goals. At age 14, I thought using drugs was alright. All of my high school associates were into black awareness and stressed that the common oppressor of Nubian people was white people … My perception of oppression at this stage only included the ways that another race of people had kept my race of people brainwashed into thinking we were inferior. I didn't perceive that my so-called friends had introduced me to a form of oppression (drugs) that would wreak more havoc upon me than any other race of people possible could.*
>
> *As I got older the self inflicted oppression of using drugs grew. The oppressing escalated to the point that I thought I couldn't enjoy a movie, party, or anything else without smoking a joint, drinking some beer or sniffing some cocaine. Using drugs, I now realize, had taken top priority over every other issue on my life's agenda.… But my definition of oppression at this point in my life was that everyone else was the cause of all my problems. I blamed the white man for enslaving my ancestors. I blamed family for being a negative force.…*
> *Today my perception of myself and oppression has changed, thanks to my fellowship. Yes, there are still people in this world whose very existence depends on the suffering of Nubian people. But an individual can also oppress him or herself by using drugs, laziness, and self deceit. (W)*

The following paper has a very thoughtful contemplative exploration of peace:

It is July and the weather is absolutely gorgeous. Temperature around 80 degrees, the flowers are in bloom, and the sun is shining brightly. I am in a place called Peace Park located in Hiroshima, Japan. Nothin fancy, a nice picnic lunch consisting of sandwiches, a little vino, some chips, and, of course Diane. We are sitting under a tree just enjoying the day. Neither one of us speaks the language very well but that seems to be relatively unimportant.

Across from us I see a little girl playing with her doll. She is so content and satisfied in her activity. Meanwhile her mother is busy preparing lunch for the two of them and there does not seem to be any rush. I think to myself I wish this day would never end.

Switching to another scene, the time is late March 1984. I am rushing around trying to get myself ready. Damn, I am sure glad this is over. The roughest three months of my life without question. But looking back it was also the most gratifying. I have gained a great deal of discipline and fortitude. The place is Parris Island, South Carolina. The place I would not wish on my worst enemy and yet would want for my best friend. Boy that is one heck of a contradiction and yet to me it seems perfectly logical.

My drill instructor, Sgt. Messinger. Funny that I still remember his name and yet how could I forget it. He put something in my life, no not strong enough, he represented something in my life that was missing. I hated him and yet I respected him.

Finally, bringing it up to the present which is now the past. In 1987 I came into something that for me is the ultimate experience. It taught me the art of submitting myself and of understanding people in their good times and bad. It constantly grows inside you and permits you to exemplify it to others. It is called Islam which simply means Peace.

To me the above experiences all capture peace in one way or another. The first is in the park in the laid back peaceful atmosphere watching the little girl playing with her doll without a care in the world, my date and I sitting in the shade enjoying the day. That was peace. My experience in boot camp was extremely hectic and demanding. I can remember being in the bush or the field and laying in my tent thinking. It was during this time that I learned to channel my emotions and not act irrationally. This experience taught me the importance of considering different options and concentrating on my objectives. Through my drill instructor I saw how to put it all together and get that sense of calmness. To me this was coming to peace with myself. Unlike being in the park where my surroundings brought me peace, in this experience the peace came from within. Finally, Islam to me grasps the whole thing.

It allows me to see and appreciate peace which is external by way of creation and also to feel the peace within myself. I get there through prayer and meditation. By doing this, I experience peace in many ways, sometimes in solitary situations and sometimes in crowds. (EB)

In class, the student wrote the following about his process: "This paper was confusing. The bad part is that I feel my paper will lose my reader or listener. For me these experiences embody what peace is. The term is so abstract and the experiences so different, yet there is something that connects them all. Are you confused? Good. Then you know what I went through to obtain what I call peace. Peace is a lifelong experience. So two weeks from now I could expand on my definition even more. As Aristotle said, we are in a constant state of being and becoming. Everyone seems to say that this paper was decent. That makes me feel good. Still this was very unsettling because I never thought about putting something so abstract on paper, But par the course, Ms. Mennis has made me rattle my brain to see what is going to come out."

How could I, Ms. Mennis, not feel very happy with the unsettling, the struggle, the rattling of the brain, the coming to understanding, and the revolutionary and joyful nature of redefining the word and world?

Looking through a pile of papers, I find one written twenty years ago by EC defining the word "terrorist": "For many years American people have been manipulated and persuaded to believe that Asian nationalists who are not of the five superpowers are terrorist." The student then goes back to 1795 for a definition ("the systematic use of terror, especially as a means of coercion") and further back to the 15th century "to restrain or dominate by force." He then looks at history: at the British invasion of Africa; at Spain and England and their actions against Native Indians; at slavery. He looks at the word "systematic"; he writes about the action of our government in Nicaragua. He writes, "we do not think enough about thinking." He asks questions about who is called terrorist by whom. He thinks about bullies, about our use of force. And he ends his paper with "A definition is a definition. We can't change it to fit our comfort." His paper, unlike many of those who use words as a way to silence and manipulate, insists that we question our terms, question authority.

Along with the writing assignments, I continually distribute essays illustrating specific rhetorical approaches. One of the essays I have given students when we do definition papers is an address given by Clarence Darrow in 1902 to inmates in Cook County jail in Chicago. It is a socialist and class analysis of poverty, capitalism, and the church, an essay that explores "the connection between the crimes of the respectable classes and your presence in the jail." What I love about the essay is not only the political and economic analysis but also the redefinitions of crime and criminal:

> *There is no doubt there are quite a number of people in this jail who would pick my pockets. And still I know this—that when I get outside pretty nearly everybody picks my pocket. There may be some of you who would hold up a man on the street, if you did not happen to have something else to do, and needed the money; but when I want to light my house or my office the gas company holds me up. They charge me one dollar for something that is worth twenty-five cents. Still all these are good people; they are pillars of society and support the churches, and they are respectable. When I ride on the streetcars I am held up—I pay five cents for a ride that is worth two and a half cents, simply because a body of men have bribed the city council and the legislature, so that all the rest of us have to pay tribute to them. If I do not want to fall into the clutches of the gas trust and choose to burn oil instead of gas, then good Mr. Rockefeller holds me up, and he uses a certain portion of his money to build universities and support churches which are engaged in telling us how to be good.*

A present day Darrow would probably add race to the equation and include the global economy and multinational capitalism, but the essence of his "argument" would, I believe, be the same:

> *Some so-called criminals—and I will use this word because it is handy, it means nothing to me—I speak of the criminals who get caught as distinguished from the criminals who catch them—some of these so called criminals are in jail for their first offenses, but nine tenths of you are in jail because you did not have a good lawyer and, of course, you did not have a good lawyer because you did not have enough money to pay a good lawyer. There is no very great danger of a rich man going to jail.*

I, of course, am tempted to quote his whole essay because I, actually much more than the inmates/students to whom I gave this essay, find his analysis compelling, but I will stop with the following:

> *When they put up the price of gas ten cents, I do not know who will go to jail, but I do know that a certain number of people will go … Whenever the Standard Oil Company raises the price of oil, I know that a certain number of girls who are seamstresses and who work night after night long hours for somebody else, will be compelled to go out on the streets and ply another trade, and I know that Mr. Rockefeller and his associates are responsible and not the poor girls in the jails. First and last, people are sent to jail because they are poor … The more that is taken from the poor by the rich who have the chance to take it, the more poor people there are who are compelled to resort to these means for a livelihood. They may not understand it, they may not think so at once, but after all they are driven into that line of employment.*

To redefine "criminal" can be revolutionary (and, in repressive countries, can actually be labeled "criminal"). I remember walking the street in Montpelier, Vermont, noticing a few storefronts with large signs about "Welfare Recipients and Welfare Frauds." Underneath the sign there were photographs, a bit like mugshots, of very wealthy CEO's, listing the huge amounts of government subsidies each has received. It was very effective in terms of challenging people to think who are the frauds and criminals, who should be in jail. I think, again, of the inmate/student saying that the teacher who shamed the second grader over her drawing of her snowman was a murderer and should be in prison.

When I was young I lived near the Bronx zoo and would often go there by myself to visit the animals. One cold day I was walking in the great ape house. It was winter and the animals were all inside, in small confined spaces, heavy glass between me and them. I was alone in the large concrete area, moving from one "cell" to another, viewing the animals and reading what was written under each cage. At one point I read: "You are looking at the most dangerous animal known to live. At this point of time he is threatening whole species with destruction." I looked up expectantly to view this dangerous animal. What I saw was a mirror, an image of me behind steel bars. It was totally unexpected; it was totally accurate, and powerful.

It's interesting that the sign was taken down soon after it stopped me in my tracks.

Chapter Twenty:

A very long way into "Comparison"

It has been two months since I have written the previous chapter on definition. During that time I have started teaching again and been busy in the world. I had a resistance to returning to what I feared might be an empty space in my own mind, feeling disconnected from this book and from my own thoughts. But this last week, during this presidential primary, I was struck, again, by the importance of the preceding chapter on definition, on how essential it is to really stop and question, to look closely, specifically, slowly, and experientially rather than repeat formulaic abstractions. I thought, again, of George Orwell and his "Politics and the English Language," about the incredible gap between what is said and what is real, between the concept and the experience, about how words have lost meaning and how language is used to manipulate rather than express. It was my political anger at lies and propaganda which brought me back to this book, back to definition, back to my sense that education (as I would define true education) deepens consciousness. But I was still stuck, not knowing how to move from definition into comparison.

I began to think of creative and critical writing, to "compare" the two seemingly opposite ways of perceiving and being. I found myself more clear about what creativity was not rather than what it was: creativity was not dogma or absolutes, not will and control, not habitual and linear thinking, not obedience to an outside authority or external judge. Creativity had something to do with spontaneity, extending possibilities through play, imagining, something about the energy that connects what is seemingly disparate, the energy created by surprising leaps of understanding. I thought about some of the distinctions made between critical thinking and creative thinking, and that the line drawn between the two might really be more flowing, more permeable and complex, more like the Yin and Yang symbols, each partaking of the other. Critical and creative—both were, to my mind, not only not in opposition but close friends, and both were essential to freedom. Their common enemy, I was beginning to see, was the constricting bars of unquestioned authority, dogma, absolutes, and habitual thought patterns, of fear and the need to control, of the control that limits and destroys both critical and creative thought.

Looking through some possible handouts on learning and education for my advisee group at Vermont College, I found a chapter I had copied from Freire's *Pedagogy of the Oppressed.* Reading it again, I remembered that I had used it in the prison to illustrate the technique of comparison, Freire distinguishing between two systems of education: banking and problem posing. In that chapter, Freire speaks of "the point of departure" for all teaching/learning:

> *The point of departure of the movement lies in men themselves. But since men do not exist apart from the world, apart from reality, the movement must begin with the men-world relationship. Accordingly, the point of departure must always be with men in the 'here and now,' which constitutes the situation within which they are submerged, from which they emerge, and in which they intervene. Only by starting from this situation—which determines their perception of it—can they begin to move. To do this authentically they must perceive their state not as fated and unalterable but merely as limiting—and therefore challenging.*

I started to think of Yoga, of awareness of the body, and how it is that awareness that creates the possibility of change and transformation. Calisthenics is one way of building muscles; yoga is another. The former, it seems to me, works from the outside, a pushing of the body through strenuous exertion towards an external goal of where the body should be. The latter, rather than pushing the body, asks where the body now is, asks the mind to reenter the body, like getting acquainted with an old friend (or, for some, a possible enemy) after a long absence, observing the experience, noticing the boundary where pain begins, relaxing in that very space, accepting rather than pushing that edge, staying present in the body at that boundary. And what is quite amazing, in both yoga and life, is that relaxation in that space rather than the will to be somewhere else opens what had been constricted, acceptance rather than the judgment allowing one to grow and change.

So much of education, especially now, is concerned with external evaluation, with outcome assessments and standardized tests, with rewards and punishments, with making students learn information that others consider important, with drills, calisthenics, and muscle building. And why does my mind now shift to those body building magazines showing men and women with enormous biceps and bulging leg muscles, people seeming more bound than freed by their muscles? I think of my slender T'ai Chi teacher who, because he is so aware and so centered, merely shifts his weight, and those who are "attacking" are flung (or fling themselves) across the room. He tells the class that what he is teaching us is only the external "house"—that which can be shown—but what we need to learn is the deeper knowledge of mind, breath and awareness that happens within us and is "rooted in the breath." How did we get so far that the outside show has became more important than the inside knowing?

In his *Pedagogy of the Oppressed*, Paolo Freire talks about "banker education" where the teacher deposits more and more facts into a passive student who is then asked to repeat back what s/he has memorized. Freire compares this banking education with problem posing education where the student is actively engaged in learning, reading texts and viewing the world closely, coming to understanding and meaning through his/her own mind questioning assumptions, challenging authority, and taking action to transform the world. Education as a vehicle for consciousness, power, and freedom. For Freire, the form or process of educating is essential. I think of Audre Lorde's saying that we cannot tear down the master's house using his tools, and of Martin Luther King, Jr. and Ghandhi, both knowing deeply that *how* we get to our goal determines whether we really achieve that goal. We become whatever passes through our hands. For Freire (and for me) one cannot teach radical theory through the banking system of education; one cannot educate people into consciousness if the method of education is one of dominance and submission, of authority and obedience, of control rather than freedom. For Freire, pedagogy is either an exercise in oppression or in liberation, either suppressing or expanding our human spirit: "Apart from inquiry, apart from the praxis, men cannot be truly human. Knowledge emerges only through invention and re-invention, through the restless, impatient, continuing, hopeful inquiry men pursue in the world, with the world, and with each other."

According to Freire, "Banking education begins with a false understanding of men as objects. It cannot promote the development of what Fromm calls 'biophily,' but instead produces its opposite: 'necrophily.'" Freire then quotes Fromm: "'While life is characterized by growth in a structured, functional manner, the necrophilous person loves all that does not grow, all that is mechanical. The necrophilous person is driven by the desire to transform the organic into the inorganic, to approach life mechanically, as if all living persons were things … Memory, rather than experience, having rather than being, is what counts. The necrophilous person can relate to an object—a flower or a person—only if he possesses it; hence a threat to his possession is a threat to himself; if he loses possession he loses contact with the world … He loves control, and in the act of controlling he kills life.'" Freire continues: "Oppression—overwhelming control—is necrophilic; it is nourished by love of death, not life. The banking concept of education, which serves the interests of oppression, is also necrophilic. Based on a mechanistic, static, naturalistic, spatialized view of consciousness, it transforms students into receiving objects. It attempts to control thinking and action, leads men to adjust to the world, and inhibits their creative power."

Towards the end of his second chapter, Freire moves skillfully comparing the two systems:

> *Once again, the two education concepts and practice under analysis come into conflict. Banking education (for obvious reasons) attempts, by mythicizing reality, to conceal certain facts which explain the way men exist in the world; problem-posing education sets itself the task of demythologizing. Banking education resists dialogue; problem posing education regards dialogue as indispensable to the act of cognition which unveils reality. Banking education treats students as objects of assistance; problem posing education makes them critical thinkers. Banking education inhibits creativity and domesticates (although it cannot completely destroy) the intentionality of consciousness by isolating consciousness from the world, thereby denying men their ontological and historical vocation of becoming more fully human. Problem-posing education bases itself on creativity and stimulates true reflection and action upon reality, thereby responding to the vocation of men as beings who are authentic only when engaged in inquiry and creative transformation. In sum: banking theory and practice, as immobilizing and fixating forces, fail to acknowledge men as historical beings; problem posing theory and practice take man's historicity as their starting point … Whereas the banking method directly or indi-*

rectly reinforces men's fatalistic perception of their situation, the problem posing method presents this very situation to them as a problem. As the situation becomes the object of their cognition, the naive or magical perception which produced their fatalism gives way to perception which is able to perceive itself even as it perceives reality, and can thus be critically objective about that reality. A deepened consciousness of their situation leads men to apprehend that situation as an historical reality susceptible of transformation. Resignation gives way to the drive for transformation and inquiry, over which men feel themselves to be in control. If men, as historical beings necessarily engaged with other men in a movement of inquiry, did not control that movement, it would be (and is) a violation of men's humanity. Any situation in which some men prevent others from engaging in the process of inquiry is one of violence. The means used are not important; to alienate men from their own decision making is to change them into objects.

In prison human beings become objects to be controlled. The Composition class, in its very humble way, asks students to engage in that humanizing "movement of inquiry." It nurtures and demands both creativity and critical thought. It is a tool for trespassing across borders of disciplines, of moving between creative imagination and analytic reflection, between our inner and outer world. It is revolutionary really, like meditation, because if we really do observe closely and are mindful, if we really begin to question assumptions and authority, we would transform both the world within us and the world outside of us.

And so the class continues, slowly developing the muscles of the mind. After writing description, narration, and definition, it is mind stretching to begin to compare two concepts. One could compare two very different terms—like banking education and problem posing education. But what I have found even more challenging is to look at words or concepts that seem, to the superficial eye, quite similar, perhaps even the same, forcing one to slow down in order to be more aware of what is subtle and deep.

The Buddhists use a term "near enemy" to describe mind states that seem close but are really "enemies" in terms of their essential nature: detachment and indifference, for example, or compassion and pity, or Elizabeth Minnich's distinction between "exclusive" and "excellent." I think of other terms that have some of the quality of near enemy: shame and guilt; pride and arrogance; justice and law; strength and power; hate and anger; suffering and pain; religion and spirituality; happiness and joy; medicine and healing; solitude and aloneness.

The list increases as I read the words of others, and as my students explore their own words. A few years ago, I had my mind ignited into thought by Erich Fromm's distinction between selfish and self-full in his essay on "Selfishness and Self-love." A few months ago, it was Sharon Salzburg's distinction between remorse and guilt that made me see something from a whole other angle. And more recently it was a section in Avivah Zornberg's *The Beginning of Desire: Reflections on Genesis* where Zornberg explores Jacob's deception of Isaac using Lionel Trilling's distinction between sincerity and authenticity.

I had always loved sincerity, like loving innocence, and had not thought of "dissembling" in any positive way, so it was with a whole other set of values and assumptions that I came upon this chapter in Zornberg's book. The following is only one small section in which Zornberg refers to Trilling's distinctions:

> By deploying texts from Diderot, Hegel, and Shakespeare, Trilling proposes to us the 'dismaying thought that sincerity is undeserving of our respect.' The disintegrated, alienated, and distraught consciousness—which Hegel calls 'base'—represents a higher mode of freedom than that of the 'honest soul,' the condition of 'nobility,' which is committed to accord with the external power of society. To detach oneself from imposed conditions, from the roles assigned by birth and social rank, is to lose one's self, but thereby to gain access to a new authenticity of self. Trilling uses Hegel's paradoxical analysis of the 'honest soul' and the 'disintegrated consciousness' as the basis for his study of the historical movement from the admiration of 'sincerity' to that of 'authenticity.' I should like to use this model to suggest a reading of Jacob's entry into the world of 'authenticity,' the world in which he will look 'like a dissembler,' and leave behind him his primary sense of himself as "ish tam," a 'sincere,' 'noble' man. Like Hegel's heroic individual, Jacob must become 'base, alienated a player of many roles, before he can redefine in his life, the meaning of 'nobility.' A kind of freedom has to become his, before he can indeed to 'his own self be true.'

Reading this chapter, my own love of simple "innocence" was jolted, and I was forced into a more complex sense of what it means to be human, a journey that involves a descent, a break up of an ideal image of self, a movement into the shadow, a putting on of masks, a dissembling, perhaps a recognition of one's own ability to do acts of malevolence, in order to move into a true authenticity. Sincerity isn't enough in a world that is complex; there is something richer and deeper, that partakes of art and play and God. Zornberg's close exploration opened for me a whole other way of reading the Biblical text, of "judging" Rebecca and Jacob, and of seeing my own life and actions. That deeper seeing is what I want students to feel in and through their own writing.

The following papers are a few that I have saved. Some of the students had difficulty in moving from the experience to the definition, but all had a quality of close observation and honesty. Some of them may seem "simple," but all of them, I believe, show active thought and an honest widening of the lens of understanding.

Pride and Arrogance by K.J.

> *Pride and arrogance, although very closely related, are very diverse in the act. By looking closely at an experience in my past, I hope to clarify and deepen my own and the reader's understanding of each.*
>
> *When I played basketball in prep school, it was a very good time of my life. One particular instance stands out in my mind. My team was playing for the North Carolina State championship. My parents flew down from N.Y. to see me play. I really wanted to do well because this was the first time they had come to see me play at this level. I was interviewed before the game and dedicated the game to my parents and had them appear on T.V. with me. At this point, I felt a sense of pride because my parents loved me enough to get on a plane to come and be a part of my place in the sun. I was so filled with the love I felt for them, but the main part of the feeling was I just wanted to show them off to the world.*
>
> *Once the game started, it was like I could do no wrong. Everything I did that night on the court in N.C. came up aces. By halftime I had 19 points, 10 rebounds, and 11 assists. At this point I was very proud of myself in that I was showcasing my God-given talent to the world with over 100 college scouts in the audience. But I was also doing it in front of the people that made it all possible, my parents. These people stuck by me, sent me to the basketball camps, understood when I didn't want to run the family business so I could play. On a larger scale, they were the people that put me on the planet.*
>
> *Coming out of the locker room after half time and seeing the pride in my parents' eyes did something awful to me in that at that point I crossed the line and arrogance reared its ugly head. When the second half started, the feeling of magic was still there, but also there was this feeling like I had to display my dominance over all the others on the court. When I got the*

ball, not only did I continue to score at will, but I tried to utterly humiliate those that had to guard me. I said all types of demeaning things to them and instead of showcasing my talent, I was tainting this very special moment with these very base acts. At this point I would describe arrogance as a total feeling of one's own importance or accomplishments, a total feeling of dominance over others. My coach called a time out and asked me what the hell was wrong with me. I was at a loss for words because my arrogance had consumed my entire being.

That was enough to snap me out of that feeling. The game went on and the magic continued. I won the MVP award, having scored 52 pints, grabbing 16 rebounds and dealing off 20 assists. Pride filed my very being, but it was different this time in that my pride came from the tears that now flowed freely from my mother's eyes. These were not tears of pain but of joy. When I got the trophy at the ceremony, I gave it to my mother, saying, "I dedicate this to the person that made it all possible" which drew a thunderous standing ovation from the audience. My feeling of pride was the most complete of all, an elation in that I gave something back to the person that sacrificed for me to make this magic possible.

Another student (AT) wrote about his changing definition of pride. In the beginning of his paper, he describes what it took—guns, girls, fancy clothes—to make him feel "proud" and then continues:

As I matured, though, my definition changed and I learned that my definition as a kid for pride was actually the definition for arrogance because if I had pride I would have never stolen from somebody, nor would I have punched a man in the face for making fun of me. If I had pride, I would have worn the clothes my mother was able to afford and been thankful for them.

My mature definition of pride has helped me to walk with my head up and chest out without a Fila suit on, gun on my waist to show I was tough, and some cute big butt girl on my arm which means, now, I won't have to do crime to feel good about myself as a man. It also has earned me respect from people with self respect and dignity.

When a man stands up for what's right and what he firmly believes in, he has pride. When a mother sacrifices an important part of her life for the welfare of her child, she has pride. When someone strives to make the best of their lives without hurting or taking from others, they have pride. But when someone hurts another to feel tough, takes from another to look better, or abuses a woman or man for self gratification, that's arrogance.

In some way this is a very "simple" realization; in another way, however, it is profound, especially when one thinks how many adults—many of them leaders of powerful countries—never reflect on the meaning of concepts, misnaming their arrogance, their acts of violence and abuse, "national and personal pride." I think, again, of what it means to look closely and honestly at one's own experience and to struggle in order to come to a deeper understanding of self and world. I think of the humbleness that is required and of the compassion that comes from that humbleness.

The following papers are a few of the many that showed that struggle to distinguish and to understand:

Compassion and Pity by C.G.

>A friend of mine invited me to visit his beloved mother at a nursing home. There I met my friend's mother and some other elderly ladies whom, obviously, no one was visiting. The place was very neat and clear but full of sad faced marked by loneliness.

>I almost cried when one of the ladies asked me if I were there to see her. I mumbled for a moment. Then I looked at her and pictured my own mother's face, which made me aware of the great respect I have for womankind. Then I said to her,"Yes I am here to see you, mom!" She held my hand and she smiled. She told me that she has three sons and a few brothers and sisters but that they do not visit her. When I left, she was very happy but I was sad.

>To me, places like that are not for a mother who cared for her child until he or she reached maturity. Our mother suffered for us; therefore we should treat her with more kindness, compassion, and dignity.

>As I write this essay I realize that compassion is reaching out to another human being's heart. When some one shows compassion toward another person, that individual's desire is to alleviate the sorrowful condition, to make that person feel secure. Compassion is something that has a special place deep in one's consciousness which compels humankind to act accordingly.

>When I left that place my heart was full of disappointment. I was silent for a moment, then asked my friend, who is a doctor, "How do you feel about your mother's condition and living in a place like that?"

>He smiled and said, "There is nothing I can do for her to change her condition." Then he asked me, "What would you do?" I told him honestly,

"I would never put my beloved mother away from me, especially in her old age." He went on to say, "That I don't understand. This is the way people live here in America." I looked at him and said, "In my country it's the opposite. We have great respect and consideration for the elderly people. We treat them with love and compassion."

There were some visitors screaming at their suffering mothers and fathers and some arguing over money and other things. They were more concerned about material things than the feelings of their loved ones. They showed no concern or compassion; maybe some pity.

Pity is a conditional feeling. It is momentary and selfish. One shows concern but it is limited. One shows kindness, but expects something back, something like recognition or any other reward.

Justice and Law by B. H

Justice is to treat people fairly in all aspects of people's activity—social, political, and economic. That is why the symbolic Lady of Justice (the lady found on police hats, correction uniforms, and in front of courthouses) is blind. She (justice) is not supposed to consider race, social class, gender, etc. when judging a person's fate or making political decisions.

Perhaps justice can be readily defined by first defining injustice—the diametric opposite of justice.

An example of injustice for me was on November 24, 1991. As I was going to a court hearing at Coxsackie Correctional Facility, a correction officer tripped me while in leg and hand shackles because I did not feel like answering his probing questions that I felt invaded my privacy. This officer tripped me while in handcuffs, then falsified a misbehavior report stating that I spit in his face unprovoked. Later on I was admitted to Coxsackie's Special Housing Unit where I had to defend myself against five correction officers who attacked me in retaliation for the earlier incident. These officers, just like their colleague, falsified the misbehavior report. The only significant difference was five officers stated I struck out at them without provocation. On November 27, 1992, I was placed before a Correction Lieutenant who reviewed the misbehavior reports and, without being fair and impartial, sentenced me to 820 days box-time. The Lieutenant would not listen to logic and refused to part from his predetermined view that the officers were right and I was wrong. I was not allowed to call witnesses and the lieutenant curtailed my right to speak out against the charges.

The blind sister Justice finally worked some of her magic thirteen months later on December 20, 1993 when an appellate committee in Albany reversed the decision of that unjust lieutenant and released me from the box. After thirteen months of writing, having hearings and hoping, somebody decided I was right and treated me fairly. Though it was very late, justice was served.

Law is much more complex to define. Ideally, law is supposed to regulate the behavior of the masses and, in doing this, serve justice. Law is comprised of rules and regulations, codes and ordinances, that are supposed to uphold justice. Law (righteous law) prevents injustice.

Law, if properly adhered to, can achieve justice. A case in point is my experience with the guards in November of 1992, the unjust hearing by the Correction Lieutenant, and the subsequent reversal of the hearing decision by the appellate committee in Albany. The hearing decision was reversed because the Correction Lieutenant refused to follow the rules and regulations (laws) of the State Legislature.

Certain rules and regulations were drafted and passed by the State Legislature to insure that prisoners facing disciplinary hearings receive "due process of law." Due process has been defined as fair procedures that insure prisoners do not lose life, liberty, or property unjustly. Some of these laws enacted by the legislature are the opportunity to speak out and defend against the charges, the right to call witnesses, 24 hour notice of the charges against the prisoner, and the right to an assistant.

The Correction Lieutenant did not abide by the laws and, therefore, obstructed justice. He refused to let me call witnesses, speak out against the charges, and exercise my right to an assistant. He was biased and partial toward his colleagues.

The reversal of the lieutenant's hearing decision was a proper decision on the law and justice was served. This experience and writing this paper about it has shown me that the difference between law and justice is that law is, or should be, the man-made protector of justice. Laws are drafted, or should be, to achieve justice. Justice is the final goal, that "thing" that we want to accomplish.

The similarities between justice and law are that, in a just and freedom loving society, the two abstractions work for each other and for the people. Law protects justice; justice protects the law by showing all the people within said society that the law works for them, thereby raising people's respect for the law. The two abstractions work for the people by protecting everybody's right to adequate food, shelter, education, security, and other liberties and human rights that determine meaningful livelihood.

Hate and Anger

Throughout the years the words anger and hate have become less meaningful in that the use of these words has become so loose that we've lost sense of their true meaning. These words are important because they express some of the basic human emotions. How many times a day have you used the expression "I hate this" or "I hate that"? We have come to see these two as meaning the same thing when in fact they have completely different meanings.

To me the word anger is used to describe the everyday happenings that disrupt my personal goals. It's the way I feel when one of the guards changes a particular rule around in order to meet the needs of a specific situation. I feel the complete helplessness I feel over my own life. I can be angry with the rotten food we're forced to eat everyday while being watched to make sure that we don't take an extra slice of bread. I get angry every time I use the bathroom, being forced to relieve myself in the complete view of anyone who happens to walk by at the time. The list could go on forever, but the point I'm trying to make is that anger is a passing feeling. You can be angry at something when you're in the position but as soon as the situation is removed the feeling of anger is relieved.

Hate, on the other hand, is something altogether different. In order for me to hate something I need to feel the same way towards it all the time. I cannot hate the way a guard changes the rules, the rotten food, or even the lack of privacy I've taken for granted all my life. I can hate the entire structure of this system. I can feel this way towards the prison system as a whole, not the specific points that stand out. To me this hate is pure; it consumes me on a daily basis. This hate has almost become a form of lust in that it grows within me at such a rate that I could easily be consumed to the point of compete abandon if not for my better judgment. I could not feel any different towards this because I have been a part of it for too long and have seen the results of its abuses. I live with this hate everyday; it's all I can do to keep from reacting in an unfavorable way. I live to see this system destroyed. This feeling to me is hate.

Anger is but a fleeting emotion, whereas hate is, in essence, part of you. Anger can be a part of hate and is, in many cases, a result of hatred, but hate, because it is permanent, cannot be part of anger.

Hate/Anger by H.A.H.

Anger brings about hate. We don't simply start out hating anything or anyone. There is a cause and then there is an effect. The effect in this case is hate. What caused hate? Anger. The anger becomes, in a sense, an obsession. It (anger) took control totally which led to hate. Anger is a lesser form of hate. A smoldering brush fire (anger) compared to a 5 alarm fire burning out of control in the dry forests of Southern California. Anger may take you to small claims court, but hate is going to the highest court in the nation to have your case heard. Minor vs. Major. Anger is being intoxicated while driving. Hate is killing a lot of people on a freeway while driving intoxicated.

My personal experience with these two reactionary words comes in the form of me as a proud, intelligent black man whose history (ancestry) goes back so far till it cannot be traced. What started out as anger has now become deep rooted. It cannot be supplanted nor uprooted. Anger began after being out on my own and seeing that all I had learned from proud, upstanding parents and other non-immediate relatives was, to my astonishment, in no way respected or cared for by the outside world. As I embarked on a social and political, as well as historical, consciousness during the turbulent '60's, the anger at seeing everything as it really was started the brush fire I spoke about earlier. It all made me angry: Abbie Hoffman, H. Rap Brown, Huey Newton, Malcolm X, Martin Luther King, Joanne Chesimard (Assitir Shakur), the Panthers, Weather Underground, F.A.L.N., the B.L.A., Jane Fonda, The Ku Klux Klan, George Wallace, Ronald Reagan, Jessie Helms, Strom Thurmond, Mississippi, Alabama … The match was lit and thrown into the brush..

I joined the service after college and, to this very day, still see the picture of me as a recruit in full dress uniform, 21 years old, a large picture of the American flag behind me. The flag I pledged allegiance to growing up. After studying the "science" of the flag and its actual representation, the true meaning of "the stars and stripes" and the red, white, and blue. Deeper study brought on the revelation regarding the King Alfred Plan, the military and political stratagem devised to ward off any threat by the black race to seriously revolt. A very disturbing piece of info, if you just so happen to be of Nubian ancestry.

I look at the map of the world, and Africa is larger than so many other continents. Here it is, my country, ruled by people who propagate racism. They also happen to be living where all the gold, diamonds, silver, *platinum, and numerous other precious elements are. The brush fire is spreading.*

Here in the United States of South African America, spelled Roxbury, Howard Beach, Atlanta Georgia, and Selma Alabama, I watch as my people made and still make fools of themselves. Uncultured dress, male species acting like the female species, Gherry culrs, tight pants, short short dresses, lightening of the skin, refusing to be who they are, Diana Ross, Tina Turner, Lionel Richie, to name a few. Those types would never believe our culture was stolen, hidden, and changed. I am in a Western Art class here and I watch the proof of who the people we are watching on the screen actually are: 1500 B.C. Egyptians, Black. I ask the professor certain questions. That person has been taught the secret too. Never reveal the truth. So I sit and endure the "course," knowing the truth. No one sees the fire burning in the brush. It's spreading fast.

I wind up in prison. The prison population is predominately black. The prison guards are predominately white. The majority of prisons are in areas far from where the predominant prison population is from. I am stripped of all possessions (just like the service). I am given a number (just like the service). I am dressed in a green uniform (just like the service). I march in a company (battalion style) to work, chow, etc. I hear nigger jokes, I see double standard practices being employed. I feel the hate from the guards and "civilians" towards me. I take orders from young kids fresh out of high school whose only perception of me was when they, as little kids, ran around a lamppost of a man holding a light. The face was black who held the light attached to the lamppost. Or maybe it was of the "negro" lady who came to clear their homes. They probably called her Sarah or Mattie. Her name probably was Mrs. Jones or Mrs. Smith. I "obey" the rules handed down from people who are really inferior to me mentally and physically. They treat me as if I were the lowest form of life. Not only because I am in prison, but also because of who I am man to man. I could take their lives with two well placed blows. Crippling blows. All the anger that turned into hate would be behind the blows. All the years, 35 to be exact, of seeing how my people are being worked on mentally and physically as well as spiritually. All the years of fights in the streets, in the rings, in the courthouses, and with myself to stay strong, don't bend from the winds of the machine that is geared to break me.

One sharp crippling blow under the heart of the machine and another to the solar plexus, causing the machine's heart to burst, and all the filthy oxygen gushes out through its mouth and nostrils. As it falls to the soil it came from, I stomp and stomp and grind until there's no doubt the machine is dead. I savagely spit the disgust, frustration, anger, and hate into the severely battered face of the machine. Only then will the fire that burned so wildly for so many centuries be doused. Doused when the machine, for sure, is back in the ropes that bind the valley.

The similarities between these two words are amazing to me. One almost always leads to the other. If not suppressed, it will lead to the other. If suppressed it will lead to the other. There should have been a word to describe the two if combined together. By that I mean, what will happen when you cross anger with hate. Angate? Hatang? Nitro and glycerin. My point is to show that these two words are so closely associated with one another due to the fact that one of the two words automatically increases (rises) or decreases (lowers) to the other. Always be denied something that is rightfully yours and see where the two words come into play.

Typing their papers, I feel, again, the power of thought and feeling. Students, through the act of writing, clarify and strengthen their understanding of specific words. Through the act of sharing their words, others grow in their understanding of self and other. And I, as teacher, learn from my students about their definition of two words, about their experiences and their perceptions of self and world, and reexamine my own definitions. I think how many people have lost their capacity to reflect on their own experiences and/or to hear another. I think how I have grown from listening to the thoughts of another.

In her essay "Eye to Eye" in *Sister Outsider*, Audre Lorde explores the difference between anger and hatred: "Anger—a passion of displeasure that may be excessive or misplaced but not necessarily harmful. Hatred—an emotional habit or attitude of mind in which aversion is coupled with ill will. Anger, used, does not destroy, hatred does." She continues:

Racism and sexism are grown-up words. Black children in america cannot avoid these distortions in their living and, too often do not have the words for naming them. But both are correctly perceived as hatred. Growing up, metabolizing hatred like a daily bread. Because I am black, because I am woman, because I am not Black enough, because I am not some particular fantasy of a woman, because I AM. On such a consistent diet, one can eventually come to value the hatred of one's enemies more than one values the love of friends, for that hatred becomes the source of anger, and anger is a powerful fuel. And true, sometimes it seems that anger alone keeps me alive; it burns with a bright and undiminished flame. Yet anger, like guilt, is an incomplete form of human knowledge. More useful than hatred, but still limited. Anger is useful to help clarify our differences, but in the long run, strength that is bred by anger alone is a blind force which cannot create the future. It can only demolish the past. Such strength does not focus upon what lies ahead, but upon what lies behind, upon what created it—hatred. And hatred is a deathwish for the hated, not a lifewish for anything else. To grow up metabolizing hatred like daily bread means that eventually every human interaction becomes tainted with the negative passion and intensity of its by-products—anger and cruelty.

In another essay, "Uses of Anger," Lorde continues to explore these two words/emotions:

Anger expressed and translated into action in the service of our vision and our future is a liberating and strengthening act of clarification, for it is in the painful process of this translation that we identify who are our allies with whom we have grave differences, and who are our genuine enemies. Anger is loaded with information and energy ... Hatred and anger are very different. Hatred is the fury of those who do not share our goals, and its object is death and destruction. Anger is a grief of distortions between peers, and its object is change.

Lorde's distinctions have been honed and chiseled from her sharp and honest exploration of her own experiences within this society. It is that close looking at the painful areas that have enabled her to grow into her wisdom, a wisdom very apparent in her writing and politics. Her distinction between two other near enemies, pain and suffering, makes clear what she sees as the path to freedom:

There is a distinction I am beginning to make in my living between pain and suffering. Pain is an event, an experience that must be recognized, named, and then used in some way in order for the experience to change, to be transformed into something else, strength or knowledge or action. Suffering, on the other hand, is the nightmare reliving of unscrutinized and unmetabolized pain. When I live through pain without recognizing it self-consciously, I rob myself of the power that can come from using that pain, the power to fuel some movement beyond it. I condemn myself to reliving that pain over and over and over whenever something close triggers it. And that is suffering, a seemingly inescapable cycle. And true, experiencing old pain sometimes feels like hurling myself full force against a concrete wall. But I remind myself that I HAVE LIVED THROUGH IT ALL ALREADY, AND SURVIVED.

How clear her words, how liberating they feel to me. But how is it, then, that when I taught *Sister Outsider* for a seminar all the men in the seminar were outraged at what they saw as her racism and sexism—against whites and against men. A good lead-in to the next chapter on analysis.

A Brief Interlude:
losing one's way and
how to return

Although Great Meadows, a maximum security prison with iron doors and gates, bars on each cell, and total control over all movement, was more oppressive than Washington's medium security correctional facility, it was, in a strange way, the easier one in which to teach. Although it is true that inmates could be transferred against their wills at a moment's notice and that every few years there would be the tension of a parole hearing and the usual despair when, after months of anticipation, they were dismissed after a few moments of inattention to all the documents they had so painstakingly gathered together, they were, mostly, there, and there for a long time: in Great Meadows, in their cells, and in the classroom. Nowhere to go and nothing to do. There were the obstacles of continuous noise, lack of privacy, inability to control journals, papers, and books, interference by both correctional officers and other inmates, and, of course, all the emotions with which everyone struggles, probably amplified because of the isolation and the powerlessness. But still they were, for the most part, very present within the classroom, receptive and focused. In Washington prison, across the road, more open and less restrictive, students always seemed less centered, more in limbo between two moving points, harder to teach. They were there for shorter periods, coming from somewhere and leaving for somewhere else. It's hard to keep one's mind on writing or literature or school if one is thinking about the possibility of going home soon. The tension, fear, and hope for the future take one away, very understandably, from being where one is. The difficulty and challenge for those men but, really, for all of us, is how to be where one is, present in the moment rather than thinking of the past or the future—regretting, planning, worrying, expecting, anticipating—all the places we all go when we watch our minds during meditation, our bodies sitting in one still place while our minds travel on and on.

In some way I have been like the men in Washington, my mind going in many different directions. I have been away from writing now for six months, teaching and working, and it is not easy to come back. I look at the moats and the towers of Great Meadow, thinking what I always think when I pass there: How can someone survive in that sterile and oppressive environment? How could I? It is summer and everything is in bloom. Everything in me calls me outside, to flowers and gardens. Unlike the men in prison, there against their wills, I need to consciously choose this path—the discipline to come in when most of me wants to go out. And I have been away for such a long time. Clearly, I need to start slowly, to not expect myself to be here, now, but rather, to arrive through a slow process of intention and, then, attention. Like getting into the cold water of Lake George, you can't—or I can't—just dive into coldness. It's a slow immersion. What I know is that once I am in the water, I am joyful and remain immersed for a long time. But as with many things, I need to consciously remember the past experience in order to choose it again and again, to remember how much joy I felt when I was writing, the focused energy when I was swimming in that deep water. And I need to remember why I began this book last Autumn, so that I can, again, choose to be here, in this room, while everything outside blooms.

And so I remember, again, the reasons: because I am free to be outside, amidst garden and flower, privileged, while so many are confined and denied light in all its forms; because the voices of the men and women in prison are silenced by those in power and I have learned so much from those voices and want to give to others the gifts I have received; because many of those in power lie, and people believe those lies, both those in power and those that are powerless; because the only way we (and even they) can see past the lies—even the ones we tell ourselves—is if there is consciousness, if light is brought into darkness, not just new information and knowledge but a knowledge of the process of awareness; because analysis is one of the processes that enable us to see beyond what we have been taught, beyond what we think we know, what we think we feel; because analysis allows us to explore the different layers, to dismantle lies we tell others and ones we tell ourselves. Because analysis of cause and effect, which is the very place I stopped in late Autumn, is so difficult and so necessary and so important to remember.

A Passing Thought

I thought I lost it all
which is what they must all feel
all the time, guilty or innocent,
all the life they thought they would lead
in a world beyond the bars in front of them.
To come down to this:
what is still here
in my life, now,
in the present,
continually
unfolding,
even here.

CHAPTER TWENTY-ONE:

ANALYSIS, PART ONE

(with no idea how many parts there will be)

Students (and probably it's much more widespread) often have a strong reaction when you ask them to "analyze." It's almost as if analysis means dissection, the breaking apart of wholeness, the disconnection from feeling and intuition, the removal of the subjective "I," the invalidation of personal experience. And the truth is it often does. No wonder, then, there is resistance—if analysis means the loss of what one experiences, what one feels, and what is mysterious and beyond reason. Or if analysis means that we are stupid, can't see what should be obvious, can't "reason." Students have the same reaction to "critical thought," the word "critical" immediately creating the constriction that comes with the judging eye, the critical voice, and criticism.

The teacher of analysis has to move slowly, carefully, since the ground is filled with landmines. Students are hypersensitive because they have been wounded. A teacher needs to redefine analysis and critical thought so that they are seen as friends helpful to our growth rather than enemies threatening our being. But even as I write this, I think that maybe I need to pay more attention to what students fear, to let in their words as "reasonable." In some way our ego is totally right about being threatened by analysis. All careful and deep thought does and should shake the foundations of the ego's constructed concepts of self and world, undercutting established boundaries and making those boundaries permeable to new truths. Perhaps what we need to do with all teaching, then, is to consciously create an environment in which fear, chaos, complexity, contradiction, ambiguity, and not knowing are seen not as problems, indications of something wrong, but, rather, as signs that we are on the right path and need to continue.

This is especially true with analysis where all those feelings will come up again and again, where students will want to stop in defeat or close off the complications that threaten simple and safe understanding. As teachers and as guides, we need to say, at those difficult and confusing junctions of possible trails, "Good, very good. All this seeming "lostness" is because you are expanding, growing beyond what is known and familiar. Very good, very good."

Once one opens oneself to the process of analysis, it is ongoing, each fold revealing another fold, each question leading to more questions. When we allow the "wild" animals within our own mind and heart space to wander, they are no longer willing to go obediently back into their master's cages, even if the master offers them food and shelter; they begin to find their own deeper thirst and search for ways to quench that thirst, to look beyond the small occasional pools in order to find the richer sources. In my mind, that is what analysis is or should be: the looking for the deeper sources. It is "radical" in the sense of going to the roots. And images, like the above—images of animals, cages, and pools—are part of the path of understanding, as are dreams, associations, connections, experiences.

When we do definition papers, I tell my students not to go to *Webster's Dictionary*, yet that is where I am now, looking up "analysis," just to see what the "experts" say. They say a lot: "Separation of a whole into its component parts; an examination of a complex, its elements and their relation; the identification or separation of ingredients of a substance; a method in philosophy of resolving complex expressions into simpler or more basic ones." Critical thought isn't in my dictionary, but critical is: "Inclined to criticize severely and unfavorably; consisting of or involving criticism; of or relating to the judgment of critics; exercising or involving careful judgment or judicious evaluation ..." Synonyms are the following: "Critical, hypercritical, faultfinding, captious, carping, censorious, exhibiting the spirit of one who looks for and points out faults and defects." Reading these definitions, I am stopped in my tracks. Maybe my students are right. Maybe this critical thought and analysis are not so good, not only for the ego but for the spirit. Maybe they are tied too closely to Ursula LeGuin's "father tongue" which insists on the separation that is so destructive to human beings, other animals, and the environment.

I think of a student who was extremely articulate with both words and paint, could capture nuance, feeling, complexity, could see relationships and trace them clearly, could go to the source in her writing, could, by my definition, engage in deep critical thought and analysis. Despite all I could see in her ability to reason, despite all the mirrors I offered reflecting back her clarity and depth of thought, she saw herself as someone who could not think, could not reason. Her self doubt was the legacy, I believe, of a very limited definition of analysis imposed on her by her philosopher father. Connected as my student was to her own natural tongue, she could not speak his language. *My kids*

I remember her walking into class having just read Elizabeth Minnich's *Transforming Knowledge*. With tears in her eyes, joyful and radiant, she declared, "I can think." Here was Minnich, a philosopher speaking about education in a way that was very clear, deep, connected and accessible. The student could understand Minnich's ideas fully. And knowing she was capable of thought, she was able to silence the anxiety that prevented thought. In teaching, I have to remind myself, again and again, that it is often the anxiety, the feeling of being stupid and incompetent, the fear of making a mistake that cause the problem. The seeming inability to think is an effect of constriction. Criticizing, judging, making someone feel incompetent and stupid are not helpful, do not free a person to think more clearly, to break out of the prison of limited thought, but, rather, reinforce the enclosure. What we need, always, is to find the key. Unfortunately (and fortunately) there is no one master key that fits all doors.

I often begin classes—whether in the prison or in Vermont College or in my community—with a short in-class writing as a way of centering a person within themselves, allowing them to follow their own channels before those channels get dissipated or diverted by louder voices. As a lead into analysis, I sometimes ask students to begin a paper with: "I am here, now, because ..." A simple "analysis" of cause and effect. What is quite wonderful is how these few words allow the mind to travel in so many different directions. It is interesting to think which direction we would follow.

Some students will give a chronological sequence of the events leading to their trial or imprisonment; some might go back to their childhood and some of the factors—like drugs or poverty—that led them to crime; others might talk about the politics of prison and the racism which lead to the incarceration of so many people of color; others might think of "here" as being the classroom and talk about their choice of education and why; some might go back to their birth, the sexual act which led to their conception and to their being "here" on this earth; others have gone further back, to God and more cosmic beginnings, to questions of existence and the meaning of life. What is clear is that each of us has a way of seeing and understanding that shapes our analysis, a framework for viewing and finding meaning—political, psychological, philosophical, spiritual. There is no one right analysis but, rather, different paths through which different individuals can more deeply and thoughtfully understand cause and effect. We animals do not all yearn for the same food, go to the same sources, have the same hunger. What we can teach is not "the way" but, rather, a way for exploring cause and effect, for distinguishing between what is superficial and sequential and what gets us closer to the source.

Hearing the writing of others—both published authors and others in the class—students get a sense of the range of possibilities. But while this sense of expansion is exciting, the process of letting out our own thoughts and hearing the thoughts of others can also be overwhelming, our thoughts like stampeding horses finally freed from their enclosure. No wonder there is a temptation to herd them back into the narrow gate, to keep them tamed and controlled.

I often ask students to write, at the end of their paper, what happened in the process of writing. The following is one expression of the chaos that can happen when we let the horses out of the padlock:

> In the process of writing this analysis paper, I had a lot of trouble staying focused on my main topic. When I started looking into my thesis, I saw that there were many different routes I could have taken. My thinking became confused. I became frustrated with myself and with what I was writing. I saw that my remembering things made me upset, so I would try to push it out. I was basically talking about my childhood in the paper and that made my thinking more confused because I would start going off on a tangent of what happened—who, what, where and how. At a point I just had to stop writing and just take hold of my thoughts. I even tried to change the topic in hopes that it would be something that was not so personal and so complete, but that didn't work. It did work in some way because I was able to see many, many things that have touched and/or affected my life.
>
> *a Catharsis*

Clearly the process is not easy, but what is also clear from the above is that it is meaningful labor, this birthing, this creation which shakes the narrow frames of our thinking and allows in what we have tried to keep out. But still the questions: how to stay with what is hard and confusing and often painful; how, in writing, to rein in what has been let out, to organize and edit, in order to write a clear, well developed, focused paper rather than one that rambles and confuses. How to harness rather than suppress and dissipate that alive and vibrant energy.

Sometimes in class I will do a brainstorming "analysis" of something seemingly simple, like "Why do people litter?" It is a question I often ask as I pick up, with anger and judgment, all kinds of garbage strewn along my dirt road, a road that leads to many hiking trails and a beautiful lake. I really do not understand how people could just throw beer bottles, packages from McDonalds, plastic soda cups, potato chip bags and just about anything from their car windows. I want to understand rather than just continually rage. I ask students to think about their own experiences, about friends and family, to make connections and associations, to think. As students speak, I take notes on the board, making lists of the possible "reasons" expressed. I wish I could reproduce the blackboard, the "chaos" of mind as they pondered the "why": laziness, not caring, not being conscious, the attitude of parents or peers, imitating others' actions, hostility, anger … And then the raising of questions. Where do they litter? Where would they not litter? The mind naturally begins to think of actions which are somewhat similar but slightly different : graffiti, defacing property, violence. The conversation often expands to the much larger litterers who pollute our world with no compunction to clean up their mess: companies dumping waste in the water and in the air; pesticides leaking into the earth and water; toxic byproducts of nuclear energy. We speak of who receives the litter, of poor neighborhoods becoming waste sites, of third world countries becoming the dumping ground for the garbage of richer nations. After the brainstorming, we, as a group, attempt to bring some order to this sprawling list, to categorize these very different "reasons," to reflect on how we might organize these different "causes." We talk about developing ideas, about trying to distinguish superficial and simpler causes from what might be more fundamental and basic.

I remember the first time I did this exercise, where I, for the first time, came to my own understanding of a possibly deeper "cause" of littering: the feeling (conscious and unconscious) of disconnection, an alienation from an environment and a form of passive aggression as a result of that alienation; a feeling that "this is not my home" and, therefore, I can do anything to it. Littering was, I was coming to see, an unconscious and habitual response of alienation and powerlessness. If my "analysis" had any truth to it, the best way to stop littering would be through an awareness of one's connection to one's environment and one's world. And that might require not only a shift of the mind but also a shift in power—in who "possesses" the earth and who is dispossessed, who has power and who is powerless. For me, the political layer would be very important: the major polluters whose greed for profits litter our earth, their crime going unpunished, the unbridled capitalism that dispossesses beings from their land and makes our land uninhabitable, the dumping on those who are poor and powerless. But I could also feel the importance of the more immediate layer—the littering on my road. If I saw someone throwing McDonald's wrappings and Budweiser cans from their car, I would rush in hot pursuit to take their license number and report them. I'd want them punished. But, even more, I'd want them to be conscious of the effects of their acts. Perhaps "restorative justice" would "work": If one had to pick up garbage along this road for a week or a month, one might make the connection between cause and effect, might see how garbage disrespects the environment, would become conscious. On a national, global, and very local level, I want the polluters to feel the consequences of their deeds. I want consciousness and action.

Clearly my "analysis" would be different from others' who might look from the lens of psychology or history, who would see other "deeper" causes. Why people litter, like any question when looked at closely enough, is not so simple after all. What I want to do in the classroom is, again, not give students answers but, rather, habituate them to the process of inquiry and reflection, to the process of analysis which leads, naturally, to consciousness and responsibility.

Blake says, "To see the world in a grain of sand." Perhaps that is what I am trying to do in teaching. Perhaps it is too much. Students often joke about my almost unintelligible marginalia which repeat a few basic statements: Say more, go further, go slower, go more deeply. And of course I know there needs to be an end to each journey, a stopping place. I accept and welcome limitations and want a satisfying ending to an essay. But why not continue our journey as far as we can, layer by layer, exploring, unraveling, and feeling the excitement of discovery? If the desert fathers define sin as the refusal to grow, the process of exploring and discovery is the opposite: the desire and will to grow.

Loren Eiseley ends his essay, "The Golden Alphabet," in his The *Unexpected Universe*, with an understanding of how we, as individuals, can either deepen or denude the world of meaning:

> *Man, since the beginning of his symbol-making mind, has sought to read the map of ... (the) universe. Do not believe those serious minded men who tell us that writing began with economics and the ordering of jars*

of oil. Man is, in reality, as oracular animal. Bereft of instinct, he must search constantly for meanings. We forget that, like a child, man was a reader before he became a writer, a reader of what Coleridge once called the mighty alphabet of the universe. Long ago, our forerunners knew, as the Eskimo still know, that there is an instruction hidden in the storm or dancing in auroral fires. The future can be invoked by the pictures impressed on a cave wall or in the cracks interpreted by a shaman on the incinerated shoulder blade of a hare. The very flight of birds is a writing to be read. Thoreau strove for its interpretation on his pond, as Darwin, in his way, sought equally to read the message written in the beaks of Galapagos finches. But the messages, like all the messages in the universe are elusive.

Eiseley then tells the tale I retell in my earlier chapter about the "expert" labeling his precious shell "conus spurious." He concludes his essay with the following:

We live by messages—all true scientists, all lovers of the arts, indeed, all true men of any stamp. Some of the messages cannot be read, but man will always try. He hungers for messages, and when he ceases to seek and interpret them he will be no longer man.

The little cone lies now upon my desk, and I handle it as reverently as I would the tablets of a lost civilization. It transmits tidings as real as the increasingly far echoes heard by Thoreau in his last years.

Perhaps I would never have stumbled into so complete a revelation save that the shell was Conus spurius, carrying the appellation given it by one who had misread, most painfully misread, a true message from the universe. Each man deciphers from the ancient alphabets of nature only those secrets that his own deeps possess the power to endow with meaning. It had been so with Darwin and Thoreau. The golden alphabet, in whatever shape it chooses to reveal itself, is never spurious. From its inscrutable lettering is created man and all the streaming cloudland of his dreams.

The question, then, is whether we approach the world with curiosity or arrogance, whether we imbue our world with value or divest our world of its richness, seeing "value" only in terms of monetary worth. It is whether we follow our dreams or, cynically, dismiss them as "spurious."

Students are right not to bring their precious shells to the grubby shopkeeper. But if the process of analysis can make more rich our treasures, if it can make us explore what is inscrutable rather than reject it, then surely education is a place of light. That is how I approach education. That is how I define analysis. That is why I trust that students can bring what is precious into the light of exploration and begin to love, even more deeply, what they have always loved, adding now the light of consciousness. I believe that education is a way of making even more radiant the golden alphabet and that analysis is part of that "way."

CHAPTER TWENTY-TWO:

ANALYSIS, CONTINUED

Perhaps I went off a bit too much in terms of the radiance of analysis for the individual self and too little in terms of the necessity of analysis for the preservation of the world. Perhaps I have been seeing freedom, also, in too subjective a way: freedom from the bars of imprisonment of mind or body, freedom to choose our own lives, freedom for an individual. Of course there is a direct connection between individual freedom and societal freedom, but this morning, while jogging, I was thinking about analysis not so much in terms of freedom but responsibility of the individual, the responsibility that comes when we really analyze the layers of cause and effect, when we become conscious of the effects of our actions.

I have always had a reaction against a "new age" assumption that our minds create our world, its implication that we create our illness and, therefore, can create our wellness. My political consciousness knows that there are causes in the larger world beyond our own individual psyche and individual control. None of us exists apart from our world: our environment affects our health (and we, as individuals affect our environment). There are earthquakes and hurricanes, drought and starvation; there is poverty, racism, sexism, and patriarchal power; there is the globalization and free trade with its destruction of local, subsistence economies; there is the power of the wealthy to influence policy; there is injustice and inequality. Some children are born hungry, others are born with illness. We are not all handed an equal bag of goods. What is true, however, and this is where Buddhism, new age, and existentialism come together in my mind, is that no matter what we are given, we still have an ability to choose. And it is our choices, our attitudes and our consciousness, that affect the quality not only of our lives but of our world.

What has always seemed essential to me is to know what we are and are not responsible for: to not feel guilt or self blame for what is beyond our control and what has been done to us, nor complacency and passivity about what is within our control for which we have responsibility. For many years I have recited, almost like a mantra, "We can only do what we can do, and we can always do what we can do." My other "mantra" is that there is no real difference between our real self-interest and the interest of the entire world if we could only see far enough and long enough; no disconnection between our individual needs and world needs. But, of course, the problem is in seeing far and long. Because our society affirms as "good" and as part of "freedom" the satisfaction of all our immediate and never ending desires, particularly for material goods, it often seems like our self-interest is in direct contrast to the interest of others, that we must choose between our own desires and a more altruistic gesture of generosity, between self love and love of others.

I think of the Erich Fromm essay I wrote about in an earlier chapter comparing two terms. In that essay Fromm shows how self-love and love of another rather than being in opposition come from the same source. It is really the lack of self-love which results in selfish grasping, our real hunger never satisfied despite all the "food" we consume. Rumi has a poem capturing that entrapment and the possibility of change:

all my activities, Don't fill the void

> *This is how a human being can change;*
> *There is a worm addicted to eating grape leaves*
> *Suddenly he wakes up*
> *call it grace*
> *whatever, something*
> *wakes him*
> *And he's no longer a worm.*
> *He's the entire vineyard*
> *and the orchard too*
> *The fruit, the trunks*
> *a growing wisdom and joy*
> *that doesn't need to devour.*

(trans. Coleman Barks)

If we could see ourselves as the entire vineyard, we would not need to devour.

Native Americans speak of looking at all our actions in terms of their effect in seven generations. If seven generations were as immediate in our consciousness as tomorrow, or one hour, the distinction between self love and love of others would, I think, disappear. From that conscious perspective, much of our grasping and addictive actions would seem pathological, acts of incredible denial and self-destruction. What is so strange is the incredible myopia of almost all of our actions today: we cannot even see the connection between dumping poisons in the air and water and the destruction of our very source of life.

I'm not sure at what age children are able to develop a concept of time, to have a sense of a few hours, or a day, a week, a year, but in terms of most of our politics, we are like little children wanting immediate satisfaction, having no wise adult to look after our real self-interests. In fact, as we get older and more "productive," we tend to get more and more myopic. It is only later, and sometimes, when we have gotten out of the "rat race" or been stopped in our track, that we actually begin to have the larger perspective, to become wise, to think of seven generations, to see the whole vineyard, and to question what is really important. Much of our consumer economy is based, I believe, on our not understanding our deeper needs and hungers, our inability to go to the real source of either need or nourishment. So, I get back to importance of analysis, of really being able to explore the multiple layers of cause and effect, not just in terms of our own happiness but in terms of the survival of all beings on this earth.

There is the Buddhist story, or it could be a scientific fact, of a butterfly, the movement of whose wings cause, in a distant land and at a distant time, the strong winds of a hurricane. There is a parallel story of the erosion of a mountain caused by the unconscious killing of a mouse. Both capture, albeit in extreme ways, the concept of every action having a reaction. They speak of the need to contemplate consequences of our actions for many generations, to see how fossil fuel emissions add mercury and sulphur dioxide to the environment creating acid rain and dead lakes, how the nitrous oxide and carbon dioxide accelerate global warming and how global warming results not only in the melting of glaciers but also the increase in extreme weather patterns—earthquakes, hurricanes, cyclones, floods, and drought. Clearly it is impossible to ever know every cause or every effect. What we can do, however, is cultivate and affirm the importance of understanding rather than denying interconnections, of exploring cause and effect, defining that process as a necessary component of being an ethical person in this world, responsible not only for his/her life but for the life of the world. Consciousness allows us to choose and choice creates responsibility, and both are components of freedom.

Earlier in this book I wrote about the importance of looking to our own experience as a path of knowing. But, clearly, it is not enough to believe that all knowledge is within us. We do not know enough; we need to read, to research, to inquire of others in the past and present. I think of James Baldwin talking about those who do not know and do not want to know. I think of Adrienne Rich's answer to an arrogant student who dismissively asked her, "As an upper middle class white, Christian man how can I possibly know the reality of poor people, people of color, gays and lesbians?" and Rich answering, as if he were asking a real question rather than acting contemptuously, "Listen to their voices, read their words, explore their experiences *and* also look to your own experience of pain and powerlessness." Viciously attacked by corporations, Rachel Carson needed to fully investigate the effects of DDT on the environment, to scientifically prove what she saw and experienced. We need to research the causes of global warming; the effects of pesticides; the increase in autism and Alzheimer disease, the clusters of leukemia, breast cancer, brain and prostate cancer. We need to explore the causes of poverty and violence, the effects of past colonialism and imperialism, the continuous and denied interference of our country in the affairs of other countries, the effect of the "free market" and of globalization on subsistence economies, the privatization of water, the dumping of toxic waste. We need to read ancient and contemporary history, understand other cultures and other ways of being, read scientific and political essays, read literature and listen to music and be in the presence of art ... In other words, there is so much we need to learn in order to be conscious.

I pick up my TIAA-CREF pension plan and think of my stocks that are making money, think of money making money, and think of the relationship between high profits and exploitation. I need to find out whom I am supporting and how I am making my money, where products are made and who is paid what for their labor. To decide whether to buy New Balance or Nike, whether to buy organic eggs down the road or pay much less for eggs in the supermarket from chickens caged and inoculated in factory farms. To shop at the farmer's market or the large supermarket. Whether to pay more money in a small mom and pop hardware store or to shop at Lowe's or the even more recently built and bigger Home Depot or the large Walmart that has effectively closed down the small stores on so many Main Streets. What to charge for rent in the house I own, whom to go to for repairs, where to buy my plants, whether to eat organic meat or no meat at all, whether to put fertilizer in my garden or use poisons to stop animals from eating my garden crops and flower bulbs. Whether to give money to the homeless, to bring blankets and clothes, to welcome those who need shelter into my home. How much to give to organizations and what organizations are most needing my money, or my work. To think about the distribution of wealth, land, power. Clearly, to be a moral being in this world is not easy. But, really, what is the alternative? It is this process of questioning and analyzing which feels fundamental to education and life. And while it not easy, it is a totally natural process.

Children are constantly questioning why, why, why. When I would ask my students to close their eyes and picture how children approach their world (either remembering their own childhood or just imaging children in their mind's eye), almost all mention curiosity and questioning as fundamental to childhood. In an earlier chapter I explore how that curiosity gets dampened and how knowing becomes more important than exploring, answers more important than questions, being right more important than almost anything else. As teachers, what we need to do is rekindle the excitement of exploring the unknown. And as adults, we can do what children cannot do: see larger patterns, make more complex connections, see cause and effect on deeper levels. While it is true that some of our discoveries—whether psychological or political—might be painful, the seeing of the pattern has its own joy. It changes us, as Paolo Freire expresses in his *Pedagogy of the Oppressed*, from passive objects into moral human beings creating our life through our action. It gives us our humanity.

I think of some of my early "analysis" assignments within the prison: to explore why they are in prison; to look at the effects of being in prison; to look at some attitude or belief, or part of their personality and try to understand some of the causes within their background; to take one experience from their past and explore some of the possible effects of that one experience. What I tell students is to open themselves to a wide range of causes or effects. To welcome confusion, paradox, contradictions. To not try to reconcile or merge or universalize too soon. And to chose something that they really want to understand for their own life. Adrienne Rich says, "Truth is not one thing or even a system. It is an increasing complexity." I want them to welcome the complexity and the confusion as indicating the breaking up of an old order, the old truths no longer large enough to contain the new realities. Life constantly challenging concepts, deepening our humanity, our heart and mind.

I think of the understandable reluctance of students, experiencing the very real pain and oppression of prison, to allow into an essay (and into their consciousness) the possibility and reality that prison actually had "good" effects in term of emotional, psychological, political, ethical and spiritual growth. How to allow in that something so unjust, wrong, and terrible can be good in any way. I think of Audre Lorde ending her *Cancer Journals* with "I would never have chosen this path, but I am glad I am me, here, now." She is talking about her cancer—as others have talked about their own illnesses—but it is not that different from how some inmates view their imprisonment: I would never have chosen this path, but ... The following is a paper a student wrote in class in response to Lorde's quote.

> *"I would never have chosen this path, but I am very glad to be who I am, here."* Why should I have chosen this path which has led me to prison? I am unable to move about freely like I had in society, and I'm unable to be with my family, friends, and associates, etc. I've had to lock in a cell everyday and night for ten whole years. It's not a pleasant feeling; yet in some way, I know that I was saved by coming to prison.
>
> In the street I was reckless, careless, foolish, and I didn't value the things I should have, but instead I had taken them for granted. Today I am a changed man because my trials and tribulations have enabled me to take a deeper look into myself, whereupon I realized that I had to really get to know myself. Who I am, what I am and why I am. Why did I do the things that I did out there, and why do I do the things that I do in here today.
>
> I'm glad I am me, here and now, because when I was out on the street, I'd never really taken time to read and write, or spend enough time with myself to think and plan. Everything was so swift and spontaneous; it was as if I were acting merely on impulse.
>
> Now I've settled down and searched and thought, and really taken notice of my feelings and emotions just as well as others. I notice a big difference in my attitude towards life and people. I had been a victim of peer pressure in the street. Not saying that I followed everybody or just anybody, but I did some things that I know weren't comfortably my own decisions.
>
> I'm glad I am who I am now because I would never do anything that isn't clearly a decision of my own, or if it is someone else's decision that'll have some bearing on my life, I will not readily agree until I have thoroughly weighed the facts, circumstances and consequences of their decision.

I have much more control over my life now despite my predicament. I realize I'm stronger now, mentally as well as physically.

I've been involved in several different groups and organizations of which I won't reveal but only say that each of those groups and organizations has helped me to see just how strong something negative could be. What I mean is, some things appear to be so intangible if they are perceived on surface value; yet if one really searches deep, he or she would see that it's not as intangible as it appears to be. That's why I've stepped away from those groups and organizations, not only because I've seen the falsity but mainly because I realized I needed overall to be dependent upon myself because my strength lies within my own ability and all I had been searching for was always within myself. If I have to depend on someone or something else to program me or direct me, I may as well be dead. That's not to say that I can't be shown something by others; I'm merely saying that once I'm shown, that's all it takes, so let me handle it from there on.

See how I'm thinking now? On the street I probably never would have taken the time out to think like this. Although I would never have chosen this path, I have to admit that it has enabled me to take a look at myself closely and from afar.

The way I am now is, I let people see only what I want them to see about me. I don't reveal most things I used to carelessly reveal, because I realize that it's not wise to be too open with anyone; even someone you believe you truly know. I've learned that no matter how well you know a person, you never really know them. Why? Because many people don't even know themselves. Just like I didn't know myself, and it took confinement to force me to learn, to search to know who I am and give myself direction.

Have you ever made a move spontaneously without knowing what made you make that move? Well then that's another reason why I said, no matter how much you know someone you never really know them.

I'm positive that upon my return to society, if nothing fatal happens to me, that I'll be a beneficent person who is caring, knowing and understanding, who shines with love and strength.

I would never have chosen this path which has brought me so much pain, misery, despair and isolation. No way could I have chosen this rotten path for myself. Yet because of this gloomy, man-made hell that I've winded up in, I've seen light within this darkness. I know what love is now. I realize what suffering is. But I also realize that one's suffering could bring peace and contentment.

It took prison to open my eyes and replenish my dreams. I am indeed glad I am me, here and now. They might have my body in prison but my mind, thoughts, soul and spirit ascend safely beyond any chains, cells or prisons that could ever be built or will ever be built. Now that I know and understand that, I'm definitely glad I am me, here and now. (DM)

Typing this paper, I feel, again, the honor of teaching such students. I hear, in the papers, the willingness to allow in truths even if they seem to give weapons to enemies and are capable of being misunderstood and misused. I hear students trying to make subtle distinctions, refusing the simple black and white "reasoning," using writing as a way of thinking. They are willing, as one of my students said when he had finished his essay, to find out that what they thought they believed was no longer true for them, that they were replaying an old tape and needed to revise or at least amend a great deal of their essay in order to speak from a place of truth.

One of my students in Vermont College had written a very moving essay about her experience with a wounded heron. She loved herons, felt intimately connected with them. This particular essay was about a dying heron that she and her friend saved from a frozen pond but, ultimately, could not "save." Her essay raised questions about rehabilitation and the saving of wildlife, about our animal-human connection, about life and death and suffering. It captured the depth of her connection to and love of herons. When T. read her piece, everyone was very moved. One student, however, felt compelled to speak about her family's small fish hatchery. T's beloved heron was this other student's enemy, the main predator threatening her family's livelihood. The student talked about her family's struggle to keep herons out of the fish hatchery and, finally, how they had to kill herons in order to survive economically. It was clearly difficult for the student to say what she knew would be judged negatively by others. I could see the expression of horror in T's face.

On one level T's essay was complete; it was a beautiful essay. But now there was another possible level. Her choice was to keep the essay as it was, holding fast to her clear concept of right and wrong, or, in some way, widen the circle, bringing in the questions posed by this more complex reality.

T. continued to work on her essay. I quote from her original ending where she and the wildlife rehabilitator are about to kill the heron in order to stop her suffering:

I spent half an hour alone with the bird. Silly, but I told her what we were going to do and why. I cried, laying my body over hers, and felt her breathing. When my father was dying of cancer two years earlier I had done the same thing—laid my body over his chest, which labored so hard, hoping it would stop him from breathing and release him. Nita came in and I just stayed where I was with my face tucked into the wing of the heron, as if I were sleeping. Within moments the heart, beating so furiously, stopped. I had held my breath and now exhaled with deep relief. Once more, a part of my spirit was set free.

That night, I dreamed of flying, as I so often do. I fly—feeling my arms extend—my bones going hollow—my hair transforming into feathers, gray and brown and white. Legs lengthening behind me, eyes sliding back on my face and my mouth and nose merging, reaching out into the air before me, hardening, strengthening. My neck elongates, then settles back into an S curve. The heron's voice squawks through my own, longing to be heard.

She then continues:

Soon after this experience, I tell it to a friend whose family, unbeknownst to me, owns a fish farm. She hesitates after I finish the story and tells me she cannot relate to it. In her family, the Great Blue Heron is the arch enemy. A single bird can destroy almost an entire crop of fish in one sitting with its sizable appetite and cunning fishing skills. She tells how her family has tried everything to stop the raids; but herons are smart, tenacious, hungry and adaptable birds. Netting over the waters and all other deterrents fail to keep these birds—who nest at air force bomb training sites— away from an easy dinner. As a last resort, the birds are shot. She tells how her mother keeps a feather from each bird in reverence for its life.

I want to be furious with this woman. I think of the wolf population— decimated by ranchers to protect their cattle, their cast. But this is not a large, beef industry we are talking about. This is a family-run business and their only source of income. This is someone I know. I understand well the human instinct of survival and protection. I find myself hesitant to judge her.

Instead, I think about how we humans, as a species, relate to our fellow earth dwellers. I think about our connection to the natural world and our habitats. I think about the animals killed in the development of the medications that saved and prolong my sister's life. Would I trade her life for theirs? I don't want to romanticize the animal kingdom. But, I ask, are we not animals?"

She continues, asking more questions, coming to her own moral choices based not on what is clear and obvious but what is complex and muddy with contradictions and ironies. Her essay gets less simple and more deep.

This is the same student who talked about having had a psychological breakdown years before, the psychologist looking at her and saying, "You are too smart to be a victim. You are a predator. The only question is if you can be a predator with a conscience." The quote—with its question—has stayed with me. And why do I see that as an ending to this chapter? As where I can stop before quoting from papers of men and women in prison who try to understand themselves as both victim and predator, who try to be, as we all are, predators, but ones with a conscience? And how does this circle back to an earlier chapter on the possibility within each of us of being both the betrayer and the messiah and how our ability to imagine that possibility shapes both our own lives and our views of others?

CHAPTER TWENTY-THREE:

MAKING CONNECTION
AFTER SO MANY YEARS

I called Sandy today, the coordinator of Skidmore's UWW prison program, asking her help in locating the men whose lives touched mine during those twelve years and whose papers I wanted to include in this book. I needed to write them a letter, telling them what I was doing, asking their permission to use their words. As I talked to her, I realized that the process of communicating with them would be a whole other story, one still unknown in terms of content. I have no idea where they are physically or mentally and emotionally, no idea where my writing to the students will take either them or me. What I feel is curious: where are they now? Still in prison (and where), or out on the streets (and where), or dead (as I know that at least two are)? And where will my knowing of "what happened after" take me, and where will the reminder of their words, my having saved their papers and my now wanting to publish them, take them? It has been over twelve years since most of the writing. Where have we all gone since then?

I know that reading their papers has taken me to an unexpected place. I am not reading them for the first time; I saved them because in some way I found them "good," and I have read some of them aloud to other classes and in talks I have given. They are familiar. But still I had forgotten how thoughtful they were. Now, sitting on the porch in the sun, having the space of time, not having to correct or comment, able to just be there with them, I am surprised at my strong reaction: I am very moved, very touched, both emotionally and mentally. I find myself in tears, wanting to read their papers to my partner, to my meditation group, to anyone who will listen, wanting to print all the papers I have in their entirety, knowing that the ones I happened to Xerox and save were only a very small portion of the ones I received.

My reaction has to do with their clarity and depth of thought but, even more, with their honesty and authenticity. I think, again, of Avivah Zornberg's discussion of Jacob and Essau, how she uses Lionel Trilling's distinction between sincerity and authenticity to show how Jacob needs to grow from simple sincerity to a more complex authenticity, his "dissembling" ironically part of his path of wholeness. I think of the men in prison. As opposed to the people on the "outside" who might feel the goodness of their simple sincerity, many of the men behind bars know they have done acts of harm. In their willingness to look closely at what is painful lay the possibility of the authenticity of which Zornberg writes.

Their language is the opposite of what is glib, sentimental, romantic, different from the voices I hear all around me in the media, in advertisements, in the political presidential campaign, in the presidential conventions now being broadcast everywhere, voices which repeat the soundbites and formulaic phrases, voices hard to listen to because I know exactly what they are going to say and because there is such a gap between word and reality, nothing real except the attempt to create an image, to sell a product. It is language used to deceive, not communicate. In their papers, even when they stumble and are anxious and confused, I travel with them, attentive and listening.

Elizabeth Minnich has an essay "Why Not Lie" which I often distribute when we begin to do "analysis." Her ability to follow cause and effect is clear and deep; I have never had a student who has not been stirred into thought through her clear thinking: the asking of essential questions, the close observation, the distinguishing between different categories of lying, the precision of words and thoughts.

Minnich begins her essay by distinguishing three different kinds of lying: "I can lie to myself; I can lie to those with whom I live and share a set of meanings; and I can lie in public, to those I do not know. There are personal, social, and political lies." She then looks at the consequences of each, beginning with the personal lie:

> *That I can lie to myself is really rather odd, since in that case I am myself both deceiver and deceived. Not only can I choose to lie, I can choose to be*

lied to. If I do not want to remember something, if something has become more complex than I like, if I do not want to hold myself to an obligation I have made, I can simplify, I can persuade myself I didn't really promise, and I can do so without admitting to myself that I am doing it …

Socrates spoke of thinking as a dialogue with oneself. When I think, I am not simply following the stream of my consciousness: I interrupt myself. I say, "No, that's not right." "But what about …," "That doesn't make sense." I converse with myself through my other voices, as if I always lived with friends who are ready to talk with me even when I am absolutely alone. …

When I lie to myself, I risk shutting off future conversations with my own other voices. I am trying to make things simple, to free myself from self-consciousness by choosing one voice over others. But what happens when I have silenced some of my other selves? It becomes necessary to keep them silenced. If I persist in this stubborn repression I may finally lose the ability to think. If I have shut off the voice of my memory, I lose all I have learned from the past. If I shut off my learned sense of the complexity of a situation, I also shut off the chance of understanding it. If I shut off my reminders, my internal friends and critics, I become less powerful and free. I need those other voices; they help me make sense in a world in which meaning is a shared reality. One definition of madness is being closed into a private meaning system: madness is a private language, a monologue …

So one critical reason not to lie to ourselves is not an external one or even, in the usual sense, a moral one. It is that you cannot think well when there are things you cannot allow yourself to think about, and you cannot communicate with others when you have stopped being able to communicate with yourself.

Minnich then explores the effect of the "social lie" (i.e., lying to others), as well as the political lie and continues:

If I lie to myself, I risk losing the ability to think (which requires that I be my own friend), and consequently the ability to be with and make sense to others. If I lie to others, I risk losing the ability to be with them as an equal, because I must either hide from or manipulate them. If I lie politically, I risk losing the ability to persuade people and to keep them with me working willingly. I risk being pushed toward violence to make public reality conform to my private view.

She concludes 'Why Not Lie" with words about truth, complexity, justice, and what it means to create a "humane world":

Simply to be in the world with others as myself takes constant effort and attention—and real courage. It requires openness and vulnerability—to my own other voices; to new and entirely different voices; to change as well as continuity, to a reality that I affect and for which I am responsible but that I do not make and cannot fully control. No wonder that lying appears as an immense temptation. Why not have done with all this interaction, this complexity, and make my own world? But that "why not" is treacherous. It contains, "Why not create my own world—why not create a cult, a sect, a Never-Neverland?" "Why not make people do what I want—why not become a tyrant?"

Truth, because it is complex, time-bound, multi-faceted and rarely clear, requires constant effort and is not in our control. But it is in our keeping. It is up to us to choose to remain our own friend, and the friend of others, and that, finally, is what makes this not just a world we share with others, a human world, but a humane world.

The following papers from the prisons show some of that openness and complexity, that dialogue with self, that honesty, vulnerability and humaneness of which Minnich speaks. It's interesting that now, ready to type up their papers, I think again of Eiseley showing his treasured shell to the shopkeeper and having it labeled "conus spurious." Clearly I am still worried that a reader will see very ordinary freshman compositions, nothing special, and I feel protective. I also feel the danger of including too many papers. I remember a student telling me of her excitement seeing huge whales off the coast of Massachusetts, and how she kept taking pictures of them. When the photographs were developed, she showed her friends hundreds of pictures, the huge whales now small black dots in the middle of a vast ocean. I am like that student: my awareness of the power and beauty of each paper parallels her sense of excitement with the beauty and power of the whale. But she and I both had the actual experience. Her photos and these papers do not have that live context. Still, I am compelled. The ordinary is extraordinary. So I say to the reader what I say to my students when I give them feedback: take what is useful.

Why I Came to Prison:

There are many complex causes behind why I am in prison. From as far back as I can remember, I will try to draw and outline a clear picture of some of these causes and their effects upon me.

Let's go back to my early years, when I was five. My favorite television shows were <u>Mission Impossible, It Takes a Thief</u> (starring Alexander Monday), and <u>The Wild, Wild West</u>. Little did I know, at that age, that watching these shows constantly planted a message deep within my subconscious mind which would express itself later on in life through my actions. It was the thrill and excitement of danger and taking risks that appealed to the unconscious aspect of my being. This was one intangible force which was to affect my destiny.

Second, my exposure to racism and the euro-centric concept which makes one race feel superior and the rest inferior. Their subordination through religion, school, and my own parents' instruction was to gradually build up an anger in me which was to affect me in several ways.

During the early years of my youth, I used to find myself feeling ashamed of being the darkest child. I was the blackest out of all my friends and one of the darkest in my classes. I used to envy the attention that the lighter children would get and how they were looked upon as being better. At that time, that anger was more painful. As a result, I used to find myself in corners crying because I couldn't understand it, and no one seemed to have any meaningful answers.

My last year of junior high school, I found myself openly rebelling against what seemed like prison. I rebelled without having a conscious cause or set motive. I was angry; controversy and rebellion were my ways of telling the world to kiss my ass! A statement that to me meant no submission, death before dishonor.

My first year of high school was extremely rewarding and wild. I came in contact with some eloquent brothers and sisters my age who were members of the "Nation of Gods and Earths." They were unlike your typical contemporary Negro who was only conscious of an aspect of history which cast or represented blacks as people who passively submitted to conquest and colonization and who were meant to be slaves. These brothers and sisters were conscious of our history from a time that not only predated slavery, but also predated the six thousand year history of european conquests. This history (oral tradition) presented black people in a light that no religion or school curriculum ever presented. The knowledge and wisdom which they brought with them was truly what my inner being sought to free it from all the blurriness of being ignorant and confused about my own identity.

Instead of the usual history of slavery and the subordination of my people, I came to learn of times predating slavery. A time when my people had produced, managed and maintained the first civilizations which introduced the sciences to the world. (The student then mentions figures in that history—their discoveries, their accomplishments. He follows that by talking about his realization of the lies he had been taught, all of which fueled the anger inside.)

Finally, I had a reason to express my anger: "I'll pay them back," I thought, and I chose to do so through burglarizing jewelry and fur warehouses. In venting my anger in this manner I became elated. The more I completed an impossible mission, the more I felt like I was better at it than Al Monday. Not being skilled or aware that in high places people enforced laws and plans that would create an economical, social, political, and cultural climate that would entrap ghetto and urban youth and bring them to rural environments to provide careers for unborn generations of rural people, I continued slowly gravitating towards prison.

The criminal justice system was, I see now, a plan for the perpetual enslavement of a third world people who did not fit in the mainstream of the american social order. Not only was this plan to affect minorities, but poor whites as well.

Do not, for one second, think that I am using my blackness as a crutch. I acknowledge the fact that I still had the choice to apply myself in a better way. Yet, we must realize the truth that the system has the black community under siege and that the incorporation of racism in the political, social, economical, and cultural spectrums does have a lot to do with why I, along with countless others, have come to prison. This also has to do with why I became a product of my environment in a negative sense. (N)

The Effects of Being a Prisoner:

The effects of being a prisoner are wide and varied.

The first effect in my case was a loss of identity. I realized who I was but I experienced a sense of being two separate entities. In one case, I was R.D., the warm, likable, flesh and blood, easy going, giving individual. Now, I was R.D. the outlaw, cold, calculating and dangerous. I was now a case history, docket number, and a few simple sentences in a computer's memory bank or in a file.

My life was reduced to a person's 15 minute interview of me that was the now sworn fact of who I was. There was no resemblance to the real me. Now I realize in such cases there rarely is. I was a faceless mannequin parading before these somber men and women of the penal system.

Through all of this, I was treated with contempt by the judicial and correctional authorities who acknowledged me with disinterest, if at all. I paraded before these sophisticated people in court proceedings and for the most part I was ignored—except for the personnel in charge of security. I felt like a child at his own birthday party with plenty of toys, games, cakes and presents and he can only look on. If I spoke up in court there was always a short embarrassed silence as the judge and D.A. looked at my lawyer, as if to say, "Can't you control your client?"

The contempt and disinterest left me feeling bitter and I lost all the respect I had held authority figures in. Wherever I went I kept these feelings, whether it was to another courtroom, prison or cell location, I despised the people running the show. I saw people strutting around heralding justice and yet flaunting it at every turn. This left me feeling very cynical towards anyone in authority.

I was affected by this cold and callous treatment and I lost touch with my real feelings. Sensitivity went south the moment the handcuffs first rode my wrists. (Warmth and sensitivity are two very human emotions, and I do deeply crave the return of these emotions in my life.)

I lost my sense of individualism. I had uniformity brutally thrust into my life. This was a very new feeling and not much welcome. Now, instead of being the machine, I was a mere cog tooled with no less precision than any other.

I grew to feel at odds with society. For some reason I felt stigmatized. I felt as though society and I were two armies deployed and lusting for battle, not knowing why nor caring. This feeling of two armies lusting for battle, I didn't truly understand; I merely accepted it.

I experienced a lowering of self-esteem. Being a prisoner, I must deal with the frustrations involved: harassment, contempt, disinterest, lack of concern, hate—all I directed at me simply because I am a prisoner. I

somehow felt these feelings of myself and prisoners in general were justified. I felt I was treated in the manner because I was less of a man due to
my arrest and imprisonment. In my mind I felt I somehow deserved what
was happening to me simply because it was happening.

Being a prisoner has had many effects on me, but I have been able to
overcome most of these effects. I have come to realize that because someone holds me in a certain light does not mean I need to see myself in the
same light.

When I came to prison I was relatively young and naive. When an
authority figure treated me in a contemptible manner or spoke to me with
contempt it soon started to affect my opinion of myself. I had held authorities in high regard and if they called me an asshole or told me I was dumb
enough, I tended to believe them.

Through the years I've been held in prison I've grown in age, maturity,
and intelligence. I've learned to examine any manner of behavior or situations I find myself in and I base decisions on the evidence I gather. I've
gathered and weighed the evidence of my status as a prisoner vs. my opinion of myself, and I realize being a prisoner does not lower my intelligence,
pride, ambition or feelings—nor should it ever lead me to believe others'
opinions of me. I've learned to rely on my instincts which I now value;
they have not let me down yet.

So, there are many drawbacks to being a prisoner, aside from the more
noticeable ones: loss of freedom, major choices, distance from family, and
missing most of life as society knows it, but with a positive outlook, time
and determination, these drawbacks can be overcome. (RD)

Another paper, also on the effects of being in prison, repeats the theme that "A person who enters this system basically a mild mannered, easy going individual may
leave a hardened, cynical, or even potentially violent, resentful individual due to the
treatment that person received while in prison." This student continues:

I for one have felt many of the things that I've mentioned almost daily.
It has become an exercise in will power not to turn around and beat a
Correction Department employee senseless for making a derogatory
remark concerning the color of my skin, my religious beliefs, etc. This goes
on daily, at least at this prison. When I've spent hours studying for an
exam and my notes are confiscated during what is called a "shakedown"
for no apparent reason other than to harass me, I feel like striking back,

sometimes quite violently. I realize that to resort to violence would be the worst response I could possibly give in this situation. I am outnumbered and more importantly I should never allow myself to be brought down to that base level of existence where those in power are considered right regardless of what they may do or have done. I have considerable pride in myself, who I am, what I am, and what I hope to be, and I care for others in my life who would be affected by a foolish response like that. I have never allowed such a mistake to happen thus far.

These same detrimental and extremely aggravating situations that hinder an individual are, for some, the same situations that drive a person to a point where he or she resolves to overcome these obstacles and beat them, the system, if you will, at its own game. A person may delve in a diverse range of studies and research projects, attend college or some other program academic/vocational that that person intends to pursue when eventually released. A person at times (hopefully) learns to be friends with him/her self, which is a major accomplishment in this situation and in life in general. To be friends with yourself is for the most part to be at peace with yourself and that is extremely important during your entire life. A person also learns how to be alone, to be confined without the option of moving where he/she desires, when he/she chooses to do so. That is a difficult thing to do since we are basically social creatures and we are inquisitive by nature. A person who is incarcerated learns to appreciate and value things that he or she might not have given a second thought to before being incarcerated. A simple walk in the woods might seem like one of the finest joys to be experienced in life, or walking hand in hand with a person you love, with no particular destination in mind, a joy to be savored. A person who is incarcerated learns a new meaning to the word "hope." It becomes an emotion that is very real and part of your very being. I like to think that I have overcome many of the obstacles that have been set before me and I believe I have. I do have to work more on myself because that is my hardest struggle, to be free inwardly.

In conclusion, I must state again that for the majority, prison is quite detrimental to their mental, emotional, intellectual, academic development and they leave prison, many times, bitter and resentful because of what they have been subjected to. There are those who appear to have overcome the adversities that they have been confronted with and rose above it, so to speak. But what are the psychological effects or scars that that individual has that you cannot see that may not be manifested outwardly for some time? To think that prisons are a way to change those

*who have violated society's laws for the better is like believing in the tooth
fairy. I cannot offer an alternative because I do not have one, but I can say
for certain that prisons do not rehabilitate, they humiliate, degrade and
are detrimental to the individual incarcerated and society as a whole.*

During the semester, I have, on occasion, given students a poem, "Abutilon in
Bloom," by Irena Klepfisz, a poem that captures what it means to be confined to
an environment not of one's choosing. "Abutilon," as Klepfisz says in the beginning of the poem, is a "flowering indoor maple; houseplant":

> *Cultivated inside out of the bounds*
> *of nature it stubborned*
> *on the windowsill six winters and springs*
> *resisting water sun as researched care.*
> *It would not give beyond its leaves.*
>
> *Yet today in the morning light*
> *the sudden color asserts itself*
> *among the spotted green and I*
> *pause before another empty day*
> *and wonder at its wild blooming.*
>
> *It leans against the sunwarm glass*
> *its blossoms firm on the thick stems*
> *as if its roots*
> *absorbed the knowledge*
> *that there is no other place*
> *that memory is only pain*
> *that even here now*
> *we must burst forth with orange flowers*
> *with savage hues of our captivity.*

The students I quote above are able to see, understand and express clearly
the detrimental effects of prison on the individual, the anger, pain, and terrible damage. But what is also clear from their writing is the ability of some to
choose to grow, to choose *their* growth over their "stubborned" refusal to "give."

To gain deep awareness and, through awareness, to be free—even here, perhaps because it is here, in the unwelcomed, unchosen, and hated place.

I think of Pema Chodron's saying that it is often through what is most unwelcomed—in terms of people, situations, feelings, thoughts—that we are offered the greatest potential for awareness. When we are successful, happy, in control, the impetus to awaken is not always immediately present. I know that I met many "free" people within the prison and many entrapped people outside the prison walls. I think, again, of Lorde's "I would never have chosen this path but I am very glad to be who I am here." No one would chose imprisonment, yet the struggle with what is hard leads some individual to deep understanding and open heart, while many people who "succeed" have no such awakenings into consciousness.

Wes Nisker, in an article in *The Inquiring Mind*, writes about a tradition in Japan "among poets, artists, and Zen monks, of writing a 'death poem' as one approaches the end of this life" and then selects poems from Yoel Hoffman's book *Japanese Death Poems*. Since prison is, for some inmates, a form of death, I have given students some of these poems as an impetus for writing longer essays:

> *Moon in a barrel:*
> *you never know just when*
> *the bottom will fall out.*
>
> > *(Mabutsu)*

> *Now that my storehouse*
> *has burned down, nothing*
> *conceals the moon.*
>
> > *(Masahide)*

> *The thief left it behind*
> *the moon*
> *at the window.*
>
> > *(Ryokan)*

In one class I asked students to write a responsive essay to "Now that my barn is burned/I can see the moon/more clearly," an unconscious combination of the three above. The following is one essay that resulted from the assignment:

I can relate this quote to the life I lived in society and the life I'm presently living. When in society, I took everything for granted. I was so lost within myself, I actually started believing the world owed me something.

I had a beautiful wife that really loved me. Once I was certain she loved me, I took her love and abused it. She stuck around for a while, even while I treated her bad. I used to yell and instill fear in her. She finally got fed up with the abuse. She tried to tell me how she was feeling, but who the hell was she to complain?

I once had expensive clothes and drove expensive cars. Nobody could tell me I wasn't what was happening. My mother used to repeatedly tell me my criminal activities were gonna catch up with me. I shrugged it off—nothing can happen to me, I'm too smart to get caught. All that changed over a short period of time.

These people got me in a cell, locked away from society. I now know I have no friends or any of the things I took for granted. I can't even voice my opinion without facing disciplinary actions. I'm told where to eat, when to wake, when to shower, how to walk, talk, spend money, practice religion. These people reach out and deprive me of all the things I used to take for granted.

The picture is clear now. I'm not important and I'm not smart enough to succeed continuously testing the system. The problem is me, all other mitigating factors are to be forgotten. I created the life I live. I know I have to change my ways. I'm ready to face what must be done. If my barn wouldn't have burned I might not be alive to see the moon so clearly.
(RJ)

One can, again, feel the honesty, as in this next paper, written later in the semester when we began to explore, through writing, issues of race, gender, socialization. By looking at his own experiences with women, this student was able to see not only his own abusive attitude and behavior but, also, the pervasive sexism of society where abuse of women is acceptable behavior. In her "Why Not Lie," Minnich writes about societal prejudices which exist "like a subterranean stream. They are always there, stubborn and persistent and often unaffected by our efforts to bring them to the surface." Through reflection and writing, this student, quoted below, was able to bring this "subterranean stream" into consciousness, to recognize his internalized and habitual attitude towards women, and to take responsibility for his thoughts and actions:

It was about 1:30 at night. I was sitting in the solitude of my cube. I was staring at a picture of my girlfriend, thinking about the times we spent together. I thought about all the warmth, caring, compassion, and unrestricting love she has always given to me. I asked myself, "What did I give her." I gave her abuse, neglect, and I gave her all of the bad characteristics that lay deep within myself. I don't want to sound like all I did was slap her around or beat her senseless but I know I abused her physically and emotionally.

There were times when I would force her to have sex with me. I wouldn't hold her down with my hands but with the power of my words which in her mind were just as strong. I don't think I would have thought I was forcing her when I was doing it.

I never appreciated my relationship with her or any other women outside of my family. The respect for the women in my family was there because they were family. But to me women were objects to be toyed with at my will and whatever the game I was ready to play. When a new woman came into my life, I was like a five year old boy with a new toy fire truck. I would hold it close and cherish it, show it off to all my friends. I would brag about all the things it could do and all the fun in the world I could have with it.

But once I got used to having the toy, I began to abuse it. I treated all the women in my life the same except I treated some worse than others. This is because I had three classes of women: bitches, hoes, and hoebitches. I showed no respect for them by calling them these names to their faces without regard to their feelings.

Now that I'm thinking about this, I was a prime example of a womanizer. I was an example of what a woman would not want in a man, but if you would have asked me then if I abused women, my reply would have been, "Damn right and they deserve it."

I can't say why I thought like that. I grew up with women all my life. I didn't have my father around and most of my family consisted of sisters, aunts, grandmothers, godmothers, godsisters, and a host of female cousins. You would think with all these women in my life, I would have had a positive attitude toward women. Still I thought women were good for one thing and that was pleasure. Of course I needed more than one because the more I had the more pleasure I could have.

All this is my former thinking pattern and a total opposite of what I think about women now. Being away in the confines of prison, away from women and with time to think, I have changed my thinking pattern. I have come to appreciate women and what they have to offer.

I do regret what I have done in the past to women. Being away from women I have begun to miss all of the external things about them—the soft, smooth skin, hair, and voice of a woman. I miss pretty eyes and bright smiles. I miss long fingernails painted and soft lips, short skirts, silk blouses. But most importantly I miss the internal things. I miss the companionship of a woman, the way I can honestly talk to a woman. I miss these things but even more so I have learned to appreciate these things. Mental stability, a caring heart, deep sensitivity, these things I have realized that I had in all of the women in my life.

I can now fully understand what it is I was really missing when I was abusing and taking women for granted. I know now that I must never take a woman for granted. I will treat women with the utmost respect because it is these women that I look to get all that makes me whole. I have come to see that it is women who really bring out the real joy in my heart. (JW)

Of course one never knows what happens after—after prison, after being out in the world for a period of time. How long does consciousness last? I think of Dostoyevsky's *The Idiot*, where Mishkin is told about a man who is about to be hung. During his last minutes, the man becomes totally present to the beauty and meaning of the world, feels a deep appreciation and gratitude, thinks how much he will honor life should he be saved. And he is saved, right before the execution, and he does, for awhile, keep that consciousness. But as time passes, the awareness gets less strong and he returns to his old ways. Perhaps these students when and if they get out of jail will return to their old ways. Perhaps I will find that out if and when I write them. Perhaps rehearing their words will return them to their point of awareness, will allow them to see again what they came to understand so deeply, to remember their points of consciousness.

And of course this is also true for all of us living our lives: the necessity of continually remembering what we have learned, of not returning to our habitual responses, especially those reinforced by society and by the speed of life which undercuts our ability to remember what we know to be true. I think of Oliver Sacks and his work with people with encephalitis and how the discovery of dopamine enabled some of those who had been "sleeping" for twenty or more years to suddenly wake up. Many of those who had a periods of consciousness later returned to their former state. In the conclusion to his book, *Awakenings*,

Sacks answers the question whether it is worth waking up if we are only to return to sleep. Honoring the struggles, courage, honesty, and pain of the patients whom he had grown to love, he writes:

> *They may still (or again) be deeply Parkinsonian, in some instances, but they are no longer the people they were. They have acquired a depth, a fullness, a richness, an awareness of themselves and of the nature of things, of a sort which is rare, and only to be achieved through experience and suffering. I have tried, insofar as it is possible for another person, a physician, to enter into or share their experiences and feelings, and, alongside with them, to be deepened by these; and if they are no longer the people they were, I am no longer the person I was. We are older and more battered, but calmer and deeper.*

No matter where the students with whom I worked and from whom I quote are in their lives and in their consciousness, I answer in the exact same way in terms of both them and myself.

CHAPTER TWENTY-FOUR:

STILL ANALYSIS, BUT MAKING THE WEB MORE INTRICATE

I keep upping the ante in class, moving from a seemingly simple cause and effect—the cause or effect of one variable—to something larger and more complex. Of course, even one variable has a web of interconnection. Exploring the effect of moving from a small rural town to a large city or having an alcoholic father or a parent die or coming to prison is not simple at all, has layers that keep unfolding, and could become a whole book. But at least one has the illusion of following one thread. Some questions, however, are, from the beginning, almost overwhelming: What are the causes or effects of hunger, poverty or violence, or drugs and crime? Or, on a whole other level, how did your socialization as a male or your ethnicity, color, or economic class affect how you view yourself and the world. Actually, I can hear the groan when those larger questions are asked, whether in a class or amongst friends. This thinking is hard, the "answers" impossible. And yet I love it—the thinking about life and meaning.

In many ways, we are all made to feel stupid about these larger issues. After all, thousands of very well educated people have done years of research on all the above topics. They are the "experts." How could I even consider asking the men in a beginner's composition course to analyze such topics. Yet I do. And they do. And in the process we all learn something about ourselves and the larger society, as well as where we need to go to learn, know, and understand more fully.

My first assumption is that just beginning to think about issues like these is very important. Part of the effect of much of our education is to make us feel that the experts know the answers and that most important issues are too complex for the common person to understand. It is the "who are you anyway" which stops all exploration and silences any answers which might challenge the status quo. The effect of the media is to further deplete our ability and energy to come to our own understanding. Sitting hours in front of a television where people are talking at us renders us passive observers, not participants. And much of what we passively observe and hear trains us to be glib, funny, superficial, to speak in short sound bites, to lie, to not really think about what is most important, and, if we do think, to not share those thoughts. On the "news," we hear disconnected "facts" and "information" with no attempt to make connections or analyze cause and effect. Much "news" is totally omitted and much that is reported is irrelevant to our lives. When I would visit my mother in the Bronx, I would sit with her as she watched the "news" on the major channels and find myself screaming at the television, at the misinformation and lies and, even more, at all the information that was never given, information that would have enabled me to understand the demands of a strike, the issues involved in a demonstration, the different participants involved in a civil war within a country, the longer and larger history of cause and effect. I would try to stop myself, saying, "Bernice, this is your 84 year old mother watching the news. Let her watch it in peace." But what is clearly true of my reactive self is that dishonest and manipulative words are almost painful to me; I get enraged at the large gap between what is said and what is real. And the corollary, and why I teach and why I am so moved by my students' papers, is also true: when people speak and write with honesty, struggling to understand, their words always move me deeply.

There are certain "ground rules" that I find useful before even beginning to explore the larger questions. To really understand layers of cause and effect, not in a simple linear way but in a larger, more comprehensive way, requires, I think, a humbleness, an avoidance of the quick and easy, a recognition of complexity and the need to struggle with what is hard, a realization that one will never know the complete "answer" and that whatever truths we discover are continually subject to revision based on new experience, more information, and deeper consciousness. We need to remind ourselves, as I do continually throughout this book, that confusion and contradictions are not a "problem," but are, in fact, essential to the journey of understanding, and that when we don't know enough, rather than giving up in frustration, we need to go to other sources, find out other information, read more, ask more questions. If we approach any subject with that open, humble, and accepting attitude, with curiosity, questioning, interest and the desire to understand, we will always learn, and continue to learn. So I give my students these very difficult topics and they, starting with their own experiences, begin to learn—about themselves, society, writing, analysis, research. They begin to understand that thinking and writing are hard, and exciting, and liberating.

One of the essays I sometimes distribute to students is a transcript of a talk I heard on public radio by Joseph Collins on "World Hunger: Myths and Solutions." What I remember is my own shift from casual listening to rapt attention when, many years ago, I heard Collins on Public Radio. I trust that response: pay attention, someone is saying something you do not know; they will teach you.

Recently I felt that switch from casual listening to total attention when I heard Linda Gordon's discussion of the "adoption" of babies taken from poor, unwed, Irish Catholic mothers in New York City by an order of Catholic nuns who brought the babies to Mexican Catholic families living in Arizona. According to Gordon, Protestant women, seeing Mexicans as "unfit" to parent "white" children, organized their men into vigilante groups who kidnapped the children so that they could be raised in Anglo ("good") homes. Each group of women, according to Gordon, saw itself as "good," as working for "the best interest of the child." But each group did great harm—because of their unquestioned assumptions and prejudices. As Gordon spoke, I could feel myself opening to a new understanding about the danger of seeing oneself as a moral agent doing God's work, could see the implications in many diverse scenarios, and could actually begin to question some of the arrogant (and incorrect) assumptions of my own "good acts."

I should try to get a copy of that talk, as I did of Collins' speech. That is, actually, how I have gathered an enormous selection of essays, poems, stories which I then give to students when the context seems appropriate—words that have a clarity, depth, and honesty, that (in their very different forms and voices) can become models for clear reasoning and thoughtful writing. It is not just that the content is "good" or, even less, because I agree with the position of the speaker, but, rather, that the author engages in the process of making connections; it is that process that I want the students to see, to imitate. That is what

Collins does when he talks about world hunger, the media's portrayal, and the "causes" that are given:

> *For many Americans, world hunger, much of the world's environmental destruction and these mushrooming populations are all part of a seamless web, namely the threat of poor and hungry people. For they believe that the pressure to feed the world's one billion hungry people is already destroying the environment, indeed, depleting the very resources needed to grow food for everyone. Clearly, they conclude, we face an ugly tradeoff between feeding the hungry and protecting the world's environment. Moreover, they warn, mushrooming populations in many countries spell ever more hunger and more devastation, and therefore, they say, family planning, that's the priority, as Lester Brown says.*

And that is exactly what I had thought, which is why I began to pay close attention. Clearly Collins was going to contradict or supplement my "analysis." He continues,

> *At the Institute for Food and Development Policy, at Food First, for the past twenty years, what have we learned from our efforts to understand the root causes of hunger as well as rapid population growth and of environmental destruction? Starting with hunger, and most basically, we have learned that hunger is not able to be explained away by a scarcity of food. In fact, if anything, abundance, rather than scarcity, characterizes the world food situation.*

Collins then gives facts and statistics about India and Mexico and Africa—what they are able to produce and how they produce enough to feed their population. He then distinguishes between "natural causes" and "human made policies," and asks: "So if scarcity is not the problem, what is?" I remember listening intently:

> *People eat only when they have control over enough land and other productive resources to produce and keep enough food to feed themselves or to have a livelihood that gives them enough money to acquire the food and*

other necessities they need. Failing both, they go hungry, even in the face of abundance of food, unless they have the political power to lay claim to subsidized or free food. The chronically hungry are those who are deprived of land and other food producing resources, those who cannot find regular employment at adequate wages, those who cannot keep enough of what they produce due to excessive rents or taxes, those who get prices too low for their produce or for their handicrafts. That is the best summary statement I could make from years of looking at why people go hungry in the world.

Yes, that's true, I thought, but I needed him to "prove" what he was saying, needed facts, figures, evidence. Collins does not deny that production is important or that family planning is important, but he talks about land used for cattle rather than human crops, about the feeding and overfeeding of the rich, about land distribution, the World Bank, the status of women, ... putting every fact and reality within a larger context, making connections and showing (in my mind) how

for the hungry what makes the difference is how democratically or tightly concentrated is the distribution of economic power.... Indeed, hunger is at root a problem not of supply but of distribution. The solution, however, lies not with redistributing food, but with redistributing economic power. The maldistribution of food is simply a reflection of inequalities in power on a local, national, and an international level. What the world's hungry need is a democratizing of power.... No food aid program. No escaping into a research laboratory. No purely individual change of lifestyle. No avoiding of the fundamentally political nature of hunger.

These are his generalizations, but the whole paper was really his "proof." His information was specific and informative, his analysis of cause and effect very clear. Collins talks about the "inequalities that result in a billion or more human beings being dispossessed ... since the 1950's (because of) food resources being used to produce feed for animals." He probes the root causes of environmental havoc and destruction, talks about unsustainable agricultural technologies, multinational agribusiness, the World Bank, megaprojects of irrigation that have depleted water sources, increased emissions of greenhouse gases. He talks about high birth rates not only reflecting "the survival calculus of impoverished family but quite often the disproportionate powerlessness of women vis-a-vis men." For Collins: "Hunger, environmental destruction, including the destruction of food producing resources, and rapid population growth often do occur together because they have a common root cause, namely enforced powerlessness."

Collins' essay is rich with information, statistics, and facts. While it is true that I agree with his analysis of cause and effect, that is not really the main reason I use his essay, or Minnich's, or Gerda Lerner's "Why History Matters," or countless other essays. What draws me is not the conclusion, but the process of getting to a conclusion, allowing me to understand certain issues in a whole other way, making me rethink my usual assumptions and question my own unexamined prejudices.

I know how easily I can fall into my own self-righteous repeating of opinions even while observing people's eyes glaze over with boredom and lack of attention. It's a hard habit to break: this hearing ourselves repeat the known formulas, ending up exactly where we began. But when a student (or any person) is able to explore in a way that widens my own narrowness, taking me in a different and unknown and even unwelcomed direction, that's exciting. And when I do it myself, in talking or writing, I feel the same excitement of traveling to a new place. What makes Collins' essay good—and makes all writing good—is the nature of the deep questioning, exploring, researching, and making connections. The honesty of careful and clear thought, the movement from passive acceptance and recitation to active reflection. It is, on another level, the movement from "enforced powerlessness" to a sense of one's own power to think and understand. It is Freire's "problem posing" education rather than banking education. It is Fromm's "active thought."

Much of our academic schooling trains us to exclude our best resource, ourselves and our actual experiences, under the illusion of objectivity. My retraining is to have students look more closely at their actual experience, to begin with what they know when they try to analyze violence, poverty and racism. Sometimes I quote from Thoreau in the beginning of *Walden*:

> *In most books, the I, or first person, is omitted; in this it will be retained; that, in respect to egotism, is the main difference. We commonly do not remember that it is, after all, always the first person that is speaking. I should not talk so much about myself if there were any body else whom I knew as well. Unfortunately, I am confined to this theme by the narrow-*

ness of my experience. Moreover, I, on my side, require of every writer, first or last, a simple and sincere account of his own life, and not merely what he has heard of other men's lives; some such account as he would send to his kindred from a distant land; for if he has lived sincerely, it must have been in a distant land to me.

The following are sections from papers from the prisons that show that "simple and sincere account." The first looks at poverty and graffiti as a way of giving voice to self:

Poverty

A poor young man who screams for identity writes his name on the subway trains demanding that pedestrians see him through his graffiti. The world is wicked to him. He isn't recognized as a person and is bypassed everyday like the garbage on a busy midtown street. Unnoticed.

Damn it! It isn't my fault that I was born onto poverty and lacked an education. Harvard and Yale were as far as the moon to me. But if all my expectations of life were material they would fill a room.

My parents worked hard to make ends meet. My mother would have to travel to Manhattan from the Bronx to work part time in the Garment District and also baby sit children other than us while my father worked in factories, supermarkets, and other odd jobs. I know for a fact that it is rough now as it was then because I can still see the pain etched in my mother's eyes.

Poverty is mightier than the Bubonic Plague for it maims our spirits and crushes our hope to the effect that we abandon our wishes of maintaining a solid career and a beneficial education and surrender to the cancer like grip of poverty. It is a travesty that we are caught up in a life of desiring and substitution. Such a vast majority of us who are deprived of the riches and fame and happiness that come along with clout and capture of our dreams. It's so far away....

Aldous Huxley, an English Biologist, once wrote: "Every man who knows how to read has it in his power to magnify himself, to multiply the way in which he exists, to make his life full, significant and interesting." What a wonderful way of saying, "Yes, you can."

I know for a fact that when poverty gets you down that there won't be any rules in which to abide by. It is especially hard to control a youth who was brought up having nothing. Soon this child will see how unfortunate he is. He will see others sporting the latest fashion and look upon himself with shame. He will eventually realize that he must continue to go to school poorly dressed without those fresh Adidas sneakers or without those Calvin Klein jeans. It is very unlikely that a job will solve the problem. Usually our egos get in the way and we fall into the cycle of crime. I know. This is only an example of the pitfall life of being poor and desiring too much. I know. It's a shame how one travesty follows the next.

Mother fuckin'right I'm mad. Can you hear me scream? I'm aggravated, disappointed, torn between dreams. Nothing is right; everything is wrong. My tension is building and my sanity is gone. I've been frustrated for quite some time, living in a world unproud, unmotivated, and discontent. I'm confused and used—now I feel as if I'm being abused.

Poverty is a story untold in a land of misfortune. YES I'M MAD. CAN YOU HEAR ME SCREAM? (WG)

At the end of his paper he wrote "Graffiti lives forever." I think back to the class discussion on "littering" and how some students brought up "graffiti." Both littering and graffiti could be considered "statements," both could express hostility, but what is clear from this students and other writings by graffiti artists is that graffiti is an art, a way of expressing self, a way of communicating and trying to connect. This student asked me to "share this essay with (my) next class if it is good enough." And so I am—sharing his essay, allowing his voice to be heard—and sharing the following papers on poverty, drugs, and racism, all "good enough."

Poverty

I was a ghetto child when introduced to the drug culture so that my acceptance of this microcosm of society was deemed as a way of life, not so much the abuse aspect of drugs but the economic reality that is associated with this way of life. In those early formative years, learning the trade of the "drug game," as I would later come to know it, was an accepted and necessary practice in my niche of the world. This way of life was, at this point in my life, the only beacon of light, the only ray of hope, to escape the deep dark bowels of the ghetto and the poverty associated with it.

Poverty had the uplifting effect on me of giving me the determination to make a way out for me and mine. I know this is very contrary to the rule, but the way I saw things was that if you didn't gain the intestinal for-

titude, the will to endure, you would definitely live a very bleak existence,
an existence very much in evidence around me.... There was no such
thing as crime, just the drive to succeed, whatever the cost. You did what
you had to do or forever be damned to a stifling, unbearable existence that
would make you a very broken, stunted human being with a life time of
unfulfilled dreams. None of the good things in life ventured, none gained.

It should be very easy for you to imagine the measures that would be
used to protect what you had once above the poverty level. Violence in
this sub-culture is a way of life, whether it be to protect what you have
struggled to achieve day to day, inch by inch, in this almost jungle envi-
ronment, or to insure the proceeds from the business which you now so
staunchly defend with your very life, if necessary. Whether it be simple
violence in the form of a fight or the strongest form where you guide the
hand of the grim reaper, you will do these things without a second thought
or backwards glance because you know that the poverty of the ghetto just
bides her time and awaits her chance to embrace you.

For me, violence, crime, and, on a larger scale, the drug culture was
my way out. Although at present I still struggle to regain some sense of
what society deems to be "normal," given the same circumstances I would
do the same thing over again to keep from being consumed by an utterly
stagnant and hopeless existence. (KJ)

What is so interesting is to hear the perseverance, the hard work and struggle,
the drive for success—all of which are the backbone of the small entrepreneur
beginning a new business. Here is world where crime is the way out, the beacon
and light. The "morality" preached by "the other world" has no connection to
the morality of the ghetto which defines success as being able to escape the
stifling and hopeless poverty. Substitute the word "drugs" for a more acceptable
"product" and you would be praising the pioneering spirit of a young capitalist
pursuing a goal affirmed everywhere in our society: to be rich. The pursuit of
money is, for most Americans, the goal of school, work, and life. The deeper
question is why some are in prison and some live in mansions, why some are
powerless and others control our political process and our world.

Another student focuses on the escape aspect of drugs:

Sometimes when I am laying in bed, looking at those cold and forbidding
bars, I ask myself why. Why do people use drugs? One reason is escape.

Escape from the daily pressures of life, from the insanity of the world. But if daily life is reality and the world is reality and people use drugs to escape from the pressures and the insanity, then I would contend that people are escaping from reality.

Let me support this through an example. In prison when a man wants to get high on drugs, he may use the phrase, "I'm going to New York." Examining this phrase tells a lot about the idea of using drugs as a means of escape. Prison is a form of physical and sometimes mental incarceration. It keeps your body and your mind away from friends and loved ones. So a man may use drugs as a means of escaping from the confines of prison, allowing one's mind to relive old memories or imagining one's self somewhere more desirable than prison. Granted prison is harsh and sometimes and intimidating condition, but nonetheless it is reality.

When I am laying in bed, looking at those cold and forbidding bars, I ponder the effects of drugs. I read the newspapers and they talk about children getting shot by stray bullets being fired by rival drug dealers. I read about mothers living in fear of their own children, afraid of coming home and finding the drug addicted child has stolen the material possession in the home to trade for drugs.

The student then writes of his very close friend. Both of them were on a basketball scholarship, both of them joined the military. His friend, married and a parent of three, is "now doing fifteen years in a federal prison in Kansas ... convicted of selling drugs on a military installation." He continues:

When I am laying in bed looking at those cold and forbidding bars, I hear my fellow detainees. They are talking about all the fun, the good times, the money, and the cars they used to have while involved in drugs. But that is only part of the story. The ending goes something like this: "Now I am doing five years laying in bed, looking at those cold and forbidding bars."

Another writes about the ability of the mind, under drugs, to rationalize and deny:

I tried cocaine for the first time after work one night at the club. I was twenty four years old. After that first use, the power of the word switched from the unknown to the known. All those questions I had were answered and new ones formed. My self-talk kicked in and I was asking myself: Why did I think this was so bad? The feeling it gives me is great; why didn't I try this sooner? At the time I thought that I had the power. I was to find out later that the power had me. The power of the cocaine.

As time passed and my use increased, little by little other things didn't seem to matter. The first thing that wasn't important any longer was going to work out at the gym. Why lift weights? Coke makes me feel like superman. After that, I started to slack on my job. Work? Why? I'll stay home and sell a few grams, make the money up. Then I would think, Man this is great. I'm never hungry anymore; I'm saving money on food.… When it had gotten to its peak I was saying, "Sleep, why sleep? I might miss something. Sex? Who needs a girl? For what? As long as I have the coke and pipe who needs anything else. To hell with the women. To hell with the world. (FD)

I do not have the papers that analyzed drugs from a more political perspective: that looked at the world drug traffic and our government's complicity in that "trade"; that wrote about our drug policy as a conscious move to imprison a large segment of the black male population; that questioned the draconian sentencing for drug usage while alcohol, a "drug" that causes greater damage to self and others, is totally legal.

One student, writing about violence, captures precisely the way our values are formed:

Children in the ghetto are brought up and taught one set of ideas in the home and school. Between these two learning environments, they come in contact with yet a third, one that contradicts the other two: the street experience. They in time will learn to accept Mrs. Green's black eye that she received from her husband when he was drunk, the butchering of a prostitute by a john, and the execution type murders of rival drug dealers. A large percentage will even be exposed to some sort of violence in their own homes, at times directed directly towards them.

It's my opinion children, during their formative years, learn certain behavior and emulate adult behavior. The young display behavior that is learned through a conditioning that is so complete that it is accepted in this type of environment as "normal," and so there isn't any thought of doing wrong or any remorse felt when they finally do commit a violent act.

The next question that comes to mind is why am I violent? It's hard for me to answer this. As far back as I can remember it's always been around me. Like myself, my home, my school, and the mole on my thigh; it was just there. Whether violence was right or wrong, it never crossed my mind. As I got older violence became a tool. When cunning and intimidation didn't work, I would go into my tool belt and pull out some violence. I was taught at an early age that force only respects greater force and I learned how much and when to use it to achieve my goals.

What this student says about violence is really true for all of our socialization: We imitate what we see all around us. The norm makes it normal, whether it is violence, drugs, prejudice, sexism, homophobia, specieism, whether we see it in our homes, our community, our media, our country, our world. Most of us continue to follow our own footsteps unless something happens to throw us off our track. Prison, clearly, is one way of stopping us, and writing is a way of getting us to actually ponder and question accepted norms, as does the following paper on "Nostrand and Pacific." I quote a small section from a much larger paper:

Ever since I have been incarcerated I have been growing and thinking. I think of the things I want out of life and how to go about achieving them. As I think about goals and future plans I realize that I am truly growing into a decent young man who some day will have all that I truly value in life.

As I think about my future, I can't help but think of the future of some of my former associates on Pacific Street and Nostrand Avenue. That is a rough corner. From the time I have been hanging out there I've seen it all, from the simple muggings, armed robberies, to the addictive gambling which will go on as long as the dice can roll. Then there are the drug dealings, brutal ass whippings that are necessary at times for the disrespectful persons. But the thing that will always stay clear in my mind are the murders I've witnessed on the block.

While all these rotten things were going on on "P" street, it never phased me. Someone could get killed there tonight and I will be right back out there tomorrow like a fool. To me a gun is mandatory on "P" street because you never know what will kick off, so what I did was keep my gun on cock.

Sometimes when I talk to people on "P" street over the phone, they say that I'm acting as though jail is softening me up. They say this because I tell them I going on some different shit when I get out. I told them I'm going to college and I'll try to get a job and leave all the guns and war things alone when I come home. Nobody has a problem with me going to college; they just want me to come back out there and swing the same way I was before I left the street ... I think that they're only saying that to try and gas me to fall back into the same boat but as far as I'm concerned it ain't happening.

I really do feel for the brothers on Pacific because I now know that the badness doesn't last for long. You either die young or get an asshold full of time that you don't know how to do. Most of them don't realize this because they never had the time to sit and think about what's going on....

All in all I hope the hot steppers on Pacific Street might be able to cool down before they end up on ice or behind steel. As youngsters we get buckwild sometimes, but as we grow we must be more responsible for our actions.... (MH)

At the end of his paper, he wrote: "Please return. I would like to develop this paper into something much more."

In the following, another student ponders his journey in life, trying to understand the connection between "sex and drugs and rock and roll":

Sex, drugs, rock and roll, and violence took me on a journey, a search for myself or a search for something.

My first experience with the above was my teeny bopper days of robbing quarts of beer from the Bodega and racing up to the park with our radio and our girls. The nights on the parkside, guzzling beer, listen to rock and roll, trying to get my first piece of ass was the beginning of my journey. I didn't know it then but the life style I was living took me through heaven and hell.

Being so young and finding so many pleasures of life, I grew up fast. The special touch of a girl, the safe feeling of drugs and alcohol, the power of rock-n-roll.

The student then talks about the parties—beer, Jack Daniels' parties, Nitrous Oxide … -and continues:

> *My friends and I would, after a Jack party, go out to the local bars and cause some serious trouble. Not that we went out with that intention but the trouble and fighting would always come. I can remember for a six month period, while having those Jack parties, I and my boys would fight every night. No bullshit. Every fucking night. I used to wake up morning after the parties and wonder what the hell I did the night before. Who would be looking for me and whose head I smashed in. My girl would then ask me who I was fucking last night. What a trip.*
>
> *Amazingly I survived this phase. I still had my girl. I still held onto another job I had besides being the super of the apartment, and I didn't kill anybody. I didn't come out unblemished though. I lost a very close friend to a bullet; I smashed 2 cars, and I left a couple of dozen leather jackets in bars. In the next phase I wouldn't be as lucky. I wouldn't be as popular amongst my friends and it would be a lonely journey from then on.*
>
> *The madness of my early teens would turn even madder as I turned 19 and needed something new. But I'm going to stop at this point. I want to look at what has happened so far and try to figure out what kind of a journey I'm on, what I'm searching for.*
>
> *It was at 19 that I turned to harder drugs such as heroine. It seemed that the comfort I found in my world I could no longer find. When I didn't get the high I got with drinking and partying with my boys, I went on searching deeper and deeper into some new world. I left behind my friends, my girl and my family.*
>
> *I had rumbled through high school stoned as all of my friends. I don't think one of us got a real diploma, as my father called it; we all settled for GED diplomas. We all passed the first time with high grades. We weren't stupid, just irresponsible or self-destructive.*
>
> *I never gave myself a fair shot. I could have been anything I wanted. That goes for all of my friends; there isn't a stupid one amongst us. I think we all grew up disillusioned by our family split ups. We all came from fucked up families. We all needed an escape and we found it in each other. We shared something in common—we all had fucked up families. So together, my friends and I, girls and guys, formed our own family, a fam-*

ily that drank, smoked pot, took pills and fought together. My journey then was easy. I wasn't alone. I traveled with the comfort of my friends. I didn't realize then that my family of friends would break up, just as my real family, and then I would have to travel alone. Deeper and deeper my search went, until I lost almost everything.

When I couldn't go out and drink with the boys and raise hell, I was lost. Drinking in a bar with a band playing rock-n-roll and girls all around—like a glove that fit smug, so was the feeling I had when I got stoned with my friends.

Today I look back and realize my journey pushed me deeper into drugs: shooting drugs and slipping deep. So far that after drugs came crime, crime for drugs and crime for help. I wanted to be something in life and now my past and present were killing my future. I figured crime would sooner or later get me killed or back on the right road.

Now my journey continues. I am, to me, on the right road. Prison, another journey for a man going deep into himself ... Here and now I search alone. Deep into myself I journey. Everyday I learn. (KS)

The above student clearly sees his life as a journey towards wholeness. Despite what others might say about his "fucked up life" of failure, he sees himself as on his path, searching deeply. And he is. I think of Carl Jung, Thomas Moore, James Hillman and of the journey of the soul, the embracing of one's shadow, the owning of one's life. I honor the integrity of this student who views his life and all life as a search for meaning and understanding.

Some students, both white and black, chose to write about racism, its causes and effects. It is a topic, in both prison and in life, which is wrapped in pain, hurt, defense, and denial. While some gave a political "analysis" of racism, others looked more intellectually and psychologically. And many began their papers, as Thoreau suggests, with a simple narrative of their first experience of racism. What strikes me strongly rereading these papers is the innocence and vulnerability of those early experiences, the openness to life, the unpreparedness for hatred, and the life long and deep effects of those first experiences. I think of Countee Cullen's poem "Incident," written in 1925:

Once riding in old Baltimore,
Heart-filled, head-filled with glee,
I saw a Baltimorean

Keep looking straight at me.

Now I was eight and very small,
And he was no whit bitter,
And so I smiled, but he poked out
His tongue, and called me, "Nigger."

I saw the whole of Baltimore
From May until December;
Of all the things that happened there
That's all that I remember.

So simple, so painful, so powerful in terms of delineating the path from cause to effect. I type up some of the seemingly simple narratives below in order for us all to take in the profound effects on an individual of an early experience of hatred directed toward them. I think of Irena Klepfisz, a poet and Holocaust survivor, who questions, in one of her prose poems in her *Keeper of Accounts*, if there are certain moments in history, in personal and societal history, which hold us caught and imprisoned: "Is it inevitable? Everything that happened to us afterward, to all of us, does none of it matter? ... Are there moments in history which cannot be escaped or transcended, but which act like time warps permanently trapping all those who are touched by them?"

Time warps. Exactly. Many students wrote of those points of time, those traumatic experiences that hold us trapped. The following are a few of the many:

> *One day just before going to school, my mother said, "Son, please don't be disappointed when life becomes difficult. Your color may be a handicap." I really couldn't understand at that time the essence of it all because life to me was just fine. I had no problems at all. I had plenty of friends—black, Spanish, and some white. We played together and shared many things with each other. During school hours we had the same teacher, read the same books, and ate the same school lunch. So where was this handicap?*
>
> *It wasn't until years later I began to see signs of this so-called handicap. For example, there was this ad in the paper looking for help at a donut shop. Well, I took the ad to school so that me and Tommie (who, by the way, is a white boy) could go and check it out after class. Boy were we excited. On the bus going to the business sections (which is where the shop*

was located), we discussed all the things we could buy, like clothes and a bike. We could even take the girls to the movies every Saturday.

Upon our arrival there we were interviewed by a nice man who was pleased to see two young men willing to work. When asked how we knew they were hiring, Tommie told him how I had brought the ad to school. Well, because I found the ad, he immediately hired me to work with him making donuts and Tommie would clean the customer area and the kitchen. We both almost jumped for joy. We had gotten the job.

Just then a big white man with a bald head came in. He looked at Tommie and smiled. Then looked at me and his whole expression changed. He approached the man behind the desk and they huddled together and began to whisper. Me and Tommie fell silent. He looked at me and I at him. What could this mean? Is there something wrong? Then the man looked up and said, "Don't worry you both have the job ... however there has been a small change. Tommie will work with me and you will clean up." For some reason, even though I did have the job, I wasn't so happy anymore. A certain feeling came over me, something like anger.

From that day, I agreed 100% with my mother's theory of handicap. But it was not acceptable to me. I began to hate anyone who looked at me funny, thinking that they were focusing in on my handicap or color. I became sensitive to any form of pacification. In school, the teachers began to bore me. I was under the impression that their teaching techniques were structured to accommodate my handicap. Something of a self-fulfilling prophecy. So I left school. I was determined to be just as good as anyone else and have just as much. Which led me to sell drugs. I thought that money could be a shield to hide my color. And with this money I was to show material evidence of my existence. I bought the best of everything, drove a fine car, and was called Mr. by many white folk. However, this symbolic participation in the upper class was solely supported by drug money. My constant indulgence in drugs led to my present incarceration.

Being here has increased my insight and altered my perspective. I no longer agree with mom's theory of being handicapped. I see that believing I was handicapped made me dangerous to myself as well as others. Racism and being prejudiced are interactive and, yes, they both still exist, but being conscious is a safeguard against their destructive power. (RH)

And from another student:

We lived in a two bedroom apartment on the outskirts of Mount Vernon. I was born in the back room of that apartment by our family doctor, which at that time was the entire neighborhood's family doctor in the year 1945.

I remember loving that building, also the neighborhood. We used to swing on a car tire tied from a rope hanging from the big tree in the back yard, play "tag" in the big open field across the street located on St. Francis' Campus, raid Albino's cherry tree, have gang fights with the existing surrounding neighborhood boys, etc.

My older brother and I couldn't wait until Friday after school was out because Friday was when we could hustle money by helping people at the local supermarket—carry packages, search for 5 cent soda bottles, shine shoes, wash cars, and, some times, even work in the local candy store. After we would accumulate as much money as we could, we would put it all together, and he would hold it in his pocket; to this day, I never knew what was wrong with my pockets.

We would go home and show my mother what we had made and stick our noses up at our sisters because they couldn't hustle as well as us. Later we would change our clothing, put some of our money in our pockets, because Friday night we could stay out until 10:00 p.m.

I was about ten years old and my brother must have been about twelve. We never experienced (to our knowledge) any form of prejudice. We didn't know what that was until one day a neighborhood boy called my brother a "nigger." This boy was a white boy whose family had moved into the neighborhood not long before. He was about two years older than my brother but not bigger; my brother was large for his age.

This was the first time I ever saw my brother cry outside of the house. (Only when he got a spanking did I see him cry.) My brother was my everything, my hero, my protector, my friend, my world. He kept telling the boy to take it back, he pleaded with the boy to take it back, but the boy just laughed. My whole world was caving in. I felt helpless standing there watching my brother cry, so I began to cry also.

My brother looked at me crying, and I have never seen that look again in my brother's eyes since that day. It was a horrified look, so scary. I immediately stopped crying and fear came over my entire body. My brother grabbed that boy and went crazy, pounding him on the head, pulling his hair out, kicking him and, finally, making the boy take back what he said.

My brother's face became normal after that rage, but I still couldn't understand why my brother did what he did. I began smiling and laughing because he did. On the way home, he was trying to tell me why I should never let any white person call me a nigger and what I should do if one does. He also told me not to tell my mother he had a fight because he might get a spanking.

A couple of days went by. My brother wasn't home at the time when I told my mother what had happened and what my brother had done. My mother didn't appear to be angry. She just said, "I'll speak to him when he gets home." When my brother finally got home, my mother asked him what happened. He told her, and that was it; he didn't get a spanking.

My whole world seemed to change after that. I didn't see people as I had seen them before. There was something strange going on. Why didn't my brother get a spanking after beating that boy so bad?

I began to see "white people," as opposed to just "people." I began to think it to be right, separating my self from them, beating them up, stealing from their stores, calling them whitey, abusing their women, anything that I thought would offend them. This went on until I became about twenty five years old and began to see how my past was affecting my life and I realized that I was prejudiced.

Attempting to break away from this ignorance brought many problems into my life, such as the "Uncle Tom" syndrome. I, on occasions, associated with a couple of white male friends, which brought on a couple of white girl friends, and my brothers and sister were furious. After a while, I dropped my white associates because of prejudice I detected among them and that enhanced my deep rooted dislike towards them. I found out that the world operates on motivated thinking tied to prejudice, opportunism, greed, narrow mindedness, selfishness and a thousand other little passions that clutter up the narrow path of righteousness. "Without virtue there can be no friendship."

I went on for years looking for that some thing I could identify with, practicing TM, Yoga, and mind exercises, but some thing was always missing. This led me to be dissatisfied with ideologies, theories, philosophies, etc.

Fortunately I ventured into myself to the extent of finding a friend which some people call God, Yahweh, Buddha, Alla.... This friend I can depend on. This friend isn't prejudiced. He doesn't hate people, cheat people, lie to people, steal from people, deceive people. This friend is called Me.

A white student also wrote about prejudice, both in his past and his present:

No matter how much people in society today like to think that prejudice is no longer a factor in everyday life, the problem still exists. In every person, in every race, there is prejudice in some form, like some sort of bad disease waiting to be wiped out but growing stronger every day. When we are young we are still innocent to prejudice, until the people around us give us this disease. Some people carry it around inside them for fear it will someday be noticed. Others wear it around like a piece of clothing for all to see and have no shame at all.

When I was a kid I grew up in a neighborhood that consisted of mostly white middle class families. While going to school that would slowly change to a mixture of whites, blacks, and Spanish. By my senior year in high school, the percentage was about even. I can remember growing up and not feeling any different about people darker in color than me. If my parents were prejudiced, they never showed it in front of us kids. In fact they had friends that were both Spanish and Black, and these friends were always welcome in our home.

In my early teens I had a friend that was black. He was and still is a very good friend. The first time I really became aware of prejudice was when I went home from school with Bobby one day. Even though his mom was very nice to me and made me feel at home, his older brothers didn't. I didn't know at the time what was wrong. His brothers would leave the room when we entered, or when they spoke, it was like I wasn't with Bobby; I would be ignored.

After leaving his house and on our way to play ball, I asked Bobby what was wrong because he seemed a little quiet. He said his brothers didn't like him hanging out with me. They said he should hang out with his "own kind," that it was because of white people that his father was dead. The whites had sent his father to Vietnam where he was killed.

I didn't understand all this, so when I got home I asked my father if this was true. He sat me down and explained to me what prejudice meant. He told me that prejudice was a part of life, and I didn't have to agree with it, only learn to live with it.

One day a riot broke out at our high school between whites and blacks. It was a drug deal between a white kid and a black kid that turned into a racial conflict, forgetting all about the drugs. The police were called and they arrested about two hundred students. Bobby and I didn't get caught up in that one, but the next day going home from school we were approached by four white kids. After some words exchanged, I started to fight with one of the kids because he called Bobby "a nigger." Although I had gotten my lumps also, I broke the kid's jaw and nose in the process.

I never liked that word from the first time I heard it. But years later, when I came to prison, I found that black men called each other nigger like they were using their first names. Everyone in prison wears prejudice right out in the open for everyone to see: the inmates, the guards, everyone. We, as inmates, choose to fight with each other instead of fighting for things that would make our prison time easier. Don't eat with this one, don't lift weights with that one. Always some form of prejudice. Where will this all end? When will it all end? (FD)

What becomes so clear from these papers is the early openness to all people and, then, the seemingly small experience which creates fear, hurt, confusion, anger, separation, and hate. What is clear is the power of our personal experiences and the societal reality of racism. One student talked about listening to Martin Luther King: "I was only a child, yet even in my young awareness I was sincerely able to feel the truth of the words ... I was able to feel the fear of racial injustice." He then says: "When I used to listen to Malcolm calling the white people devils, how could I help but to believe all he said when the facts of their actions were so clearly documented and lived out." He then talks about slavery, discrimination, hostility, and says,

Naturally I felt fear and anger toward the white race, and distrust, sadness, and humiliation for my people and myself.... What type of effect was it supposed to have on me when I used to turn on the television and see a bunch of movies and t.v. shows which clearly displayed white people as being the superior more intelligent human beings ... What kind of effect did it have on me to learn that the white race's cruelty, torment and hatred of my race was all just because our skin was black? Obviously I felt terrible upon learning these realities, that people could be so ignorant as to do all those inhuman things to my people just because of the color of our skin ... How was I supposed to feel or how would any black person feel to learn that the white slave master was considered omnipotent administrator and the black slave was considered the super masculine menial? That means that the white slave master was supposed to possess a mind and that the black slave only possessed super physical strength with no ability to think. (DM)

The rhetorical questions—how was I supposed to feel, what type of effect was it supposed to have, how else could I feel—are powerful. Yes, how could one not see whites as devils? The "logic" and the writing are strong. The student ends his paper with the following: "As a black man I feel injustice, humiliation, subordination, deprived, limited, powerless and discriminated against.... That's not to say that all whites are racist towards blacks. I, myself, have come across some good white folks. But racism is just a reality that will probably continue to exist until the end of time."

That was the student's conclusion. At the end of his paper, when asked to write about the process of writing, the student wrote: "This particular writing was really difficult because it's on a touchy subject. I really wasn't sure if I should go ahead and hand it in, or read it, because I really don't want to offend anyone. I really just wanted to see what I would produced by writing on this complex subject."

And I felt, again, the integrity and courage, the pain and hurt, the consciousness which gives me hope about "the possibility of change" of both self and society. I think how these students are the "experts" to whom we should pay close attention.

One student, BH, wrote less personally but more politically about his own socialization by class, race, and gender and how he "hated all people because of their physical differences and did some very violent things." Because of his consciousness of black oppression, he "felt justified in anything (he) did to any white person": "As long as I was taking from 'crackers' it was alright. Since I wasn't doing too much crime in the neighborhood and hardly ever robed another black, I felt justified in my actions and able to feel a false sense of self-esteem. After all, whites had all the money ... This is how I thought." The student then writes about reading Marx and political theory and his beginning understanding of how "matters have been brilliantly strategized by our enemies (the ruling families of the U.S.)":

The majority of the police in my neighborhood are white. Since the police officer's job is essentially to protect property and keep the oppressed in their place, it was usually the white pig slapping me up for some offense or beating me up and calling me "nigger." Most of the teachers that taught the garbage I call his-story are white ... White people control all areas of people's activity (labor, law, economics, etc.) and since these institutions usually work against people—especially black people—black people tend to become hostile to all white people rather than the rulers.... Our rulers understand this and continue to fuel the deadly fire of racism and separatism.

He writes about his ability to rationalize his crimes:

After years of justifying my oppression of white folks, I began to move on to other crimes. Robbery was starting to get too costly for me since I had so many arrests for it. I moved on to drug-dealing and since I was accustomed to justifying oppression of others to my conscience I began to sell drugs in the community. I justified this to myself by never forcing it on anyone and vowing to never sell to babies or pregnant women. I stuck to this principle, but it's really stupid now that I look at it: What was stopping the pregnant girl I denied from sending her "man" to cop (buy)? In my subconscious I knew this shit wasn't correct but after so many years of self-justifying racism with reverse racism, I was able to do anything.

He then reflects on economic class, the media, the pressure to have name brands and consumer goods: "Since I was poor I could disguise my poverty by wearing the fancy clothes and stealing the trinkets that meant wealth ... I could have less than a penny in my pocket but as long as the exterior looked good I got attention and respect ... That sense of power and respect, along with the drive to get away from the dirtiness and the neglect of the ghetto caused me to do everything I had to stay on top."

He writes about viewing women as "sex objects and servants," a "hole to satisfy my needs ... I fooled myself into believing I loved these girls but I never had any problem using them and juggling them to my advantage ... I never physically abused my female companions but I put them through verbal abuse and psychological abuses that hurt them all the same."

Recounting all his denials and self-justifications, all his abuse of others, he ends his paper with the following: "This was the type of knucklehead I was. Being socialized on the basis of economic class, race, and gender made me unsociable—sick. It had me roaming around with a disease of the heart and mind that made prison or violent death inevitable. Luckily, through gaining consciousness, I've been able to treat this sickness and move towards a cure."

One feels the continually deepening awareness in his writing and his life. I think about one of the Eastern gurus who, when he came to the West, had sex with his students and then lied about his actions. I remember being filled with self righteous judgment until I was stopped by a friend's question: "Can you imagine how large he will become if he can incorporate his actions into his being?" Exactly. His seeming "sins" could be the very passageway to "enlightenment"—if he were able and willing to bring them into consciousness. Recently President Clinton talked about Monica Lewinsky and how it took something that scandalous to make him confront his addictions and face the harm of his actions. I remember not only judging Clinton but also feeling how terrible this all was, the worst thing that could really happen to someone, to be so exposed in one's sexual obsession, immorality and lying. Perhaps it's a bit like the barn burning—the most unwanted experience, the greatest failures, leading us to our deepest growth if we stay with rather than escape the painful feelings, take in rather than deny the actions of our own hands. I think, again, of Tom's understanding that compassion often arises from our ability to recognize our own capacity for malevolence. The men and women I taught in prison were continually confronted by the effects of their actions; they could not deny the hurt and pain caused to others (and to themselves).

In the following paper, KS writes about his legacy of family violence. What I like so much about his essay is, again, the desire to be conscious rather than unconscious and to take responsibility for one's life:

> *All my life I was led to believe that love was associated with pain, physical and mental. I was told to love when I wanted to hate. I was told that hurting was okay because it was how to show love. I grew up with this twisted conception. From the time I was little and all through the years of watching pain being inflicted on my mother. From the fighting that my brothers and I did, we showed love by hurting each other. I was also taught to protect that hurting love, as I protected my mother, as I protected my brothers from others who might inflict pain on them. I associated love and pain with protection and to protect a love no matter what kind of pain I went through.*

So then as I got older and met Laura, I knew when I heard the stories about her being a slut or easy, I knew I had to protect her because I loved her. I loved her because she needed protection, and the more I heard the stories, the more it hurt, the more I needed to love her and be her protector.

I was blinded by my love until I saw the light through a phone call. Then my hurt was too great and I lashed out and inflicted pain on her because that's the way I was brought up: to love and to inflict pain and if it hurt the other person I was indeed showing love.

Then I had to draw some kind of line. I could or would never be like my father. I couldn't inflict pain (physical pain) on someone I loved anymore. As I reached out and hit Laura across the face, I saw myself as my father, I saw the shine on Laura's face and I saw my own mother's face. I decided I could not live like that.... When I hit her I knew it would only get worse. I would resort more and more to using physical violence on her because after the first smack to her face I opened the door to the violence I saw as a kid. I could not live that way. I swore to be anything but like my father.

So even years after I left her, years after her asking me to come back, I still couldn't. I was too aware that I loved her too much to go back to her. I helped her in every way possible after I left—helped her into college, gave advice when she asked—but I could never sleep in her bed again.

I still hurt for her love, but the choices were simple. I can go back to her and love her and worry about another episode of violence or I can live the way I know best, by keeping away from the woman I love ... I never want to be like my father or like Uncle Andy. I can never live with the thought of hitting a woman for love or for hate. By choosing this path, I'm safe. (KS)

He hasn't broken free of the pattern in the sense of being able to love without violence. But his consciousness, his ability to recognize the pattern, has given him the ability to choose—to not follow his father and his uncle.

As a feminist, I feel the power of patriarchy and sexism to define what is real, natural, normal—for a man, for a woman. As a teacher, I feel the importance of having students remember and think about the messages they received as children and as adults in terms of how they should act and be as a boy/man or a girl/woman: to stand outside of cultural assumptions and conditioning, to look closely, to question. There is no other way to break out of the prison of any of our socialization except through this process, the "dismantling" (as Audre

Lorde says) of the lies we have been fed, the questioning (as Elizabeth Minnich says) of "mind-numbing concepts." In meditation, the teachers often talk about suffering and the causes of suffering. And what they always say is: don't accept what we say; always look to your own experience. Writing is one way to look to our experience in order to become conscious human beings, and consciousness is, really, a path to lessen our own suffering and the suffering in our world.

Toward the end of the semester, I let students explore any relationship they want to understand. Some chose to write about their relationship with music or art or sports. Others chose to write about their relationship with family members. The following papers touched me because of their love and respect as well as for their understanding of what is complex and, often, painful. They write of a father, a great grandmother, and a son.

My relationship with my father is a very significant one. He is a good listener and an understanding man. My father is a very quiet person, but behind that quietness, there is wisdom and love to be shared at any time …

When I was about 12 years old, I used to ask him a lot of questions, and this man was always ready to respond to my curiosity very politely and with great patience. The thing that makes our relationship very significant is his way of making me understand some facts of life that I am experiencing today. He used to tell me that the result of my thinking would be my deeds and my entire behavior. Nevertheless, for a man to make mistakes is natural, but to always correct that mistake with success, learning something from it …

My father love to play the guitar; that is all he does in his spare time. Since we lived facing an ocean, every night my father used to take his guitar and sneak out to the beach and play his guitar there by himself. I never understood why he was doing such a thing, so one day I asked him why he was so often alone in nature and he responded to me by singing me a strange song that I had never heard before; then he told me that that was his nature—and that some day I would be able to understand.

One night I decided to follow him because I was curious to find out what he was doing. When he discovered that he was being followed by someone, he surprised me when he called my name and asked me why I was hiding, and he also asked me if I didn't trust him anymore. I don't recall what my answer was because I was so scared. He noticed that I was trembling, so very gently he hugged me with his strong arms and told me not to be scared.

I will never forget that night. My father started to play his guitar very carefully. But he wasn't singing any song. However there was a very silent song—the sea waves' sound.

I stood there contemplating my father's melody. When he finished, he started to look up at the sky. Then he began to tell me the name of the stars, and the name of some planets. But at that time, I was too naïve and unable to understand all that he was teaching me. He also told me that when I grew up, that I should follow his example—whenever I needed to communicate with Bunquiuu, meaning god in Gariffuna, that I should find me a solitary place to concentrate. I asked him how I would know that Bunquiuu is there. He told me that I would feel His presence within me.

My father used to relate a lot of old historical tales to me and always told me that in any even man should not lose his values nor his dignity and to always be responsible—that by being responsible I was going to gain respect anywhere.

When I decided to come to this country, the first person to know about my plans was my father. He cried when I departed and I too cried. We loved each other very much, but I had my reasons to leave.

Now our communication is through letters, but the understanding is still there. Today my father has problems walking. When I heard this, I almost went crazy. I wrote him a letter full of disappointment. I was confused and depressed. But his reply made me feel better—as always encouraging me as if I were the one who was having paralysis problem.

A few days ago he wrote me a letter that said, "Nirouu," meaning son, "I know how you feel being where you are. But don't worry; don't consider nor picture yourself in prison but consider yourself in the best school for a man like you. Remember that most of all wise men were educated in prison. Some prophets went to prison for some reason. So do not waste your time wondering. Be patient and try to understand what is your mission. Remember that there is a reason for everything—whether good or bad. Also remember that Bunquiuu is just. He protects the righteous and teaches the weak. I know you are very strong, so please stay strong and do not stop struggling." (CG)

VB writes about his great grandmother:

I feel fortunate to have grown up in a household with my great grand-mother living and helping to instruct me while growing up. She was the inspiration and foundation of a beneficial learning experience for me, and I worship all that I have learned from her. Through her wisdom, she taught me valuable and unforgettable lessons which guide me to this day.

From the time I was born until her demise in 1987 (may she rest in peace) I will always remember her hair of silver, because it gave her a glow of wisdom and beauty.

Her hair was long, the absolute color of silver, and hung past her petite shoulders. She was small, about 5'0", and slim. To my knowledge she had never seen the insides of a hospital. Whenever she was ailing she concocted her own home remedies which I noticed always seemed to work. To me Gram-ma was the epitome of love and beauty and her patience and kind-ness far surpassed anyone else I have encountered.

When I was around her I always observed her closely because of her uncanny capability of doing things which I thought no other woman her age could manage. She washed her own clothing by hand, cooked all of her meals herself, and constantly marched up and down the immense stair-case of our house. Never once had I heard her ask anyone for assistance in any of her undertakings.

Her hobby was making all types of preserves. She would always ask us not to throw any glass jars away because she used them to preserve the fruits that made the delicious jams. One day when I was about fourteen years old, while sitting on the back porch of our home watching gram-ma rock back and forth in her rocking chair knitting a blanket for her bed, I boldly asked her how old she was, and when she told me she was ninety years old I bugged out. I would have never thought of her being so old, not after seeing how active she was.

At the age of fourteen was about the time when I was just becoming aware of my heritage and began to ask a lot of questions about the history of Black people. I went to all the members of my household posing ques-tions and looking for answers but no one really seemed to pay me much attention, that is, except for gram-ma, who listened to me and always smiled while I was speaking.

One day while she was ironing in the kitchen I started talking about some of the present day Black leaders such as Malcolm X, Martin Luther king, Jr., and Huey P. Newton. As I rattled on about these Black leaders I noticed that familiar smile on her face, the smile of love and concern. Then she reached for my head and pushed her long brown fingers through my bushy Afro and squeezed my head affectionately and asked me had I ever heard of a man called Nat Turner. I reluctantly said no, never heard of him. Sensing my reluctance she said, "Well not many people talk about Nat Turner." Then I became curious and asked, "Why? Who was he, Gram-ma?" And she said, "Oh, he was a preacher and was accused of killing a lot of white folks along time ago and he died swinging from a rope." I asked her how she knew and she told me her father told her about him when she was just a little girl. I wanted to know more but that's all I got from her before she began to hum and continue ironing.

What I gathered from her concerning Nat Turner sounded very interesting to me but I thought it was just another old folk tale. When I was a child Gram-ma used to tell me a lot of stories, some I didn't believe but later found out to be true. She once told me that she herself and her family were slaves and lived on a plantation in Georgia, and that even after the Emancipation Proclamation there were still many slaves owned by white men in the south and how when she became pregnant with her first child the owner of the plantation, who she proclaimed to be "a nice man," gave her money and clothes and sent her to New York. These were some of the things which I found out to be true. Now what she told me of Nat Turner made me become inquisitive, and I went and asked some of my older associates who at the time were members of the Black Panther Party and were educated in Black history and they immediately confirmed what I was told about Nat Turner.

I was amazed that a ninety year old woman had brought such knowledge of the past to my attention. I had no real knowledge of the past at that time. I was only conscious of the struggle at hand and the leaders of that time. So when the opportunity presented itself again, I went back to Gram-ma to ask more about Nat Turner. When I asked her about him she said, "Why you want to know so much about this man. He's dead and gone." So I asked no more. At that moment I got the impression that she feared that I would use such information destructively because she knew me better than I knew myself. I don't blame her though because I was young and definitely naïve, just becoming consciously aware of my heritage and embittered by the fact that my ancestors were taken captive in their own land long ago, treated like animals and enslaved in this country for over 400 years.

I can see her point, me being young and easy to lead, I just might have used it to add fuel to the already burning fire inside me. But nevertheless from that point on, my beloved Great Grandmother, who I truly owe much credit to, inspired me to seek out my history and from this inspiration I found the importance of knowing. Standing in the kitchen discussing the Black leader of the day, I was inclined to learn about the Black man in America and abroad.

Looking back and analyzing why I was able to learn, I see the following: the inspiration left to me by Gram-ma and the struggles of the 1960's encouraged me to pursue an education in and around this area of consciousness. I've even disregarded, at times, my scholastic lessons to further myself in the history of my people, my ancestors. Over the years whenever I found time to sit back and seriously read, I would look for material in this area. Whenever I got the chance to initiate a meaningful conversation I would try to place my listeners in a mode of Black consciousness, hoping through the exchange I would be able to advance my awareness. This is the process which I use to facilitate learning. (VB)

Rereading and typing these two papers, I think of the depth of love and respect and the vulnerability and the courage required to express that love, especially in an environment which fosters defense, coldness, protection, and hardness. In her *The Places That Scare You: A Guide to Fearlessness in Difficult Time*, Pema Chodron, a Buddhist nun, tells a story told to her by Jarvis Masters, her friend on death row, about a fellow inmate, Freddie

who started to fall apart when he heard of his grandmother's death. He didn't want to let the men around him see him cry and struggled to keep his pain from showing. His friends saw that he was about to explode and reached out to comfort him. Then Freddie started swinging violently. The tower guards began to shoot and yell for Freddie's friends to back away. But they wouldn't. They knew they had to calm him down. They screamed at the guards that there was something wrong with him, that he needed help. They grabbed Freddie and held him down, and every one of them was crying. As Jarvis put it, they reached out to Freddie, "not as hardened prisoners, but simply as human beings."

That is what I experienced in my years teaching in prison: the reaching out as human beings. In the following paper a student, CW, writes about his relationship with his son, bringing in an earlier experience with another student in the class, Sean, a man young enough to be his son. I am including the whole paper because I love how the student weaves together different experiences at different points of time in order to understand the "father-son" relationship:

> *Being an incarcerated father separated from my son Chris since '91 has caused me to search for an understanding of our relationship on all levels; from that time to the present I've noticed a constant change in his life.*
>
> *Chris stands about five feet with a snicker bar complexion, low cut hair with a quarter moon part on the left side, big brown eyes, straight white teeth, with cringed eyes and dimples when he smiles and ears he could have only inherited on his mother's side of the family. He loves to wear caps and shirts with his favorite ball team insignia on them, with rock faded jeans and an ever increasing style of foot wear. Chris resembles me a lot.*
>
> *When I was home Chris and I would spend special time on the weekends together. We would do things that would take him hours to explain to someone else. For example, he was eight years old when I took him sailing for the first time. We left Long Island, New York, sailed to Virginia Beach, Virginia with a couple of friends and their sons. We would watch the sun slice the horizon and disappear as the lesser lights claimed the night. At night while anchored we would sit out under the starry moonlit sky and tell sea stories of old pirates, man eating sharks, sea monsters and the Bermuda Triangle.*
>
> *One morning after breakfast we were fishing and Chris wanted to know whether or not the story of the Bermuda Triangle was true. I said, "Sure we were lost for ten and a half hours with no radio contact right in the middle of it." He said, "Daddy if your ship had got lost like the others ships I would have grown up and found you." I told him, "That would have been impossible, because you wasn't born yet." There was a long silence and I saw a strange sadness in his face. Looking out over the sea I asked him, "What's wrong." He said, "I wouldn't be here if your ship got lost forever." At that moment I saw tears swelling up in his eyes. I put my arms around him and pulled him close to me and heard him say, "Daddy, don't never go away forever." I said, "Never." "Promise?" "Promise." At that point our father-son relationship took on a new characteristic bond.*

This weekend when I called he was gone to summer camp with his classmates. The message he left with his mother was to tell daddy he said "Never." My eyes immediately filled up with water. She asked me, "What do he mean?" I told her, "It's just among men." At that point I felt a tear in our relationship I've never felt before. I knew he was feeling the pain and missing me more than ever because he was thinking about the good times we had in the past.

As I said, there was a time Chris and I could relate; I could look into his face and see those big eyes sparkling full of life responding to my permeating love for him. Now, it seems he's on a ship pulling away from port heading towards rough seas. I used to hear laughter in Chris' voice over the phone with the joy of knowing it was in relation to me; now I barely get to talk to him and when I do it's a distance silence saying all the things I hate. I used to give him a lecture on his behavior and get a better report; now principals and counselors are lecturing him to no avail. Like I mentioned in an earlier paper, "I'm in school, my son skips school. I'm hoping to come home, he's about to be sent away." I created his life, he's trying to give his life away." Chris may resemble me in looks, but his ways are becoming past finding out.

What is Chris thinking? I have no idea. I've been trying to reach out to him across these rough seas, to understand his feelings and show my love that is physically distant yet mentally and spiritually present with him. I'm searching for a way to unite and keep us together. It's very hard being apart from your son/from your father.

I was reading my paper in class called "Changing the Effects of the Cause," part of what I mentioned above. Another part reads: "The effects of being in prison are positive, negative, mental and physical, not only for me but for my family too. An example of negativity is not being able to see my son grow up and give him the fatherly advise needed in a fast moving world … I can already see a long term effect taking place in my son's life. Will imprisonment or death be the effect of my incarceration for him?"

After reading my paper a young man named Sean began to make comments. His comments were directed to my paper but his mind was on his father. The look on Sean's face—the words he tried to converse—all told a story. A story of wonderment, a story of thwarted love, broken promises and very few answers. His face said, "If you were there I wouldn't be here." Listening to Sean talk about his father made me see myself and hear Chris' voice crying out for me from within Sean. I hear him, but it's like dying and coming back as a fish in a bowl trying to tell someone, "This is me, do you hear me" to no avail.

I want to answer Sean/Chris' questions, clear up his doubts and know how he truly feels. Sean asked me, "Do you feel it's your fault for your son's behavior?" I simply replied, "yes." From my brief conversation with Sean I learned in part what is going through Chris' mind in this father-son relationship.

Why is our relation the way it is? Like I told Sean, it's my fault for his being the way he is. I know my incarceration is the cause for our relationship being the way it is. It's very simple: I'm here, he's there, not only as a man but bridging the gap mentally as the man of the house, meaning he knows I'm not there. He understands certain dangers at his age and he naturally protects his mother, because I'm not there.

I want to be an example of Chris even in prison and by staying out of trouble in prison, I'll be able to communicate with him regularly, continue my college education and have answers for him as questions arrive as he advances in school. I want Chris to continue to have self-confidence, but direct his energy towards getting an education. Even though I'm not there, this relationship is crucial to my son's growth. This father-son relationship hints of immortality; eventually, I would like to have grandkids with Chris' continuing my name, my line, and possibly my dreams.

I know Chris will someday become a man, a lover, a husband, and a father, maybe not in that order. I know it depends heavily upon what he learns or doesn't learn from me. How Chris behaves at home, in school, and on the streets depends on me and my examples. Our relationship has not been easy for him to see those examples and is now made more difficult by my incarceration—tearing it apart. Yet, despite such distance I will try to instill in Chris my love for him—most importantly the meaning of manhood in this father-son relationship. (CW)

The student ends his paper, "While writing this paper there should be no question to where my mind was, so I immediately wrote this missive to my son," and includes that letter:

Dear Son,

I'm writing to remind you that nothing could ever take the love I have for you away. I received your message loud and clear and yes it's still a promise. Christopher, I love you very much and miss you as well. Son, I know things are not the way they used to be and I know that I'm to blame. However I can't change the past or restore those lost years, but we can both look ahead to a favorable future together if it's the Lord's will.

Chris, I want to know how you feel about me as a father. I want you to share whatever is on your mind with me on a man to man basis and don't hold back your feelings, son—it's important that I know how you feel.

By the time you read this letter you would have just come in from summer camp with your bags still packed on the floor. Give me until six pm and I'll call just for you. I love you, son."

One feels this student's honesty, his ability to pick up threads from earlier papers and from discussions in class, to experience and express all his feelings, to make connections. He is using everything to deepen his understanding. There is, for this student, for so many of the students I work with, no separation between thinking, feeling, writing, questioning, and living. This is "education with a heart."

CHAPTER TWENTY-FIVE:

A POETIC INTERLUDE

Then today, while jogging, poems came to me that seemed, somehow, connected by some thread to this book. Now the books and poems lay scattered around me. What I see is that they all have to do with flowering, of seeds coming to life after a long winter, of our human need to give birth to what lay deep within us, to find some vehicle for our creativity, our soul, our spirit, our humanity—no matter what the circumstances, no matter what the obstacles. I think, again, of Thoreau's "Though I do not believe that a plant will spring up where no seed has been, I have great faith in a seed. Convince me that you have a seed there, and I am prepared to expect wonders." Perhaps this is, or should be, the faith of all teachers, all parents, all beings.

Here are a few poems about life emerging from seeming death. They express, through metaphor and image, the reality I experienced all those many years teaching students buried in concrete and steel whose words (and whose beings) emerged from the ground like sprouts, like life.

Lithops

> (Irena Klepfisz)
> *common name: living stone*
>
> *Barely differentiated*
> *from the inorganic they conceal*
> *their passions in sheer survival.*

It is philosophy: life's hard
growth and erosion even rocks
in the end are broken down
to formless dust.

But like all schema incomplete
for between the grey and fleshy
crevices strange blossoms grow
in brazen colors. For us it is
the ancient sign that every life
has its secret longings to transcend
the daily pressing need
longings that one day must flower.

Royal Pearl

(Irena Klepfisz)

Where do new varieties come from?
General Eisenhower is a red tulip which was first
recognized in 1951. In 1957 a lemon yellow mutation appeared in a field
of red General Eisenhower tulips. This yellow mutation
proved to be a stable sport which was called—Royal Pearl
                              —Brooklyn Botanic Gardens

In dead of winter imprisoned within
the imprisoned earth it was a leap
defiant of all eternal laws and patterns.
Beneath the frozen earth it came to be
like a splitting of an inner will
a wrenching from a designated path
a sudden burst from a cause unknown.
And then in spring it opened: a lemon yellow
in a pure red field.

Our words deny the simple beauty
the wild energy of the event. Anomaly
deviant mutant we're always taught
as though this world were a finished place

and we the dull guardians of its perfected forms.
Our lives are rooted in such words.

Yet each winter there are some
who watch the gardens emptied
only white as the snow presses
on the fenced-in grounds just
as on an unclaimed field.
And each winter there are some
who dream of a splitting of an inner will
a wrenching from the designated path
who dream a purple flower standing solitary
in a yellow field.

My glads went from
peach to white
when they bloomed
in the Spring, In the
cellar then, Planted
near the cellar wall.

And from the *Light From Another Country*, a wonderful book of prison poetry edited by Joseph Bruchac, I quote two of the many poems that express the deep longing to express one's full humanity, the challenge of holding one's dignity in the violence of a storm.

The Ritual

(Paul David Ashley)

I stand below the gun tower
in the rain. Other prisoners line up
behind me. They want to return
to their cells. "Not yet," I tell them.

"Not until the bastard
stops calling me by a number."

It is late and because visitors are present
the tower guard grudgingly calls
my name.
I walk through the gate
as if I were almost human.

Later in the darkness

he takes me from my cell.

He begins the ritual
of unconsciousness. I hear the thud

of clubs falling on flesh. When I call
out my number the guards walk
away. I shout at them.

"My name, goddamn you, call me
by my name."

And they return.

Prison

(Paul David Ashley)

If you would work one small miracle
repair one man
without violence or contempt
assemble one body
without learning on the grotesque
inventions of pain

if I could understand the mystery of rain
how it holds its dignity
in the violence of a storm
if freedom was not more important
than even god or death
you could have me I would not escape.

I think of the Buddha's teachings about suffering and the way to be free of suffering; how to have equanimity in the midst of injustice, pain, cruelty, suffering; how to be free.

Chapter Twenty-six:

My letter to them

Before I wrote to the men in prison, I did my own free writing to clarify my reasons, beginning with "I want to write to the men in my class in prison because …:

I want to write the men and women whose papers I want to use because I need to get their permission. Because I want to connect with them after all these years. Because I think about them and miss them. Because I am curious where they are and how they are and how their lives have unfolded. Because I want to see if they respond and, if they do, where their responses take me. Because I really don't know how either they or I will respond. Because I want them to know their words made a difference in my life, both when I taught them and now, that their honest and deep words have effect, that their words and thoughts and feelings are valuable, deep, worthy of saving, worthy of printing in a book. That they are worthy--despite what the environment of prison may make them feel. I want to send them their papers because I want them to remember the depth of their thoughts, the honesty of their words, the level of their consciousness. Because sometimes we need to remember what we knew so deeply, because circumstances sometimes are so harsh we forget what we know and follow our smaller, less conscious, and habitual ways. Because it's good to be reminded because memory can be short and life can be hard, and we can build up our defenses around our heart, and sometimes

*all it takes is a little air and light, kindness and compassion, for us to open
again to our loveliness.*

I then sent out the following letter to twenty five men:

Dear _____

*Years ago we worked together in an English Composition Class in
Skidmore's University Without Walls College Program. A few years ago
the college program ended because of cutbacks in funds at both the state
and the national level. Because I learned so much during those years, I
wanted to reflect on the experience and, also, honor the students whose
writing and thinking taught me so much.*

*During my 12 years teaching at Great Meadow and Washington,
I would save some of the papers that particularly moved me because of
their honesty, openness, depth of consciousness, insight, and ability to
express with clarity and power. (I probably would have saved more, but
the question was often whether I could get to a xerox machine to make a
copy of the paper before returning it by the next class.) About a year ago,
I decided to write a book entitled* Breaking Out of Prison. *I am writing
this letter because I would like to include some of what you wrote for that
Composition class within that book and would like your permission.*

*In the book I explore different ideas about freedom: my own childhood
experiences trying to "break free" from constrictions in my family; meditation as a path of awareness leading to liberation; and writing as a way
of thinking about inner and outer worlds and coming to new understanding. What I am trying to do in the book is really look at how we can move
beyond our habitual reactions, our socialization and indoctrination, the
lies and stereotypes and prejudices perpetuated by the media and those in
power, and see through our own eyes, defining the world through a close
and deep reflection on our own experiences and through seeing connections and patterns. In other words, how we can break out of the mental
prisons that entrap us. In some way, the Composition class was a way of
using writing as a path toward freedom: a way of stopping, looking closely,
reflecting, and coming to insight.*

*The book is now about two hundred pages. It goes in many different
directions (probably too many), incorporating personal experience, literature, philosophy and my many years teaching writing in different schools.*

But the center of the book is, really, about teaching writing within Great Meadow and Washington. And the center of that center are your papers that I have saved because the words in those papers were powerful to me. I want other people to hear those words—their power and insight. I would like to include, in whole or in part, 30 different papers from 25 different students.

I have no idea if the book could/would ever be published, but I would like to try to publish it and would very much like to include your writings if you would permit me. I am enclosing a xeroxed copy of some of your writing I might use, in whole or in part. I could either include your name or have it be anonymous; it is up to you. And I would certainly—if you wanted—send you that section of the book where your writing was included, so that you could see the context in which I am putting it.

So, I am writing to ask your permission to use your words, and to say hello after all these years, and to ask how you are, and if you are still writing, and if you have any memory of your own good words written during that semester a long time ago. (It's always interesting to see where we were at different points in our life, to be reminded of what we knew and what we said. It would be very interesting for me to hear some of your own thoughts in response to your writing, so please write any thoughts, questions, feelings.)

Thank you for the honesty of your words and the depth of your thoughts which taught me so much on so many different levels. I really loved teaching in the UWW program and miss that experience greatly. The writing of this book and the inclusion of your papers are a way for me to honor what was and is deep and meaningful.

> *May you have a good New Year.*
> *Sincerely yours,*

Sent Dec. 26, 2000

CHAPTER TWENTY-SEVEN:

PATTERNS

When students generalize too much, not seeing specifics, not noticing what is directly in front of them, I tell them to stop, to look closely, to describe with exact and specific details. The importance of Zen mind, beginner's mind, of seeing as if for the first time, of seeing what is rather than one's concept of what is. But when students see everything as separate and isolated details or events, then it is important to train the mind to step back, to detach, to recognize patterns, to make connections, to see things within contexts, to come to a larger understanding of relationships. Almost all of our society is geared against both ways of seeing: the specific particulars in front of us and the patterns that connect. The multiple distractions, the noise and constant sensory stimulation, the quick soundbites, the juxtaposition of totally unrelated events, the lack of any analysis, the sensationalism and romanticism and voyeurism, the sense that everything exists in itself and outside of history, that we exist apart from our environment and from other beings, that one event is isolated from what went before and what goes after, that we are isolated from the world around us in both time and space—all militate against seeing.

What would it mean if we could really see the uniqueness of each person who is incarcerated? What would it mean if we could really see the larger societal patterns? This book, hopefully, might help a reader see and hear a few individuals. In terms of the latter, the following are just a few of the statistics that many people already know: More than 2,000,000 people are serving time in U.S. prisons, 60% for nonviolent convictions. In 1980, there were fewer than 500,000 prisoners; we have expanded four times in two decades. If recent incarceration rates remain constant, an estimated one out of twenty people will serve time in prison during their lifetime. Now, one out of four African American men between the ages of eighteen and twenty-five are either in prison or in some way connected to the justice system. America spends 100 billion dollars on the criminal justice system each year. The United Sates has the highest per capita rate of incarceration in the world, 690 per 100,000, six times higher than any other industrialized nation. California has the third largest prison system in the world, preceded only by the entire U.S. and China. New York and California spend more money on prisons than on state universities. California has built twenty-one new prisons and only one college in the last twenty years. 10,000 professors and other university employees have been laid off and 10,000 prison guards have been hired.

Perhaps we can use both the closeness of "beginner's mind" and the more distant detached perspective to "see." If we were from another country, or from another world, and heard the above information, what could/would we assume about this society, about both the jailors and the jailed?

The following poem came in answer to the above question:

At first there were only a few
who needed to be put behind bars
for the others to feel safe and protected.
But then the danger seemed to grow larger,
be more subtle. Frightened eyes began to see more
enemies. And so more prisons were built.
And more. In fact, it seemed there could never be enough.
More prisons then schools, more prisons then restaurants,
than apartments in the city. Nowhere else it seemed
for the poor and black to live,
no other place to be fed, to be schooled.
Everything was turned into steel bars and concrete walls,
a strange kind of Midas curse.
And still those few who remained outside
shivered, more and more scared of the shadow
cast by the prison walls, looking suspiciously
at each other, wanting to be safe.

I wrote this chapter and all of this book before September 11, 2001. Since then, our fears have been more manipulated to give those in power even more power. We are told that if only we give up certain rights and obey those in authority, we will be safe from "them." The actual prisons, as well as the prisons of the mind, have grown even stronger and more impermeable to reason, the need for awareness and compassion even more necessary.

CHAPTER TWENTY-EIGHT:

GRACE ABOUNDING

Grace Abounding

(William Stafford)

Air crowds into my cell so considerately
that the jailer forgets this kind of gift
and thinks I'm alone. Such unnoticed largesse
smuggled by day floods over me,
or here come grass, turns in the road,
a branch or stone significantly strewn
where it wouldn't need to be.

Such times abide for a pilgrim, who all through
a story or a life may live in grace, that blind
benevolent side of even the fiercest world,
and might—even in oppression or neglect—
not care if it's friend or enemy, caught up
in a dance where no one feels need or fear:

I'm saved in this big world by unforeseen
friends, or times when only a glance
from a passenger beside me, or just the tired
branch of a willow inclining toward earth,
may teach me how to join earth and sky.

What saves us? A pigeon eating from our hand. The flash of violet and purple as it struts in the sun. A paper we wrote that someone really liked, that we really liked. A letter from someone far away. A slant of light, a mote of dust, a strain of music, a thought, a memory—suddenly appearing, just like that, a smile across our face, remembering. And little things become amplified when we are vulnerable, when we have been deprived. This week I have been sick with sore throat, headache, fever, very small compared to people who really suffer illness but enough to give me a glimpse into that corner of grace that comes, sometimes, from feelings of pain and deprivation. For me, yesterday, grace was sliding into a hot bath, feeling the warmth around me, my body stretched out rather than constricted; it was feeling clean and fresh, brushing hair and teeth—a return and a connection. I felt happy, as if I had done something quite wonderful.

> *I can glimpse grace slipping in with me*
> *into the bath, my body stretched and open*
> *in the hot water after days curled*
> *under blankets, feverish and sweaty,*
> *spirit having vacated mind and body.*
>
> *It's a small corner of a room I hardly know.*
> *Others, I know, abide here for years, for a life,*
> *the small tight space of pain,*
> *men in prison, their small cells.*
>
> *Coming out of the bath,*
> *I feel radiant, almost beautiful.*
> *I brush my hair,*
> *put on a clean shirt,*
> *sit in a chair, with a book,*
>
> *The room so clean and tender now*
> *and everything slow*
> *and filled with soft light.*

In our society of surfeit, of so much and so fast, where does grace have any space to enter? In prison, however, everything is stripped down. Grace has, it seems, more time, and those small eight by eight foot cells more air and space. It is true that deprivation can make us bitter and hopeless. But it is also true that it can amplify and make more poignant small moments of any connection—to one's self, to another, to warmth and light, to a seed or a flower or an animal, to kindness and love—grace more present when we are more vulnerable.

I think of Naomi Nye's poem "Kindness":

Before you know what kindness really is
you must lose things,
feel the future dissolve in a moment
like salt in a weakened broth.
What you held in your hand,
what you counted and carefully saved,
all this must go so you know
how desolate the landscape can be
between the regions of kindness.
How you ride and ride
thinking the bus will never stop,
the passengers eating maize and chicken
will stare out the window forever.

Before you learn the tender gravity of kindness,
you must travel where the Indian in a white poncho
lies dead by the side of the road.
You must see how this could be you,
how he too was someone
who journeyed through the night with plans
and the simple breath that kept him alive.

Before you know kindness as the deepest thing inside,
        you must know sorrow as the other deepest thing.
        You must wake up with sorrow.
You must speak to it till your voice
catches the thread of all sorrows
and you see the size of the cloth.

Then it is only kindness that makes sense anymore,
only kindness that ties your shoes

and sends you out into the day to mail letters and purchase
    bread,
only kindness that raises its head   Wow!
from the crowd of the world to say
It is I you have been looking for,
and then goes with you everywhere
like a shadow or a friend.

The newspaper article I just read showed an African American man wearing a woolen hat, eyes closed, cheek pressed to the brow of a horse, one hand reaching over the horse's neck, the other stroking his face. The caption read: "Paul Malone, an Inmate at the Four Mile Correctional Center in Canon City, Colorado, shares an affectionate moment with a wild horse that is undergoing training as part of the Wild Horse Inmate Program." The article begins: "Canon City, Colorado. Learning to tame wild horses—gently, not by 'breaking' the animals as in a wild West movie—is helping some prison inmates prepare for life after incarceration. When Randy deVaney is released from the Four Mile Correctional Center southwest of Colorado Springs, he hopes to put his new skills to good use by running a horse program for underprivileged children. 'Now I know what I want to do with the rest of my life,' said DeVaney, 42.'" The article talks about the program of rounding up wild horses and training them in the prison, often with men who have never seen a horse before. "DeVaney, like many of the inmates has fallen in love with the horses. He spends his evenings reading books and watching videos on horse training. Hardin (the corrections supervisor) acknowledges that some people may think working with horses under the crisp Colorado sky might seem more like a vacation than punishment. But he said the program teaches inmates communication skills and responsibility and gives them goals and skills. 'It also takes patience to train a horse and to train others how to train a horse,' Hardin said. 'Now maybe they'll be able to use that patience when they go home to their families.' The hard work also has helped inmates like Manual Torres, 26, acquire a pride they didn't have before. 'We're doing this for people on the streets,' Torres said. 'It makes you feel good to send home a good horse.'"

A few weeks ago I saw on PBS a program about inmates in a women's prison training dogs to work with children and adults with disabilities. They showed one woman working with her puppy; she was clearly filled with love and joy. What I saw was "grace" abounding: in her close, loving, playful, and sweet connection to another being and in her feeling that she was doing something worthwhile for another, that she was doing good work and that she was good.

Certain things, it seems to me, are so simple. We all flourish when we love and are loved. Since many of us have been hardened and damaged by our past connections to other human beings, and since the human/human connection can be so complex, animals can be the perfect vehicle for that love. Dogs—pure love and devotion—how could it not be healing to love and be loved unconditionally, especially for those who have felt unlovable and worthless? And another simple truth: it is in giving more than receiving that we most feel our own humanity, our own capacity for generosity and goodness. What strikes me as painful, not just in prison but in all of our society, is how many people are cut off from both their potential and desire to give their unique gifts to the world. I think how much good it does the heart and soul to be of service, to help, to bring laughter and joy to another, to feel a connection between the work of our own hands and the effect of that work.

It's simple, really, but clearly it is not easy. We need, as individuals, as a society, and as a world, to want healing more than vengeance, the flourishing of the human spirit more than the diminishment. With human beings, as with horses, the way to "train" is not through "breaking" the spirit, but through reviving and replenishing the spirit—a patient and slow building up of trust rather than a whipping into submission. And what that demands, I think, is a belief and faith in people's potential for goodness. While it is true that some dogs, horses, and human beings have experienced such strong and constant cruelty and damage in early years, the possibility of trust is very small, for most beings there is vast and deep potential. What is required is Thoreau's "faith in the seed."

Chapter Twenty-nine:

Where were they?
How to locate?

Where were they? On some of the papers I had saved, there was only a nickname; on some the name was cut off. Sandy tried to find someone who could track down addresses of those names I had. Out of twenty, six had died. A high statistic. I thought of those men, wondered if there were some generalization I could draw about who survives and who does not. I could learn about who survives and who doesn't: K. was incredibly bright, incredibly articulate. He was the one who wrote about anger and hate, the one filled with both, a combustion that would have to be snuffed out, in some way, by those in power. But F. wrote a paper I did not include about addiction, spoke of how an addict was like a lion prowling the streets, hungry to attack. He wrote about going to a church to steal from the collection box only to find himself asking for forgiveness, his heart stolen by God, by Christ. D. was the one who had probably been the longest in prison when I first met him, the one who wrote about the difficulty of holding onto one's self within an environment geared to reduce everyone to a number and an object, the one who wrote about prejudice and seeing beyond the blinders of his own socialization, the one who struggled so hard to be fully human, and who was so human and open and articulate within the classroom. K.S.'s papers spoke with direct honesty. He was the one who wrote about drugs and sex and rock and roll, about gangs as a substitute family, the one who explored the connection between love and violence, a connection imbibed unconsciously from his father's violence, one he felt he could sever only by separating from the woman he loved. K.S. concluded his last paper

265

talking about himself as a man on a journey, needing to stop in order to reflect on his life. I remember when he dropped out of school, how I had wanted him to come back into the program, how much I had respected him and his use of writing as a way of becoming more conscious. I never found out why he dropped out or, now, how he died. With Tom, however, I had maintained contact through letters and visits after he was transferred from Great Meadows to Fishkill. I knew he was sick and, then, dying from AIDS. I called the prison, hoping to see him on my way back from visiting my parents for the Jewish holidays in the Fall of 1987. The office said that Tom was deceased; the officer would give me no other information.

Tom is the one who did not drop out or disconnect but wrote voluminously, hundreds of pages, from the time he left Comstock to the time of his death in Fishkill. I have included some of his writings in Chapter thirty-one. But now I want to look at these other five men who have died in prison, to see if there is some way to explain their death, some understandable cause and effect, some pattern. But I do not see a pattern and do not want to invent one. I think of Irena Klepfisz's poem "Bashert" (a Yiddish term meaning "inevitable, (pre)destined") about those who survived and those who died in the Holocaust. The poem is divided into two parts, the first "These words are dedicated to those who died":

> These words are dedicated to those who died
> because they had no love and felt alone in the world
> because they were afraid to be alone and tried to stick it out
> because they could not ask
> because they were shunned
> because they were sick and their bodies could not resist the disease
> because they played it safe
> because they had no connections
> because they had no faith
> because they felt they did not belong and wanted to die
>
> These words are dedicated to those who died
> because they were loners and liked it
> because they acquired friends and drew others to them
> because they took risks
> because they were stubborn and refused to give up
> because they asked for too much

These words are dedicated to those who died
because a card was lost and a number was skipped
because a bed was denied
because a place was filled and no other place was left

These words are dedicated to those who died
because someone did not follow through
because someone was overworked and forgot
because someone left everything to God
because someone was late
because someone did not arrive at all
because someone told them to wait and they just couldn't any longer

These words are dedicated to those who died
because death is a punishment
because death is a reward
because death is the final rest
because death is eternal rage.

These words are dedicated to those who died

    Bashert

The second part of the poem is "dedicated to those who survived":

These words are dedicated to those who survived
because their second grade teacher gave them books

because they did not draw attention to themselves and got lost in the shuffle
because they knew someone who knew someone else who could help them
and bumped into them on a corner on a Thursday afternoon
because they played it safe
because they were lucky

These words are dedicated to those who survived because they knew how
to cut corners
because they drew attention to themselves and always got picked

because they took risks
because they had no principles and were hard

These words are dedicated to those who survived
because they refused to give up and defied statistics
because they had faith and trusted in God
because they expected the worst and were always prepared
because they were angry
because they could ask
because they mooched off others and saved their strength
because they endured humiliation
because they turned the other cheek
because they looked the other way

These words are dedicated to those who survived
because life is a wilderness and they were savage
because life is an awakening and they were alert
because life is a flowering and they blossomed
because life is a struggle and they struggled
because life is a gift and they were free to accept it

These words are dedicated to those who survived.

Bashert

When I teach writing, I want students to draw lines of cause and effect, to notice patterns, to try to come to an understanding of "why," to not see facts and statistics as isolated and unconnected. But what Klepfisz captures in her poem is exactly what I feel about those who survived and those who died in the prison: there is no pattern. I recognize the abuses of power, the courage it takes to resist, and the punishment of those who question and rebel, but with these five men I cannot see a way of explaining survival or death; those on one list could have as easily been on the other, the very things enabling one to survive being the same things that could cause one's death. There is no logic, no control; it is bashert. In cases like this, to try to find a pattern is to simplify reality in order to maintain an illusion of logic and control: If only ... if only ... then ... What I see here (and other times in both personal and world history) is that one may have very little control over whether one dies or lives; it does not matter what one does or does not do. What one can always do, however, is "save one's soul";

one can act like a free person even if (and, perhaps, particularly if) one is held within the most strong prison. It is possible; I have seen it. I have seen it in those five men.

I dedicate this book to those who survived and those who died and to all who struggle to be more fully human and to be free.

Chapter Thirty:

Those who survived

Of the fifteen survivors, two I could not locate, two didn't respond, but eleven responded within two or three weeks. An amazing return rate. I, unfortunately, was not so responsible or responsive. It is now July 13, the day before Bastille Day, the day before Tom's birthday. Now, mid summer, I respond to their mid winter letter and write this chapter.

What to say? First, it was amazing that they wrote at all; it had been between seven and ten years. It was amazing that they remembered, wrote specifically about the class and how much they learned, remembered small details about me—that I liked loons, did Tai Chi, was an Aries. Remembered large things—how important UWW was for them, "a bright spot in an otherwise dark period." They spoke of how writing helped them "escape" from prison and how it allowed them to express what was deep and meaningful: "Many a day has passed that I wanted to reach out to you two (Sandy and me) and thank you for helping me learn how to release my feelings and express myself through the written word." "Because of the class, I have become a much better writer and person. It not only opened my mind, but also taught me how to express myself in my writings. I always had a problem expressing myself verbally, but because of the class I have learned to express myself on paper and continued to do so after the class ended. I learned to open my mind, look in other directions, and to remove the blinders from my eyes. You started me on the path to becoming a better person; my interaction with you is the reason I have grown so much locked behind these walls for so long."

What is very strong is the gratitude. What is also strong is the fact that my having written, after so many years, allowed them to write. That is, they never assumed they could or should impose on my or any of our lives. If I had not written, they wouldn't have written, and I would have never known their feelings about the class, about UWW, about writing, about their lives after the class. What is also quite amazing, given their circumstance, is that after that initial response to my letter, none assumed they could or should continue the correspondence. My letter, coming so late back to them, perhaps will allow that door to be opened a bit more. That open door is the least I can do given the iron gate that surrounds their open hearts.

Their letters were gracious; that is the word that first came to me, gracious in their respect, gratitude, excitement. They spoke of feeling honored that I would want to include their writings in a book. They spoke of wanting the book if it ever should be published and, of course, all thought that it would be published because I was writing it and it would be very good and very important.

One theme repeated many times was their own surprise at how open they were in their writing: "I read the copies of the stuff you want to use and I only have one question to ask you: How did you ever get me to write something as personal and soul bearing as that?! I haven't been that open in quite some time." And: "Your letter did two things. Firstly, it showed me how bad my typing was and the mere structuring of words gave credence to the fact I was in the right class! But more importantly, it was like looking into one of those old view finders and the theme was Gothic B. L. The innocence between those lines made my heart skip a beat. My roots were just being planted and grown I have.... Of course you can use my papers; I'm flattered! But my ego is cryin out to give ya a more current or post education piece. But I doubt I could match these earlier papers. My heart was on my sleeve, as they say, in these writings. It's truly amazing how such naivete survived the machinations of a life in maximum security prisons. You know something, Bernice, I've only been in one fight in my life. I was 11 years old and got a black eye over a girl!" A few of the men felt a bit embarrassed at what they now saw as less developed thought and less strong writing skills. Some of them have completed college, either within and outside of prison, and felt that they could "write much better." But while the ego would have liked to have edited and revised their papers, most recognized the power of the original: the direct and almost innocent honesty, no separation between word and feeling, no protection or defense or artifice. Perhaps the papers were not "academic"; perhaps the students had no yet learned (or I had not yet taught) a more sophisticated writing style. But they and I knew that something very meaningful would be lost if they revised their work.

I think of some of my former Vermont College students who recently withdrew from a very fine MFA program. What they felt was that the program was taking them further from the heart of their writing. Instead of the faculty challenging them to go more deeply into their subject, they were continually asked to repolish their rough gems, the raw edges of power and beauty being refined out. The problem wasn't in the process of revision which they all respected and, actually, loved—where one is working with the craft, struggling to chisel the form out of the rock through hard labor, to bring into form what is deep and formless. Rather, it was the external criticism that made them focus more on the judgment of others than on giving form to what lay mysterious within the heart. One of my students said that she knew she had to quit the MFA program when she realized how much more powerful the writings of those in her women's group were. That power of the heart is, I think, what some of the men realized in their papers. What was interesting was that only one really felt embarrassed about his early work. He wrote: "I was a bit embarrassed by my own writings. As you can well imagine, that period in my life was difficult, as it would be for anyone, let alone a 17 year old kid. While I see a bit of intelligence in my young words, I loathe the majority of them. My belief in god at that time was necessary—whether god existed or not was not the question." This student continued in school, getting his Bachelors and Master. He is now working on his PhD. He asked that I not use his paper and said, at the end of his letter, "No one really knows about my past here. I think it is best that way." It is not that I don't understand, and respect both him and his words. I have not used his paper. But I think of the very different response of K.J. who wrote: "Feel free to use my name. I've learned not to be ashamed of what transpired in the past, for those experiences made me the man that I am now."

Then there were the other things that they said: "I'm writing again to send a photo of me and my daughter, just so you will have a vision to go with the words" (KJ). Another said: "I'm on a six month parole violation. I was released from Auburn 9/96. Needless to say I haven't been a stellar example for a parolee. But in my eyes I wasn't a bad one either. My violation was for going to Florida to visit my father who was in the last stages of small cell lung cancer. Some say the action was irresponsible. I look at it as being compassionate. The consequence was six months in Attica. As you know I had a lot of issue with my father and we made our peace with each other. This is a positive consequence and I'm ok with it" (BL). And another, the one who wrote about his son: "After reading my thoughts from the past, it truly stirred me and awakened old emotions within my heart. Since the printing of those seemingly prophetic words, Chris was incarcerated for six months, yet he's alive, dropped out of school, yet he's trying to get his GED. Chris has become a lover and, in turn, will be a father by April 2001, which will ultimately make me a grandfather. Am I proud for the turn of events? No. But I no longer feel totally responsible for Chris' actions. I've learned over the years, and through many emotional trials, that he will go down certain roads I've warned him against in life; however, they will gradually develop his character and help him"(CW). One man wrote: "I have to admit that many of the courses I took in college classes at jail were indeed harder than the classes I'd taken in the traditional school. Many people in jail have such low ideas about themselves that they are disbelieving and skeptical about their own ability to learn. Myself included." And another: "I still love writing but I'm in love with reading and I haven't changed dramatically in that I still believe in hope—hope for me, my future, mankind, the world. I still believe that the key to writing is to let heart and soul guide your heart" (BH).

One of the students signed his letter, "Still your student." I feel I could/should end my letter with "Still your teacher and still your student."

CHAPTER THIRTY-ONE:

JULY 14, TOM'S BIRTHDAY AND BASTILLE DAY

I wanted this to be the last chapter. I planned to take out all the letters that Tom had written and to end this book reflecting on him and what he had taught me. Time passed, and more time, and finally, on July 11, I rummaged through an old box and found twenty letters, each one eight to twelve pages, almost two hundred pages of typed and handwritten letters mailed between February 86 and September 87 from Eastern Correctional Facility and Fishkill, the prisons Tom went to when he left Great Meadows. In one of the letters Tom thanked me for a card I sent on his birthday, July 14; he was 29 in 1987. If he had lived he would be, now in 2001, forty three today. It seemed right that I should end on Tom's birthday with a kind of "Happy Birthday, Tom" letter/chapter. Then I looked at my calendar, not only Tom's birthday, but the birthday of the French Revolution: Bastille Day. Even better: to begin the book on the Jewish New Year and to end on Bastille Day.

Bastille Day, July 14, 1789, the beginning of the French Revolution, the day the citizens of Paris stormed the gates of the ancient citadel releasing all the prisoners held within, the day the French celebrate as the beginning of their freedom. I think of my bumper sticker: "No one is free as long as anyone is oppressed." I think of our society putting more and more people in prison, the illusion of many of us that we can only be free if more people are enchained. What consciousness would be needed to actually have our citizens want to free those imprisoned, to see our freedom as dependent on their freedom, to see that "they" are "us," or that we could, easily, be them? To want to break down the prison walls, what walls within us would need to come down?

Perhaps that is what Tom did for me, in ways I did not always welcome. He broke down those neat and clear walls which separate good from bad, angel from monster, sweet from bitter, repentant from unrepentant. He was not easy, which is why I want to write about him.

I have two hundred pages of his letters but no saved papers. There are quotes, though, that I remember almost verbatim, the first two from papers and the last during one on of my visits to him.

In an earlier chapter I wrote of Tom's defining "compassion" as coming from an ability to recognize one's own capacity for malevolence. I remembered his words because when I read them, I realized not only their truth but, also, the cost of denial. Unable to recognize our capacity to do harm, we are unable to experience to the remorse that softens and deepens the heart; we become imprisoned in arrogance and self-righteousness.

I think of one of the *Genesis* series with Bill Moyers, the participants exploring the story of Esau, Jacob, and Isaac, and of Rebecca's telling her son, Jacob, to deceive his father. The mothers (writers, artists, Biblical scholars) talked of the deception, reflecting on the mother's action and why, understanding the different pulls, not judging. One man on the panel said, smugly, what everyone knew—that Rebecca deceived Isaac. When asked by one of the women if he could ever imagine deceiving someone, he said no, he could never imagine. And I thought, that is the problem; you cannot imagine your own capacity to commit a malevolent act. Tom could.

In another paper, I remember Tom writing about maturity, distinguishing between fruit ripening and people maturing. Fruit and vegetables, he said, do ripen. But with people it is different: at every stage of our life we are ripe; we are who we are (as well as becoming who we will become). According to Tom, there is not one final goal to which our life is leading, everything unripe until the final ripened "fruit" at the end of our journey. Since Tom died so young, his fruit to the outside world not having "ripened" and "matured," his thoughts and words give me comfort: He was who he was at each moment, full and unique. When he died, according to his own definition and my now seeing, he was ripe and mature.

He was the only person I knew who loved Carlyle. His letters were filled with quotes from Becket, Nietzsche, Heidegger, Thoreau, *Frankenstein*, *The Brothers*

Karamazov, Heart of Darkness, The Fall, Kierkagard, Blake, Camus.... He was a philosopher who loved to discuss ideas, writing of Nietzshe's "the pathos of distance," talking about good and evil, honesty and deception. His letters bubbled with ideas. And when words weren't enough, he drew pictures with colored pencil, capturing himself teaching pottery or in a classroom. He talked about teaching, about getting better in his drawings, about playfulness and its importance in life. And he was playful in his letters, in a way I never experienced in person, playful and funny and vulnerable and open and loving. He signed his letters "your friend, Tommie." It's interesting how moved I was by the innocence of "your friend, Tommie." A student who substitutes in the elementary school recently showed me letters from her students thanking her. They ended their letters with "your friend."

Reading Tom's very long letters, I could just picture (although I could not remember) my very short replies. I thought of his isolation and clear need for communication, his love of writing and thinking, love of words, ideas and passionate debates, and my limited time, limited responses, limited giving. I could tell from his words that I must have talked about my garden and weeds, about Arizona and canyons, about love and goodness; I clearly wanted to bring some light and life into the darkness. But as I read the honesty and directness of his letters, I began to feel strangely pollyanish, naive, miss goody two shoes. But then, just as I was feeling bad, I would read Tom's words about my letter being "good, very good," and that, after nine pages, he had just begun answering the first half of my letter.

My letters must have given him something. And I know from his letters that I also sent cards and visited more than the three times I actually remember. I'm very glad I acted from my better and less selfish self, that I took the time. Small gestures are important in all cases but particularly when someone is lonely and cut off from so much of the outer world. It's important to remember and to imagine oneself in the same position, imagining as one path toward empathy.

In his letters Tom was incredibly appreciative. At the end of each letter, he would say that he had so much more to say and that he would write again soon, which he did, except when he got so sick that he was in pain all the time, losing his sight, his ability to move, his mind. His earlier letters spoke of not feeling well, of having no energy, of having terrible cysts on his backside. In March of 87, he mentioned the doctor's diagnosis of AIDS, saying he had two to ten years. His voluminous letters got less, he apologizing, saying he didn't want to write if he couldn't create a spark. He was afraid he was boring me; he was very thankful; he was very courageous. He died about six months after receiving the diagnosis.

I must have sent him books, because he refers to them. And he writes about his art in an exhibit in Albany and some of his clay sculptures. He sent me a pot called "He man." It is funny and beautiful—a well shaped pot, about 6 inches wide and 8 inches tall. The pot sits on two wonderfully shaped feet. The muscled arms rest on the nonexistent hip. There is a belly button in the center. I loved it and must have told him that; in his letter he expresses happiness at my response.

In all his letters he asks after me, wants me to tell him about my life, wants to hear my ideas, is reaching out to hear of the world as well as to speak to the world.

It must have been the last visit in which he talked of his crime. Most of the men in prison did not; I never knew what they did or for how long they were in prison. But Tom needed to tell. What I had known before was that his mother bore him when she was thirteen and that his uncle prostituted him from when he was very young, nine or ten. What he told me that day was that he was in prison for raping an 84 year old woman. It was one of those crimes I might, at another point in my life, have shaken my head over in disgust and disbelief, wondering what kind of monster could commit such a crime. I remember Tom looking me in the eye and saying that he could not now guarantee that he would never do such a thing again, that the "passion" could take him over. He could imagine himself doing such an action again; he needed to say that. He had that kind of honesty.

He knew that consciousness does not necessarily mean that one will never again do what is hated and known. In her *Woman Warrior*, Maxine Kingston talks about her mind "needing to become large in order to take in paradox." I knew I needed to become larger in order to take in all that Tom told me, to not leave out the parts that did not please me, to not not hear in order to preserve my own beliefs, values, desires.

I think of Jane Goodall and her work with the chimps. After a certain number of years she experiences, for the first time, direct aggression of one chimp against another. Was she tempted to suppress the information? I might have been in my not wanting the "enemy" to have any ammunition, in my wanting to keep the chimps "good." But what Goodall wants, it is clear, is to see the truth of what is, rather than the idea of what should be. Tillie Olsen, in her *Tell Me A Riddle* says, "Everything that happens, one must try to understand." That, I think, is what Tom tried to do: to understand without any lying or camouflaging or denying.

In imagining, allowing in, seeing what is, there is the possibility of consciously changing ourselves and the world. Imagining *both* the possible "bad" and the possible "good" within us and outside of us, we can actually bring into being our dreams and visions for ourselves and the world. Awareness, faith, freedom, they all seem inextricably bound together.

CHAPTER THIRTY-TWO:

HAPPY BIRTHDAY, TOM

I have just realized the gift I want to give you, now, when you would be forty three, fourteen years after our last contact. The gift is your words, or at least a very small portion of your words, in print. Had you the ten more years you wanted, you would have created your own book. But, as you said in your paper, we can't talk of "ripening" as if our life were a movement toward our becoming a more full human being. Reading your words again, I feel the ripeness and maturity of your words now. They are the words of a free human being.

> *I come to find that I despise the masks, and the fooling, the withholdings, the restraint that this incarceration place me in. Not only do I lose myself to the world, I lose the world. This means that I also lose real contact with reality. Not in a crazy way. I suffer from the helplessness and the violence that springs from that helplessness. Part of this violence is the abandonment of identity—self—as a defense against this feeling of helplessness. On top of that the violence becomes oppression. I do not like the oppression of myself by myself. This is incarceration at its fullest. This position I'm faced with pollutes every interpersonal relationship I approach. Just as you say you take off your button "Question Authority," I take off myself. I am too bright for the environment that I am existing in. My fear is that I would be killed if I really spoke up and out at some of the crazy nonsensical events that I have viewed directly or indirectly heard about. This sort of self restraint, killing, or putting to the side of the self, is the most extreme violence. This has made me even violent towards you.*

How? By my fear, my withholding, my niggardly approach in giving you all that Tommie is. I have nonetheless tried—but only a stunted dwarf has been able to escape the chains, the cell. Thus I not only have been violent but I have cheated you inadvertently.

From this letter onward I will have no choice but to be honest, not the half honest enigmatic spirit that I have been. There is no reason for me to fear you. This I feel from a deep part of my inner world, from within my heart.

I find that our words are often used in a rather off handed way. This is one way that all that pollution slips in and then grows out into diseased ideas such as racism and other attitudes that put one person beneath, or even completely out of the picture. But the word itself and its power as a symbol, its unspoken quiet parts that kind of lay in this silence, its like an area that turns into an echo chamber, where the actual concept of any word reverberates throughout, all the process that all words, either by themselves or in clusters, go through in order to help translate the world reality into a communicable experience that is conducive towards empathy, compassion, and even sharing. This stuff you already know. Everytime I try to write to you, I always get this feeling that it's a waste of time, not on my own part but for you. Like what can I say that you have not already been through in one form or another? I think that this is an inferiority complex in the brewing. (Smile) I know that I have no reason whatsoever to feel this way. What I would like, after careful thinking and reflection, is a response that is real. Just what this real response is I can't tell you because I just don't know what it is off hand. I will know it when I see it or hear it or feel it.

So I will say only that this is person to person, and I cannot approach this in any other way, and really what other way is there when it comes to living life. Life is a strictly personal affair, so I think.

I used to think that thinking was different from feeling. But now I come to realize that the line between thinking/feeling is very thin, very frail, and possibly an illusion. This line that separates the two for me I now see as an escape route from the responsibility. It seems to me that I would most time rationalize away an event and say, I think. I could somehow stay removed from the feeling, good or bad. This way of avoiding pain, for the most part, kept my feelings out of it and away from it. To feel is to think.

To think is to feel. There are only different ways of feeling, different feelings, different thoughts.

One day I was writing a letter to a friend and discovered that I was very much changed, that I no longer believed the fine line between thinking and feeling, and that is also when I realized that I am very much a political being. Because to feel is to be affected. I feel that it is up to each of us to educate one another, to build a pedagogy of the heart. I am, in fact, a teacher. But none in this place wants to hear what I have to say. Not that I say much; I only say it could be much more than it is. I sometimes wonder what happens to the person in the classroom. As they walk out they leave this ghost behind, like just waiting for the next class so they can haunt the others around them for two hours with their real selves.

To me this says a lot about reality and the human condition in relation to truth. All Reagan can do is work out of his premises, and he'll reach all the necessary conclusions. The answers are in it already. The logical chains do not allow for flukes of thought or, better said, flukes of reality. There is no doubt that Reagan is acting and the scripts or scenario may be all too familiar. Nonetheless, there are indeed many who share in this premise, this mendaciousness of consciousness.

Now we must look to our own thoughts and, low and behold, the same applies for us. All concept, metaphor on metaphor, all battling over electrical impulses that we assume are real. All conjectures of life on life. For shame—what truth is there? But we are still bombarded with life. We feel the primordial spirit and absorb the crass reality in a deep way. Somewhere under the skin the whole body is infested with life. Not just mind—the mind is but a toy to the greater intelligence of the body. There is an illusion that we suffer from. Somehow we tend to think that the mind is in charge of this ship? I do not suffer from this illusion anymore. I think the illusion has its roots in Aristotle. That's when it slips over us as a people. The type of illusion I'm speaking of is of the same type that slipped over the German people before and during the war. That is a very powerful illusion, so powerful that one takes it for a world reality and thus the idea becomes the reality. Yet it still does not in any way change the fact that it's pure illusion. Such as the kind that Reagan and his crew suffers from. Enough or not enough of that.

What is truth? I'll tell you some truth. It was nice, warm, and to me wonderful that you recalled me enough to write and to send me this card.

That is truth. The truth that you thought about my pottery interest and even my potential feeling about the pot. You gave me a prize today. A prize being a small gift—the gift of thought. And that to me is the most valuable gift there is. That's truth. So I want you to know that I know.

I will start with the facts as I know them: Here I was sitting in my tiny cell, as I have been doing for about 1000 days, and this feeling/thought comes to me that I am all too alone in this space and time. Alone within this body. Alone within this mind. A very alone totality of me. But don't let me fool you here. There is a lot more that goes on beside this aloneness. This aloneness is in the backdrop, the background, or maybe just ground that the further revelations overtook me in. I guess that means that while I was in this state of aloneness things came to me. The things are thoughts. The things are feelings. They coalesce into this whole they call self, me, I. This coalescence of mind—thought/feel, thinking/feeling—is more along the lines of body/mind. This dichotomy of mind out from the body is really an absurd condition for the human. As a matter of assumed fact (smile) it is outright preposterous. This dyadic existence is the most obscene crime that ever enthralled humans.

So, what am I saying? I am saying that while I have been in my cells for these 1000's of days and in my life/time, it is all too apparent that there is something wrong (smile). Well ... I am no longer concerned with what is wrong—or what is right. I have lost this part of my culture or conditioning. Somehow I separated. But not into a dichotomy or dyad of self—mind/body—but I stepped over into a multiplicity of being. I kind of stepped out—into this panoramic reality which I think is broader than psychodynamic reality. The reason I feel that panorama is a better word is that it involves an unfurling of reality, an unconcealment, and an exploration that doesn't lead directly to the head/mind. I think it leaves room for the unexplainable existence of the body.

Well, this is no great revelation within itself. This is not my complete state of mind/body that I am trying to tell you about. Wait a bit more and keep that ground rolling around near by. I will pull it all together. I have a direction into a complex labyrinth of a moment that took place in a cell in one of the 1000 of days that occurred last night in the unknown universe. This is space and time and a life/time event that is rather mystical—although I reject the idea of the mysticalness of life. Only because most people want to take the mystical for themselves and hold it as if they are the only ones alive. This is greedy, unsharing, and down right selfish. Like they are the only ones who got the handle on life. Thus is explained my reluctance to grant the premise of the mystical experience. We all live life together. I take it for granted that we all know in our hearts that life is a pretty strange event, but a normal every day event. Who doesn't know how to live? That is an impossible concept to entertain. We are all alive in the same way. There is no inside information, no handle that separates one from another. I think we covered this idea in our last class together. What outsider? What insider? ... We all share in a profusion of realities, a profusion that is the common ground that we all reach into/out of. This is how I get into the panoramic reality that I have embraced. I have not limited my choices, but I am one of the most limited of humans. Look at my situation. Is it my limited acceptance and pliableness of attitude that brings on the conflict or is it the overwhelming confines and surrounding structures of culture that accuse me of being abnormal or deviant?

But what does all of this got to do with my experience that I had last evening? It is all on the periphery of the circle playing about like children in a sand box, building little worlds at their wits' end. All this is what came to me last night. It has come to me before. It is nothing new, but is always fresh with its impact:

Unity/descension/together/apart/one/separate/two/me/you/we ... All chopped up and combined into this panoramic reality. This is my apprehension of the world. This is in direct conflict with the others. The society, the larger abstraction, the broader concept of ourselves. At a one to one level I am fine. I can cope with the multiplicities of life. But it is the abstractions that confuse the hell out of me. Thus my disinterest in politics is explained as a lack of comprehension of the larger abstractions. Not that I don't perceive the ideas. They are seemingly clear in their ambiguity; I can touch on them, I can recognize them when they come into my life/ time ... They are always there. Life is political. But I want life to remain personal and intimate—one on one. I find that in these extra-caricaturistic symbols, the larger grandiose abstractions that one must break up-into becomes a realm of anti-life. A life of pantomine. A celluloid production of Idea. This only means that one starts to live out there, on this surface plane, out there with the facades and the personas and the masks. I have little desire to dress up, to play with makeup. I am an already complete enigma full of life. I don't see the need, nor can I develop the desire to, further my illusions for myself or for others.

So, all of this came out of me last night. There is a lot more to the moment than I have covered. I will try to grasp it more in depth. I don't know if this is making sense to you.

What is of special significance is that all this comes in waves. Words are frail indeed compared with the initial experience of feeling, life, life, life.

The master of time. I know a lot about time. After watching it as I do, I think it gives me a certain perspective that not many other humans have. The workings of psychological time is what I am talking about, not the clock time which is the lesser of the two evils. "Individual consciousness is but a shadow; what is permanent is the world" (Royce). From within these walls this statement takes on the toughest. If you don't leave here knowing that, then you haven't done enough time. A new prerequisite for parole.

After a quote from Nietzche from Thus Spake Zarathustra: *"Ah, but don't you love your dirt?" It may be too much a charge for you, too much a yell or proclamation or just too hard. But that is how I feel. If you read it deeply I think you will see that it is not so much a yell or charge but more a plea to move, to move away from the old cold stones of an old cold traditional way of reacting to the world. Is it romantic? (Smile) Yes, but this is the stuff writing is made of.*

I know I'm in a period of threshold. What the shrinks call "the just noticeable difference." So I think/feel that I am becoming "just noticeably different." A new threshold and a cracking, shattering.

I love my body. Even when it's not in good shape, I find pleasure in it. I think many people forget their body and are unhappy with it. I think they put too much into the American stereotype of skinny being in. That is all a lot of bullshit if you ask me. Also I think there is a certain amount of lingering hate for the body from the medieval period. All spirit and mind and the despising of the body. Well, I think/feel that that idea is really very bad. I love all of me. The good, ugly, and the bad. I have to own up to it all. That is the only way to find peace. I have to own up to myself about myself.

But besides that I have been trying to peek at the body and how it works in space and time. I'm doing it for a philosophic view. Life is very much connected to and experienced through the body. So I have been try-

ing to grab a peek at it. I have been trying to focus in on it as it goes through an experience, such as play, and when it is playing. It is not easy and possibly impossible to see your body. There is a lack of real insight into the realm of the body.

So when Spring comes around I find that I get fervidly enthralled with life, head over heels in love with life. Even in here I tend to perk up out of my infernal brooding and join in with the rest of life. That's a pretty good thing. Spring is kind of my reprieve from a cold night.

I am concerned with the mentality that is warlike and domineering, if not out right oppressive. There is a segment that shares this sentiment and I think their stinginess should be equated with their capacity for stinging. They are ugly. I understand that the Senate may pass this Contra aide bill ...

The "pathos of distance," that's Nietzsche's idea on what type of attitude the rich have and desire to create from the resentment of the poor. In prison one is very poor. Not in the monetary sense but in the sense of life. Prison makes one empty in a certain kind of way. On the other hand, prison can also fill you up.

I am a fan of the right hemisphere. Intuition, nonverbal, timelessness, diffuse. We should learn how to use that hemisphere more than we do. If we keep this side of the brain confined to the prison of the left, we may never be able to reclaim it. I have been trying to write with my left hand for years. Also I juggle and I am a card mechanic. I do tricks and cheat, but I don't really cheat, I just know how to. I think/feel that if one uses the left hand it will bring it back to life.

I think that I am going back towards the Tao, Zen, not that I have been away. I have only been into the western stream. I think that I am coming to the same point that Heidegger found himself in. I have been like scraping the well, or my pebble has hit bottom and is now resounding throughout the water. The problem is that I don't know if it is a scraping or landing.

But I believe in something larger than even God—the human heart. And the malice that springs from it, I can cope with in all its enormity—at least we can start to finally lay the blame, the guilt and the shame where it really belongs. Not to forget the good stuff too. We are also known for some dazzling works of kindness and even works of love.

This pot is not the pot but the picture of the pot. There is far too much light placed on it. The reflection of the lip of the pot runs counter to the downward flow of the glaze. This upsets the balance of the pot in the picture. It really does not affect the pot itself, but the appearance or representation of the pot. The camera was placed too high over the pot. The picture becomes more important than the pot. That is very Western culture, always misplacing their intention, mistaking the subjects or, at the very least, confusing them. One can say that Western Culture mis-speaks.

This sort of experience is mystical. No, it's human. It's part of our condition, within our realm, so just accept that you and everyone else are a transcendent being. So? So, the world is deep.

But life is about living. That is all I really want out of/in/life: How to live a better life. To learn more and more about how to live more, how to live and become a full human, within myself and out there with all the others, that we are all together in here/out here, we are all in all mixed up. So I want to join in. I want to get involved. I want to participate.

If by chance or perhaps deliberate intent you find your self driving by this way on your way down or up from the city, or just out cruising the Thruway, I would like to see you at any chance. I would not mind this— and would even like it a great deal more than I can express.

When one leaves here it is not so much an end as it is only a completion. You can suffer many completions within a continuation, but only one end. This prison is not my end. I'm only working off a negative completion.

I have forgotten how to laugh as much as I might smile. You can only laugh when love is in the pot cooking up a meal for life.

Lately I have been fighting with the ghosts of time. They live on these peripheral shadow clouds that follow you about as if they were rain clouds looking to pee on you. But low and behold shadow clouds are not so kind; when they decide to drop their teary drops upon you, they turn out to be phosphatic warmings and burnings of both flesh and innards.

Should life be squandered? What good is a life if it is not squandered? Wouldn't that then be hoarding life? If not at the very least a miser towards life and living it? Yet one can't really hoard life, only kind of limit the experiences. But that limitation is in effect a way to hoard life. This limitation of experience creates a fear for the unexplored terrain. One sticks with what one knows best.

"Courage also slays dizziness at the edge of abysses: and where does man not stand at the edge of abysses? Is not seeing always seeing abysses?" (Nutz)

Death kind of barges right the hell into the living rooms of our dwellings. It has that kind of power and, in a way, grace. Death's reign is true and sure once its eye has settled on you.

They are still building more prisons, more beds. What will happen to this mega-system once we hit a depression? The system is already going down hill in services, security, rehabilitation. The over all trend is one of disdain and hatred. That is going to grow. Criminals will be the new niggers of our culture. (I use the word nigger in the sense of object of abuse and score.)

The bottom line on crime is either economics or illness. Which ever one is the cause makes no difference. A society cannot battle crime or criminality with vengeance. You either heal the sick or you solve the division of the pie, or you do both.

They still seek blood, at the very least pain. This is what Nietzsche says, this is what he means: society must start thinking of ways of coping with the ills in a creative fashion and not out of vengeance

Back to our visit, I want you to know that I almost cried at one point. I got real teary for a minute. I just couldn't hold it together—like one has to hold it together, like it's a requirement to hold it together. But there wasn't enough time. There was just not enough time—and most of it was spent on me, a me you know a lot about. The next time we'll deal with you.

So, I'm pretty much filled up with energy and vigor, and I can feel the thoughts knocking at my brain, kind of aching to get out. I have a lot I want to say to you.

This letter is not nearly enough. You know I'm capable of more than this and once I'm cooking up with energies again I'll really pull some interesting stuff out of the hat. Promise. I don't like to send letters if I feel less than myself or if I feel that I didn't send a spark for a few thoughts. This letter is like that. Choppy and not all that I had in mind.

First I want to thank you for your lovely letter. I found it very lively, descriptive, and very much needed on my part. You do bring some good feelings into this dull and dreary place. And for that matter into my heart. It's my heart that we are actually talking about here. A dull and dreary heart. So, that is what you cheer up, brighten up, and even inspire, and I like it a lot and enjoy every moment, every word. It's that simple. What else can I say? Thank you for being my friend.

Expiate is the word the author uses over and over. It's all self induced on Ironweed's part, as it is with all of us in some ways, at least with all of us sinners. Us, the guilty ones. Us, the not so innocent. Well, I will write you a letter on guilt, shame, expiation, purging, catharsis.... all of these concepts have been with me for a long time. But that will have to wait until I can sit and think. But I'll do it. I owe you a prolific letter on shame.

I had a super good day with you and enjoyed every minute that I had with you. Even with the things that are not so nice, but I felt like I wanted to let you know the harder, darker, and craziness. That way I can feel like a real friend, kind of out in the open, without the ghost and the monster always creeping about. So with all that kept in mind I feel much more secure, because it's honest. I like that kind of feeling—that makes me feel good.

Now about you forgiving me. The reason I said what I said is this: I feel now that it's dead … the dead past, but never really forgotten. And the forgetting is very important. The dilemma is that once a person becomes conscious, it's always there. However there is hope always of real friendship, caring, even love can grow. I value our friendship. Duration, duration, that's what I look for. A friend is a friend is a friend.

I am happy that we talked like we did. I felt that I wanted to, and that it is important to be honest and open, so I told you about the dark side, the monster, the creep. I have slayed that beast. I am learning how to love and even how to be loved. But sometimes it is hard to believe in love, in being loved. I can feel my own love cook when it's in the pot, but the other's love is always in doubt.

I kind of see it like this: So many people die in one day that my own death is insignificant, and frivolous in the face of all of them. Plus there are many children, old persons, and mid life. I'll just fit in there somewhere. It's perfectly natural to die. I just hope that I can do something of a little value, resolve a few things with my family, reach a little deeper into my mother's and brother's heart.

Freedom for, not freedom from. It's always a question of what next. Even after satori. You can take that bit of advice from a retired monk who is now going to return for the night. I have lot more to say but the nature of life is that one gets tired. Good night. Your friend, Tommie.

(Last letter, written from a hospital): Once I get back to Fishkill I am going to take on the task of writing my book. It's not going to be an autobiography but more a conversation on life, the world, and my life will be in there too, with some organization and structure. I'll be audacious, coy, and exhilarated. Dashes and all. It is the only thing I have left to do. I don't know how much time I have left and necessity has forced my hand. I

figured on 10 more years of education before I'd be able to really write well enough. However, life has its own way most time. So fatalistic it makes me sick. I have had time to learn how to will. I'm just beginning to learn and I'm cut short. I'm not crying. I realize everything has its time, so I'm not freaked out. But I want to do some good, some how.

They just played "Let it Be" by the Beatles, a very powerful song and it has been one that always makes me stop to listen. The song affects me deeply. With all my disdain for the spiritual, I'm full of it. I have just started to read Purity of Heart is to Will One Thing *by Kierkegaard. I presently have an infection in my eyes; it's pretty serious. I can go blind. So far it's not super bad. I also have pneumonia. I'm on my med and my sleeping pills so I don't know how much longer I'll be with you tonight.*

The light is still alive
demands the good fight
even when it's fading in the night
Rage is not the answer for me.

For now I'm kicking and trying to get well. A Big Hug, Tommie.

Dear Tommie,

In ten years you could have written a wonderful book. Even now, each letter has so much passion and wisdom, these letters an almost book, these brief selections just a hint of the exuberance of your mind and heart. Thank you, Tom, for all that you have taught me. You were a very good friend.

Chapter Thirty-three:

The end of one cycle

> *How*
> *Did the rose*
> *Ever open its heart*
>
> *And give to the world*
> *All its*
> *Beauty?*
>
> *It felt the encouragement of light*
> *Against its*
> *Being.*
>
> *Otherwise,*
> *We all remain*
>
> *Too*
>
> *Frightened*
>
> (Hafiz, "It Felt Love," trans. Ladinsky)

When I first came to teach in the prison, our group was told to never accept any gifts from the men in prison, that all their "gifts" were really meant to "con" us. But how could I refuse the cards, the paintings, the time spent weaving folds of

5 Love Languages,
my Stories
my Blog.

paper in and out to create a tightly woven briefcase. Perhaps one of the deeper pains we experience as human being is being unable to give our gifts, to have no place that welcomes them. Perhaps even more than in receiving gifts, there is a joy in giving. You can see the radiant expectation on the face of the one who gives, waiting for the gift to be unwrapped, and the joy when a gift is loved.

Perhaps my gift to the people I've taught through the years is in my ability to receive their gifts: my clear sense of the value and richness of their words and their being and how much my life has been enriched by them, my ability to recognize, receive and welcome what is precious. In fact, this whole book is a collection of gifts I have received during my years teaching. Now, through the act of writing this book, I feel I am, finally, giving back what I have received: I am acknowledging the givers' generosity, depth, intelligence, and wisdom, the gifts of their being.

This book, then, is dedicated to all those who are imprisoned in mind and body and to all those who imprison themselves and others. To all students and to all teachers. To all of us who walk on this earth. To this earth on which all beings walk. May all beings be free.

Acknowledgments

Grateful acknowledgment is made to the following for permission to reprint copyrighted material:

Coleman Barks, "The Guest House," "Love Dogs," "This is How a Human Being," from *The Essential Rumi*. San Francisco: Harper, 1995. Reprinted with permission of Coleman Barks.

Robert Bly, "Last Night as I Was Sleeping" (Antonio Machado), from *The Soul is Here for its Own Joy*. Hopewell, New Jersey: Ecco Press, 1995; "The Panther" from *Rainer Maria Rilke, Selected Poems*. New York: Harper & Row, 1979. Reprinted with permission of Robert Bly.

Joseph Bruchac, ed., "It Started" (Jimmy Santiago Baca), "The Ritual"and "The Prison" (David Ashlely) from *The Light from Another Country: Poems from American Prisons*. Greenfield Center, New York: Greenfield Review Press, 1984. Reprinted with permission of Joseph Bruchac.

Mark Doty, "Green Crab Shell," from *ATLANTIS*. New York: HarperCollins, 2005. Reprinted with permission of Mark Doty.

Langston Hughes, "Harlem," from *The Collected Poems of Langston Hughes*. Arnold Rampersad, ed. New York: Knopf, 1994. Reprinted with permission of Alfred A. Knopf, a division of Random House.

Irena Klepfisz, "Abutilon in Bloom," "Dedication to 'Bashert,'" "Lithops," "Royal Pearl," from *A Few Words in the Mother Tongue*. Portland, Oregon: The Eighth Mountain Press, 1990. Reprinted with permission of Irena Klepfisz and Eighth Mountain Press.

Daniel Ladinsky, "Dropping Keys," "It Felt Love," from *The Gift, Poems by Hafiz*. New York: Penguin, 1999. Reprinted with permission of Daniel Ladinsky.

Lee, Li Young, "Persimmons," from *Rose*. Rochester; New York: BOA Editions. Reprinted with permission of BOA Editions, Ltd.

Nye, Naomi, "Kindness," from *Words Under the Words: Selected Poems of Naomi Shihab Nye*. Portland, Oregon: Eighth Mountain Press, 1995. Reprinted with permission of Naomi Nye and Far Corner Books, Portland, Oregon.

And deep gratitude to the following who have made this book possible:

> my students in Great Meadows and Washington Correctional Institutions and in the Adult Degree Program of Vermont College of Union Institute & University;

> my colleagues who know the value and necessity of progressive education and who teach with heart and integrity;

> my friends who provided invaluable dialogue and feedback, inspiration and encouragement: Margaret, Ann Keller Sr., Kathy, Marian, Judith, Jan, Tania, Maida, Jill, Paula, Clara, Sharon, Raphael, Howie, Joanne, Rita, Marjorie, Jean Marie, Kay, Charlene, Fred …

> my writing and meditation groups in Glens Falls, N.Y., who nurture my continual "practice" and growth;

> Kristine Hege for her technological expertise and generous assistance;

> Ignatius Aloysius and Cynthia Kerby for their spirited willingness to design the cover and the powerful result of their artistic vision;

> my sister, Susan, whose life and death continually teach and touch my heart, and her sons, Aaron and David, whose creative expression enrich this world

> and Ann Blanchard whose deep listening and compassion have helped me break out of my own many prisons.

Thank you all.

Bibliography

(of all books quoted from and referred to in the text)

Abram, David. *Spell of the Sensuous.* New York: Pantheon Books, 1996.

Assagioli, Roberto. *Act of Will.* New York: Viking Press, 1973.

Baldwin, James. *The Fire Next Time.* New York: Dial Press, 1973.

Barks, Coleman, trans. *The Essential Rumi.* San Francisco: Harper, 1995.

Beauvoir, Simone de. *The Second Sex.* New York: Alfred A. Knopf, 1993.

Berry, Wendell. "The Journey's End" in *Words from the Land..* Ed. Stephen Trimble. Reno: University of Nevada Press, 1995.

Bly, Robert, ed. *The Soul is Here for its Own Joy.* Hopewell, New Jersey: Ecco Press, 1995.

Bruchac, Joseph, ed. *The Light from Another Country: Poems from American Prisons.* Greenfield Center, New York: Greenfield Review Press, 1984.

Bryant, Dorothy. *Ella Price's Journal.* New York: The Feminist Press, 1997.

Capra, Fritjof. *The Web of Life.* New York: Anchor Books, 1996.

Chodron, Pema. *The Places That Scare You: A Guide to Fearlessness in Difficult Times.* Boston: Shambala, 2001.

.... *When Things Fall Apart.* Boston; Shambala, 2002.

Collins, Joseph. "World Hunger: Myths and Solutions." Pamphlet of Food First.

Daly, Mary. *Beyond God the Fatehr: toward a philosophy of women's liberation.* Boston: Beacon Press, 1973.

Darrow, Clarence. *Address to the Prisoners in the Cook County Jail and Other Writings on Crime and Punishment.* Chicago: Charles H. Kerr Publisher, 1975.

Doty, Mark. *ATLANTIS..* New York: HarperCollins, 2005.

Edwards, Betty. *Drawing on the Right Side of the Brain.* Los Angeles: J.P. Tarcher, 1989.

Eiseley, Loren. *The Immense Journey.* New York: Random House, 1957, ... *The Unexpected Universe.* New York: Harcourt Brace Jovanovich, 1969.

Elbow, Peter. *Writing with Power.* New York: Oxford University Press, 1998.

Ellison, Ralph. *The Invisible Man.* New York: Random House, 1952.

Fanon, Frantz. *Wretched of the Earth.* New York: Grove Press, 1973.

Ferrucci, Piero *What We May Be.* Los Angeles: J.P. Tarcher, 1981.

Field, Joanna. *A Life of One's Own.* Los Angeles: J.P. Tarcher, 1981.

Fouts, Roger. *Next of Kin.* New York: William Morrow & Co., 1973.

Friere, Paolo. *Pedagogy of the Oppressed.* New York: Continuum, 1993.

Franck, Frederick. *Zen and Seeing.* New York: Knopf, 1973.

Fromm, Erich. *Escape from Freedom.* New York: Farrar & Rinehart, 1941.

Gilligan, Carol. *In a Different Voice.* Cambridge: Harvard University Press, 1993.

Goodall, Jane. *Chimpanzees of Gombe.* Cambridge: Harvard University Press, 1986.

.... *Reason for Hope: a spiritual journey.* New York: Warner, 1999.

Goldstein, Joseph. *Insight Meditation: The Practice of Freedom.* Boston: Shambhala, 1993.

Gordon, Linda. *The Great Arizona Orphan Abduction.* Cambridge: Harvard University Press, 1999.

Hardy, Thomas. *Jude the Obscure.* Fairfield, IA: 1st World Library, 2006.

Harris, Sam. *The End of Faith.* New York: W.W.Norton & Co. 2005.

Hoffman, Yoel, ed. *Japanese Death Poems.* Rutland, Vermont: C.E. Tuttle Co., 1986.

Hoffman, Eva. *Lost in Translation.* New York: Viking Penguin, 1989.

Holzer, Nina Burghild. *A Walk Between Heaven and Earth.* New York: Crown, 1994.

Hughes, Langston. *The Collected Poems of Langston Hughes.* Arnold Rampersad,ed. New York: Alfred A. Knopf, Random House, 1994.

Kegan, Robert. *In Over Our Heads.* Cambridge: Harvard University Press, 1994..

Kingston, Maxine. *The Woman Warrior.* New York: Vintage, 1989.

Klepfisz, Irena. *A Few Words in the Mother Tongue.* Portland, Oregon: The Eighth Mountain Press, 1990.

Krishnamurti, Jiddu. *Freedom from the Known.* New York: Harper & Row, 1969.

Ladinsky, Daniel, trans. *The Gift, Poems by Hafiz.* New York: Penguin, 1999.

Lee, Li-Young. *Rose.* Rochester, New York: BOA Editions, 1986.

Le Guin, Ursula. *Dancing at the Edge of the World.* New York: Perennial Library, 1990.

Lerner, Gerda. *The Creation of Patriarchy.* New York: Oxford University Press, 1986.

.... *Why History Matters.* New York: Oxford University Press, 1997.

Lorde, Audre. *Cancer Journals.* San Francisco: Aunt Lute Books, 1997.

.... *Sister Outsider.* Trumansburg, New York: The Cross Press, 1984.

Marshall, Paule. *Brown Girl, Brownstones.* New York: Random House, 1959.

Memmi, Albert. *The Colonizer and the Colonized.* Boston: Beacon Press, 1991.

.... Jews and Arabs. Chicago: J.P. O"Hara, 1975.

Metzger, Deena. *Writing for your Life.* San Francisco: HarperSanFrancisco, 1992.

Minnich, Elizabeth. *Transforming Knowledge.* Philadelphia: Temple University Press, 2005.

.... "Why Not Lie." *Soundings: An Interdisciplinary Journal.* Winter, LXVIII, #4.

Mueller, Lisel. *Alive Together, New and Selected Poems.* Baton Rouge: Louisiana State University Press, 1996.

Myerhoff, Barbara G. *Number Our Days.* New York: Dutton, 1978.

Nye, Naomi Shihab. *Words Under the Words.* Portland, Oregon: Eighth Mountain Press, 1995.

Olsen, Tillie. *Silences.* New York: Delacorte Press, 1978.

.... *Tell Me a Riddle.* New York: Delacorte Press, 1979.

Orwell, George. *A Collection of Essays.* New York: Harcourt, 1981.

Plaskow, Judith. *Standing Again at Sinai.* New York: HarperSanFrancisco, 1991.

Rich. Adrienne Cecile. *The Will to Change. London: Chatto & Windus, 1972.*

.... *Arts of the Possible.* New York: W.W. Norton & Co., 2001.

Rilke, Rainer Maria. *Letters to a Young Poet.* San Rafael, California: New world Library, 1992.

.... *Selected Poems.* Bly, Robert, trans/ed. New York: Harper & Row, 1979.

Roberts, Monty. *The Man Who Listens to Horses.* Thorndike, Maine: Thorndike Press, 1998.

Sacks, Oliver. *Awakenings.* Garden City, New York: Doubleday, 1973.

.... *Seeing Voices.* New York: Vintage Books, 2000.

Salzberg, Sharon. *Faith.* New York: Riverhead Books, 2002.

Shiva, Vendana. *Biopiracy.* Boston: South End Press, 1997.

Stafford, William. *Even in Quiet Places.* Lewiston, Idaho: Confluence Press, 1996.

.... *The Way It Is: New and Selected Poems.* Saint Paul, Minnesota: Graywolf Press, 1998.

.... *Writing the Australian Crawl.* Ann Arbor: University of Michigan Press, 1978.

Thoreau, Henry David. *Faith in a Seed.* . Dean, Bradley, ed. Washington D.C.: Island Press/Shearwater Books, 1993.

.... *The Heart of Thoreau's Journals.*Shepard, Odell, ed. New York: Dover, 1961.

.... "Walking" in *Works of Henry David Thoreau.* Owens, Lily, ed. New York: Crown, 1981.

Tolsoy, Leo. *The Death of Ivan Ilych and Other Stories.* New York: New American Library, 2003..

Trimble, Stephen, ed. *Words from the Land.* Reno: University of Nevada Press, 1995.

Wagoner, David. *Traveling Light: Collected and New Poems.* Urbana: University of Illinois Press, 1999.

Woolf, Virginia. *A Room of One's Own and Three Guineas.* London: Hogarth Press, 1984.

Wright, Richard. *Black Boy.* Lodi, New Jersey; Everbind Anthologies, 2003.

Yogananda, Paramahansa. *Autobiography of a Yogi.* Self Realization Fellowship, 1997.

Youngblood, Shay. *The big mama stories.* Ithaca: New York: Firebrand Books, 1989.

Zornberg, Avivah Gottlieb. *The Beginnings of Desire: Reflections on Genesis.* New York: Doubleday, 1996.

CPSIA information can be obtained at www.ICGtesting.com
Printed in the USA
BVOW04s0725240913

331897BV00002BA/5/P